WHISTLED
LIKE A BIRD

WHISTLED LIKE A BIRD

The Untold Story of Dorothy Putnam, George Putnam, and Amelia Earhart

SALLY PUTNAM CHAPMAN

WITH STEPHANIE MANSFIELD

WARNER BOOKS

A Time Warner Company

Grateful acknowledgment is given for permission to reprint the following:

Lyric excerpts of "Blue Skies" by Irving Berlin on page 66 © Copyright 1927 by Irving Berlin. © Copyright Renewed. International Copyright Secured. Used by Permission. All Rights Reserved.

Poems "To Dorothy" and "A House in a Hammock" from *Floridays* by Don Blanding, published by Florida Classics Library. Copyright 1941 by Don Blanding. Copyright Renewed 1969 by Security-First National Bank. All Rights Reserved. Used with permission of Florida Classics Library.

Photograph of Amelia Earhart at the Double Dee ranch from Jim Dunrud. Used with permission.

1940 photograph of Junie, Dorothy, and David at Immokolee and 1944 photograph of George Weymouth owned by George Weymouth. Used with permission of the owner's sister, Barbara McCallister.

Warner Books, Inc., 1271 Avenue of the Americas, New York, NY 10020

 A Time Warner Company

Printed in the United States of America

First Printing: July 1997

10   9   8   7   6   5   4   3   2   1

Library of Congress Cataloging-in-Publication Data

Chapman, Sally Putnam.
    Whistled like a bird : the untold story of Dorothy Putnam, George Putnam, and Amelia Earhart / Sally Putnam Chapman, with Stephanie Mansfield.
        p.   cm.
    Includes bibliographical references.
    ISBN 0-446-52055-1
    1. Putnam, Dorothy Binney, 1888–1982.   2. Putnam, George Palmer, 1887–1950.   3. Earhart, Amelia, 1897—1937.   4. United States— Biography.   5. Publishers and publishing—United States—Biography. 6. Women air pilots—United States—Biography.   7. Air pilots— United States—Biography.   I. Mansfield, Stephanie.   II. Title.
CT275.P8925C47   1997
070.5'092—dc21
    [B]
                                                              97-9456
                                                                 CIP

This book is dedicated to the memory
of my parents, Nilla and David Putnam,
and my sister, Binney.

And to my husband,
Jack

ACKNOWLEDGMENTS

As long as I can remember I have wanted to write this book, but often questioned whether I, a nonprofessional writer, could overcome the difficulties long enough to complete the task on my own. In the beginning I considered hiring a collaborator to assist me, but ultimately I realized that no one else could write my grandmother's story but me; so after two years I finished my book. But writing this story was only the beginning. Many talented people have been involved in its creation, and I can honestly say that the privilege of making these new friends has been my greatest reward.

Ben Forkner, my friend and scholar from Angiers, France, offered his editorial eye during the first draft. Shrinking the Atlantic Ocean was a bear at times, but we managed it. Thank you, Ben. I share the smooth and tight finished product with Stephanie Mansfield. For several months we pruned and reshaped my manuscript. It wasn't always easy cutting words and changing style, but Stephanie is a skilled professional and I am grateful for her editing.

Acknowledging a ghost is a helpless endeavor, but I want to thank my grandmother Dorothy Binney Palmer. Though her spirit is all that remains, she continues to live through her diaries. Four months after her death in 1982 I ventured into Tibet, where the first few lines of this book were written. Though I was still grieving, the mystical setting at the top of the world inspired me to begin this memoir.

Larry Kirshbaum of Warner Books first read my proposal and listened to my story two years ago. It was Larry's infectious enthusiasm that launched me headlong into the greatest challenge of my life. His guidance and brilliant attention to structure and clarity led me to the conclusion of *Whistled Like a Bird*. I could not have survived this wild adventure without him. Also to Mari C. Okuda at Warner Books, my deep appreciation for her compassion and able assistance. Not only is she an artist, but a sensitive and bold professional. To Ann Adelman, who copyedited my manuscript, thank you. Her astute discoveries were the finishing touches my story needed.

A few friends read the manuscript in progress and made helpful comments. Most notably, Anne Wilder, a writing legend in her own time. Her guidance and support from the first chapter forward were priceless. Also my love and gratitude to Olive and Pete Peterson. Their biased but fresh comments nudged me back on course from time to time. To Elaine Harrison and Bob Rodman, my very special flying friends, thanks for taking the time to read and comment on my early efforts. To Laura Evans, tentmate, soulmate, and inspiration; she has been with me over the long haul, and knows from experience the trials of writing a book. I am grateful for her empathy and friendship. A warm thanks to Kathy Weymouth without whom I would never have had the pleasure of meeting the wonderful Weymouth family. Her kindness has touched me deeply.

Since 1976, when I first began to research my family's history, a number of people contributed their knowledge through interviews and letters. Their decisive quotes have enriched the narrative. Others associated with my family over the years have opened doors and their hearts to my ambitious undertaking. I am indebted to them for their willingness to share: Janet Baldwin, George G. Barnard, Sheldon Bart, Nancy Bignell, Jerry Coe, Allen Dennison, Jim and Joan Dunrud, Tom duPont, Frank Fee, Patti Hobbs, Mr. and

Mrs. Clyde Holley, Jerome Lawrence, Robert Lee, Anne M. Lindbergh, Charles S. Lovell, Mary S. Lovell, Barbara McCallister, Muriel E. Morrissey, Claudia M. Oaks, Whitney O'Keeffe, Eric Paisley, Charles Palmer, John A. Pope, Patsy Raudenbush, George Rieveschl, Jr., Lee Rodgers, Arthur O. Sulzberger, Jr., Louise M. Thaden, Bradford Washburn, Theodore M. Wassmer, Fay Gillis Wells, and Joan and Dean Young.

Closer to home, my thanks to Sherlock and to my assistant, Lyn Lane, who cheerfully took the many handwritten drafts and made them a home inside my computer. In addition, at Immokolee there are two special people whose responsibilities have quadrupled in order to take up my slack; Ralph and Mary Jane Paul. In the midst of chaos, they made peace and comfort. I am grateful for their tireless help and devotion.

My extended Putnam family blessed me with information. To my brothers, David (the real writer in the family) and Doug Putnam, and to my sister-in-law Jan, they all know the story too well. Doug's clippings, letters, photos, and more recently, diaries, are a golden thread that bind this book. Sadly, Mom and Dad are not here to read this labor of love, but their lifetime of patience and guidance share in the birth of *Whistled Like a Bird*. Nor is my sister, Binney, here today, but her unsurpassed encouragement became the foundation from which my story grew. Thank you for the little silver fish, Binney. To Nilla Childs, Jane Portman, Dolly Dudley, and Sally Thompson, Binney's darling daughters, my love and respect.

To Uncle George and Marie Putnam, their incomparable firsthand recollections helped me paint an accurate portrait: my sincere gratitude. To Cynthia Putnam Trefelner, my appreciation for sharing the missing pieces of our grandmother's life and the collection of family photographs. Her encouragement and Immokolee's first gift of daisies will long be remembered. To my cousin and dear friend Tad

Girdler, it was like old times again, thank you for the memories.

And last but not least, I owe my deepest gratitude to Margaret "Peg" Lewis, my grandfather George Palmer Putnam's widow. Her tireless energy and dedication to my story plus her sharp memory and wealth of facts became mine for the asking. From the bottom of my heart, Peg, I thank you. This book could not have been written without her undying assistance.

I feel as though I have been seeking answers forever. During the long journey, I have been supported by my family. Most of the time my dedication to *Whistled Like a Bird* has left little of me to give back to them. Their patience and never-ending love forgave my long absences and enabled me to complete this book. John and Alex; David, Phoebe, Alexa, and Christina; Steve, Liz, Steven, William, and Maggie: I love you all.

Lastly, to my partner and husband, Jack. For years he watched me curled with Dofry's diaries, sometimes laughing, other times making notes; and many times he left me alone to cry, but he was always there. For two years Jack was "Mr. Mom," and rarely enjoyed a homecooked meal. He held our family together and became my secretary and chauffeur. In all honesty, *Whistled Like a Bird* could not have flown without him.

—Sally Putnam Chapman

CONTENTS

PART THREE
1928–1929

PART FOUR
1930–1982

INTRODUCTION

I have waited twenty years to write this story.

My grandmother Dorothy Binney Putnam's life had always seemed so ideal, without pain or hardship—I thought.

All of that changed, however, when—at the age of eighty-two—she entrusted me with her private diaries, ten 3 by 5 leather-bound books, spanning the years 1907–61. "These are for you, Sally," she told me. "You have always wanted the family history, and my place in it. I believe you are ready for them, dear." Fighting back a rush of tears, I lowered my head and felt her hand against my face. "Yes, dear, you may use these diaries in your book." The yellowed pages revealed a strong, cursive script, even though the indigo ink was often smudged, bleeding through to the other side. Amid her words, I discovered four-leaf clovers, notes, and faded photographs. It was a treasure trove of intimate memories and observations, which has become the heartbeat of *Whistled Like a Bird*. Excerpts from the diaries appear in italics throughout the text.

Simply put, she was the most remarkable person I have ever known.

The journals—complete with her own secret codes, which I later deciphered—began while she was a college student and detailed her private reflections, including the time of her highly visible marriage to America's most powerful publisher, George Palmer Putnam; her friendship with the world's most celebrated heroine, Amelia Mary Earhart; and her passionate love affair with a younger man, which ultimately gave her the strength to end her troubled sixteen-year marriage. In questioning her marital commitment, she wrote: *"Love—Why is it there are so many men who consider love outside the bonds of matrimony the privilege of the male only? There are so many."* However, while the world was aware of George and Amelia, my grandmother led a deeply private life.

Her thoughts remained within her heart and her diary. Few outsiders realized that in the midst of the record-breaking events achieved by Amelia Earhart, there had developed a poignant love story between Dorothy and George Weymouth, a student at Yale University who was nineteen years younger.

At the same time, Amelia Earhart and my grandfather George Putnam had fallen in love, and "Dofry"—the nickname we called our grandmother—chose not to fight for her husband.

Years before Dofry was willing to share the truth with the world, she wrote a brief note to me, saying: "I refused to be the workhorse in the background any longer, and besides, there was another woman in the background. A.E."

Dofry was a sensuous woman, and I remember her eyes as blue and clear as a hot Florida sky. Her figure was statuesque, her stately stride bold. But it was her words that pulled you in like a warm embrace. She had the same seductive effect on men and women alike.

She married four times and was fearless in her pursuit of passion, yet surprisingly insecure.

Fortunately for Dofry, she was a woman of means. Her father had invented the Crayola crayon, so she was not dependent on any man for her own financial security or identity.

In releasing George Putnam to Amelia Earhart, my grandmother embarked on her own flight to freedom. And while the world was showering the boyish-looking aviatrix with fame, my grandmother was equally heroic for the times. What I had never known about Dofry growing up was her fierce struggle for independence. Her pursuit of fulfillment was a risky endeavor in its own way, and an uncelebrated flight from the home-and-garden security she had treasured.

As a child, I was fascinated by Amelia and her relationship with our family. She had given my father his first flying lessons and the image of Amelia the aviator was etched in my girlhood vision. I was a freckle-faced, towheaded tomboy who climbed trees rather than practiced the piano. Small wonder—it was the famous flyer who was my idol.

Toward the end of the war, I recall my dad buzzing our house in a B-25 bomber, waving his wings. When I reached sixteen and learned to fly, I did the same thing to him, in a small yellow Piper Cub. My flying career ended, however, when I left home for college. Before long, marriage and family replaced my wild lust for the sky. Yet still today the mystery of flight causes me to look up at the sound of a plane.

Although "Grandpa George" is portrayed by biographers as a dour, insensitive promoter, interested only in pursuing his career, I remember him as a magical storyteller, who fished with me on the Indian River and climbed to the top of my rickety treehouse. He died when I was thirteen, so I was too young to know of his feelings for my grandmother. But I know now, from reading her private diaries, how deeply he loved her and how wrenching their divorce was, despite the public perception that Amelia Earhart had stolen him away from her. This was simply not the truth. In fact, quite the opposite; Amelia gave Dofry the excuse she needed.

I decided to write this book when my grandmother was still alive. Many years before her death, we spoke openly about my intentions. We talked for hours on the open loggia, she in her hammock and I seated on a blue wooden stool. I marveled at her willingness to respond, the directness in her eyes when my questions strayed into painful territories. To Dofry, I had finally come of age and was a companion more than a granddaughter. To her, I was a woman who could empathize with her past.

It wasn't until my husband, Jack, and I bought and renovated her historic Florida home, Immokolee, that *Whistled Like a Bird* began to unfold. I can feel her presence within these walls. By entrusting me with her diaries, there was an implicit understanding that her story would be told; and as the house came to life again, so did my grandparents and their dazzling array of friends and lovers.

Amelia may have inspired my dreams as a child, but it was my grandmother who led me back as an adult to Immokolee, "my home place."

—Sally Putnam Chapman

"No bird soars too high, if he soars with his own wings."
—WILLIAM BLAKE

PART ONE

1888-1927

Life.
— And so, on with the
voyage of our lives,
a voyage that we
make in general by
dead reckoning,
for we have scant
time to take an
altitude — — — — ..

Life.
And so, on with the voyage of our lives, a voyage
that we make in general by dead reckoning, for we
have scant time to take an altitude. . . .

D.B.P.

1

FRIENDS

I OFTEN DREAM I AM FLYING.

My grandmother must have felt she was dreaming that hot August day in 1928 when, seated behind her close friend Amelia Earhart, she rose up from the ground at Bowman Field on the wings of a small Avro Avian airplane. In one way, the two adventurers had much in common. In another, they were light-years apart. I love the one photo taken just minutes before they took to the sky, my grandmother standing confidently next to the silver biplane. She was a beautiful woman, tall and slim. On that day she was relaxed and radiant, her face lit up with the thrill of the impending flight.

Amelia was wearing goggles, as she peered down from the open cockpit. A silk scarf circled her long neck. A waif of a woman, both boyish and feminine, she was proudly waiting to share her skills with the elegant Dorothy Binney Putnam.

I can imagine the deafening roar of the plane's engine; the sensation of being pulled from the seat with each banking turn. My grandmother must have clutched the sides in anticipation, but she was a fearless woman, and like Amelia, addicted to risk.

They had met two months earlier when my grandfather George Palmer Putnam asked my grandmother to join him in Boston to await the departure of Amelia's historic flight in the *Friendship* across the Atlantic. The thirty-one-year-old flyer had soared into worldwide fame by becoming the first woman to fly the Atlantic on June 18, 1928. During the following six weeks she was a house guest at the Putnam home in Rye, where she was to write a book about her daring exploit. The first typed draft was finished just the night before her morning flight with my grandmother, making their joint airborne adventure a special celebration.

Speeding toward the airfield down an almost deserted road, they could taste the salty air wafting in from Long Island Sound. Dorothy had put the top down on her new yellow roadster before leaving home. She had been driving her own car for years, almost always a convertible, and loved the feeling of power and freedom, for she lived in a time when well-bred young women were afforded few outlets for such pleasure.

The pair of tousle-haired dreamers racing toward excitement were lively portraits of Americana. Dorothy, at the age of forty, was five foot ten, blessed with a strong, athletic figure and intelligent blue eyes. Amelia, at five nine, was more willowy. Both had cropped hair, as was the latest fashion, and were fond of loose-fitting, flowing drop-waist dresses and cloche hats.

These spirited young women were living proof of the thrill-seeking 1920s. Dorothy had flown many times before, but this would be the first time she had flown in Amelia's Avro Avian. However, that was not the only thing on her mind this glorious day.

Her high-profile marriage was beginning to unravel.

As far as she was concerned, it was hardly a passionate union, and over the past few years she and George Putnam had inexplicably drifted in opposite directions. *"Oh, for years, it's been so antagonistic. I can't imagine looking at him with longing or desire. And yet I am passionate and demonstrative. Why, oh why should I want another's touch and embrace!"*

George Palmer Putnam—of G. P. Putnam's Sons publishing house—was acting as agent and publisher for the young flying celebrity. Dorothy sensed that George had fallen for Amelia's youthful charm and carefree good looks, a suspicion that raised a mixture of jealousy and relief. For she herself had fallen passionately in love with her son's tutor over a year ago. She and the younger man had been able to keep the affair secret, but the strain of leading a double life was beginning to wear on her.

On this day, the exhilaration of flight masked any uncertainty she felt about her future. The flight at dawn was a memorable occasion. Riding in the open cockpit with the sun's first rays warming her face, Dorothy wore a windblown grin. Peering down through airtight goggles, the two flyers studied the patchwork of farms and pastures below, passing directly over the rooftop and gardens of Dorothy's Rye home, the very house where only an hour before they had shared a cup of hot chocolate.

Dorothy describes the scene in her private diary:

AUGUST 17, 1928 *Took my first flight in a small plane in Amelia's "Avro Avian" her English Moth plane which Lady Heath flew from South Africa to London. A small silver darning needle, with a glinting blue back. G.P. and A.E. off canoeing for hours after their time at field. I met Larry G.* [Gould, noted geologist and family friend] *and went to beach for a swim, tea, etc. In p.m. after dinner, Larry read Amelia's manuscript in studio while I played the piano. She's practically done a whole book in one month—with Fitz* [Fitzhugh Green, writer and assistant to George] *and G.P. helping.*

After landing, Dorothy and Amelia drove back to Rye, their silk scarves streaming in the wind. Amelia left the house with George to go canoeing and to discuss the finished manuscript, while Dorothy took her younger son,

George Junior ("Junie"), to the beach for a picnic and an afternoon swim. They all met again later in the day and continued to discuss Amelia's book.

George Putnam was an exacting publisher, not satisfied with simply printing and releasing a book, and his name had become synonymous with marketing genius. Only months before, he had published Lindbergh's *We*. The book sold over 600,000 copies and helped the lanky, handsome pilot become financially successful. George was hoping to repeat Lindy's literary success with Amelia's story.

That evening, Dorothy was exhausted, but she spent an hour at the piano playing the latest show tunes for the usual group of writers and artists who congregated at the publisher's home. Finally, she left her music and wandered off to bed. An hour later, Amelia made her way to Dorothy's bedroom.

"Dottie," Amelia whispered. *"I want to dedicate my book to you."*

My grandmother was half asleep and unable to show her surprise or gratitude, but months later, she recorded the scene in her diary and wondered if there might have been an underlying reason, other than friendship, for such a gesture:

> *"I'd like to dedicate my book to you, Dottie, if you think it's good enough, and if you don't, I won't. But I'd like to." This was a surprise, does she really want to? Or was it a sop to me because she monopolized George all summer? She's deep and silent, one phase of her life all hidden.*

Dorothy lay awake for hours after Amelia left the room. It was an odd expression of insecurity on her friend's part. She worried in the dark, wondering about the relationship between Amelia and her husband. She had begun to question whether it was entirely professional. George had a reputation for turning explorers into writers and becoming intimately involved in their lives, and Amelia was no exception.

Still, Dorothy and Amelia had formed their own bond, and my grandmother enjoyed the companionship of this celebrated young pioneer who almost overnight had become the most famous woman in the world. Both women considered themselves feminists and welcomed the chance to engage in spirited debates: about the future of women in business, politics, and especially aviation.

They had shared many experiences such as that morning's flight and were equally independent and strong-willed. Dorothy, more socially adept than Amelia, had become a mentor of sorts, and they often shopped together in nearby Stamford, with Mrs. Putnam assisting Amelia in selecting a wardrobe for her endless speaking engagements. Self-assured and self-sufficient, Dorothy was everything Amelia had aspired to.

Amelia, on the other hand, had something Dorothy envied: Independence. Amelia's image as the modern woman forced Dorothy to reassess her own unacclaimed life.

AUGUST 1, 1928 *The days seem to flit by without my accomplishing anything! No practicing, no books to speak of— nothing. Am I ambitionless? Lazy?—a "waster"? Inwardly I wish to accomplish much or at least contribute something of* me *to what others do!—to help. Yet days pass and I seem idle, ineffective, almost useless.*

Dorothy was the product of two strong-minded parents. Her mother, Mrs. Alice Binney, the daughter of Mr. and Mrs. William H. Stead, was born in London on July 8, 1866. Highly cultivated in the arts, Alice had benefited from a traditional English education and was a college graduate, an unusual accomplishment for a woman at the time.

Dorothy's father, Edwin Binney, was born in Scrub Oak, New York, on November 24, 1866, to Joseph Walker Binney and Annie Elizabeth Conklin Binney. Though Edwin's formal schooling ended with high school, he was brilliantly inventive. At the age of fifteen, he was hired as a bookkeeper for his father's company, the Peekskill Chemical Works; and at seventeen he joined a paint concern in Springfield, Massachusetts, as a traveling salesman. When Edwin turned nineteen, his father retired, handing over the company to his son. Shortly thereafter, Edwin and his cousin Harold Smith changed the name to Binney & Smith. The new firm specialized in carbon black made from natural gas. Edwin was instrumental in organizing the Columbian Carbon Company, a firm that later became the largest producer of natural gas in the world. At this point, the family had modest means.

Shortly after Dorothy's birth on July 20, 1888, the Binneys moved to the country, some fifty miles from New York City. They discovered a beautiful stretch of rocky beach on Long Island Sound, in Sound Beach (later renamed Old Greenwich), Connecticut. The land they purchased had been farmland and people could not understand why anyone would want to establish a residence in such a desolate part of the country, or as close to the shore as they had chosen. At that time, the family could only afford to build a one-room house, but with the clever use of an extended curtain, one room became two. The square, peaked-roof cottage was surrounded by pastures, punctuated by stone walls to scramble across before reaching the water's edge. There were apple orchards nearby and lush hillsides leading to the secret hollows of Laddin's Rock Farm.

In 1890, after the birth of a second daughter, Helen, they hoisted the building up on rollers and moved it closer to the massive gray rocks that jutted out of the Sound. With the birth of their third daughter, Mary, in 1892, a two-story wing was added. Over the years, the family home (Rocklyn) expanded into an impressive vine-covered estate. A conspicuous lighthouse, about a mile out from the beach, would become the famous turnaround point for Dorothy, who as a youngster swam out and back effortlessly. The seaside was a private playground for all the Binney children, and diving into its chilly waters was as comfortable to them as the sandy beaches were to their Florida cousins who often came to visit.

When the fourth and last child of the family, Edwin Binney, Jr. ("June"), was born in 1899, Dorothy finally welcomed the baby brother she had always wanted. Eleven years apart, June and his oldest sister, Dolly, shared many childhood adventures together.

Dorothy's parents took opposite sides on the subject of child rearing. Edwin raised Dorothy and her sisters with the belief that nothing they desired was beyond their reach. In contrast, her mother was more demanding and more critical. I remember as a young girl my grandmother's lingering sadness as she recalled her mother's heartless remark, "Dolly, dear, because you are not a particularly pretty child, you must strive harder than most to accomplish something with your life. For girls without beauty must rely on assets other than a pretty face in order to make their way in the world."

Though my grandmother blossomed into a beautiful woman, she was burdened by this early insecurity and would spend her life struggling to overcome her lack of self-esteem.

Closely supervised by their mother, Dorothy and her two sisters spent their first three years in a private one-room schoolhouse near Rocklyn. On many mornings, before the school bell rang, the girls walked two miles to the train with their father and then back again. My grandmother's earliest brush with nature began there, as she listened to her father identifying the birdsongs they heard along the way.

In 1903, Edwin Binney invented what would eventually

become one of the most recognizable products of American ingenuity: the Crayola crayon. Little known to historians, it was his wife, Alice, who thought of the name for the now-legendary coloring sticks. As a schoolteacher, she had a trusted sense of what would excite and stimulate a child's imagination. Binney & Smith had already developed black crayon markers from carbon black when Alice asked her husband to create them in colors.

One evening at the dinner table Edwin announced that he had developed the oil markers for her. She suggested combining the French word *craie*, for "chalk," and *ola*, from the Latin root for "oil." The family company first marketed its crayons at five cents a box, which included eight sticks of brilliant colors. They were produced in a small stone mill; at night, workers carried them to private homes, where they were labeled by hand. (The employees referred to the different homes by color: Blue crayons were labeled in what was known as "the blue house," reds in "the red house," and so on.)

The Binneys were now quite financially prosperous. In the ninth grade, Dorothy transferred to the Catherine Aiken School in Stamford, Connecticut, where she graduated in 1906 with honors. She entered Wellesley College, on the outskirts of Boston, and proved exceptionally skilled in music, theater, and swimming, which immediately set her apart from most of the other girls. She said later she chose the college because it was the only one with a women's crew team. Her college diaries reflect an exuberant person armed with a wide range of athletic and scholastic achievements. *"First crew practice. Oh, my shoulders ache!"* At the same time, she was never at a loss for male or female companionship. *"No social meeting last night; walked. Basketball. Kate and I maids at a man party of 18 down at Shakespeare House. Fussed to death! Prize to man who could make us smile!"* Over the course of four years, Dorothy exhibited the joys and concerns of every student away from home. *"Glee Club and it was simply splendid. College Hall never looked more attractive than with myriads of men floating about."*

My grandmother's earliest diaries exude a passionate love affair with the outdoors, and with birds in particular. *"Interesting lecture on birds in Zoology this morning. Math, German, English. Gym. Fudge. Worked. Bed early."* She never ceased to appreciate wildlife, and later taught me to recognize the songs of birds before I had learned to identify them by sight. *"Saw some new birds today—the oriole, among others."*

Binney vacations were spent at home, or in Carthage, North Carolina, where the family owned a pre–Civil War plantation, Binneywood. The children also traveled to Paris and London to visit relatives. From the time Dorothy learned to walk, her father Edwin (or "Bub," as he was known to his children) had taken her along on camping trips. He passed on his skills of setting up camp, and the art of both salt- and freshwater fishing. "With us," Dorothy recalled, "there was no generation gap. He taught me to fish when I was two; when I was four, he said I was old enough to bait my own hook, and when I was six, he said, 'You're old enough to take the fish off the hook by yourself.' "

Bub's gentle guidance gave his daughter an unusual confidence in the wild. From the family's backwoods North Carolina retreat over the Christmas holidays in 1908, Dorothy pursued a typical, lively swirl of winter activities: " *'Binneywood,' N.C.—Up at dawn to go wild turkey hunting. Home at nine, then chopped trees, then quail hunting—good luck. Made fudge and sipped chocolate by fire."* And on another winter day: *"A bully long horseback ride. Dressed in p.m. Roasted peanuts. Mother read Kipling aloud to us. Made hot drink, roughhoused."*

During her four years at Wellesley, she was also known as an overachiever. *"This afternoon I tried out for the part of Demetrius in the Shakespeare Society June play. In p.m. the Glee and Mandolin Clubs gave a concert at 'Denison House' in town."* The Boston settlement house would reappear twenty years later in an ironic coincidence. It was where Amelia Earhart was working as a teacher when she was asked to fly across the Atlantic. The day after Dorothy's visit to Denison House, she continued to anguish over the underprivileged children: *"Have not yet got over my heartache from seeing those poor little street waifs last night. A Springy day, early flowers and a robin! Tried again for my part."*

At the end of my grandmother's sophomore year in 1908, she and several friends from college traveled across the country by train to join a Sierra Club outing for a two-month camping trip. *"Left Boston, 10:30 a.m. for trip West. Russian nobleman and a lot of fellows on the car."* The goal was to climb to the summit of Mount Whitney, the highest peak in the continental United States at 14,495 feet. *"The mountains and oh, how wonderful, the deep canyons and gorges, high snowy peaks and big trees. Hot at Sacramento. Arrived on time."*

George Palmer Putnam had joined the Sierra Club outing as one of several guides for Dorothy's group. He was an impressive figure, dark-haired and ruggedly handsome. He also was a young man with aspirations. At twenty-one he was already working in San Francisco as a writer and reporter, having moved to the West after completing a year at Harvard. He later transferred to the University of California at Berkeley, but stayed only one term.

Given all that is known and has been written about my grandfather, it is not surprising that the young George Putnam was in a place where few of his college contemporaries in the East would have ventured. He was born in Rye, New York, on September 7, 1887, to one of the great publishing dynasties of America. His parents, John Bishop and Frances Faulkner Putnam, created an intellectual atmosphere, and exposed their son to a rich and literate boyhood. George's pure pleasure in the woods and open air are reflected in the colorful tales described within the pages of his own books. A voracious reader and a shy student at the Gunnery School, George viewed himself as nonathletic, and later recalled: "Most of my small activities, I realize in retrospect, were lonely."

Though he was guaranteed a career in publishing, he had a restless soul. At the tender age of eleven, as the Spanish-American War was brewing, George was looking for a way to help raise money for the Red Cross. He later recalled the episode:

> Being then all of eleven years old, and son and grandson of a publisher, it seemed high time I published something. Which I told father. "A book?" he asked discreetly. I had not thought of that. "No. A newspaper." Father said we would discuss it after dinner. We did. The upshot, creation of labors during the months that followed, was *The Will O' the Wisp*, a paper "published semi-occasionally," its slogan said. The little paper was a financial and possibly a literary success. Under the circumstances the trades-people took advertising space, although the butcher with whom Mother did not deal would have none of it, with a profanity which in retrospect compels me to admit was justified. I delivered a net profit of eighty-six dollars to the Red Cross. And my name had been on an editorial masthead.

It's no wonder the Wild West of stagecoaches and frontier towns seduced him as a young man. As he explained in his autobiography, *Wide Margins*, academia could not satisfy his aspirations: "Following the Berkeley college term I set out to seek my fortune. Exactly that. There I was, an easterner in the far reaches of the roaring west. I wanted to hear it roar." An expert outdoorsman and fly fisherman, George had struck out on his own and was the perfect choice to be a Sierra Club guide.

Shortly after the trip began, Dorothy and George became inseparable. On July 1, 1908, she writes: *"Up at 3 a.m.—35 mile stage ride, 8 mile walk. Putnam with me most of the time—I like him!"*

And on July 7: *"Made my 'bed' in early a.m. Then all after-noon fishing upstream with George Putnam. Caught a trout 2-3/8 lb., the record. Our own little campfire in the evening."* Breakfast was served at sunrise, followed by a bathe in the nearest stream before the group headed off for the great Mount Whitney.

One morning, several newcomers joined the group, among them the legendary John Muir. The indefatigable naturalist and walker of the wild woods had become a one-man force determined to preserve America's wilderness. Muir was largely responsible for the establishment of the Sequoia and Yosemite National Parks, and was the founder of the Sierra Club. He was a leathery seventy-year-old when he joined my grandmother's group. In a letter she wrote to me sixty years later, Dofry recalled her encounter with the great spokesman:

> John Muir the great explorer, naturalist, joined us (on donkey-back, with Chinese boy on foot). Because I was (probably) the youngest member in the big Sierra Club group (19 yrs), Muir took a "shine" to me, and always along the trail (if he saw me) he urged me to stop "to have a cup of tea with him." And the Chinese boy would brew it on a little fire (two tin cups). Stupid me, though I didn't realize till years later what a *marvelous* experience it was for me just to have *John Muir* urge me to "visit" with him.

Approaching the initial stage of their climb, Dorothy was stunned to learn that a girl in another group had fallen to her death. She decided to make the ascent anyway. Wearing a long skirt and petticoat, with boots laced to the knee, she staggered breathless to the summit with her new beau, George Palmer Putnam. *"Started ascent of Whitney—U.S.'s highest mountain—by moonlight. Reached top at 9 a.m.— lunched there. Glorious view over Owens Valley."* In a letter to me, she recorded the difficulties encountered during her final ascent:

The Whitney Trip; bled at the nose at 10,000 feet, staggered and couldn't breathe, etc. It *shook* me a bit, yet I continued with 4 men, the only ones of a big mountain crowd who'd been approaching, mile by mile, entirely on foot for over three weeks! Enough. It was a staggering and frightening event, adventure. Plenty.

On July 20, 1908, Dorothy had much to celebrate, including her twentieth birthday: *"Twenty years old today and oh, such a day. Fourteen of us had lunch down on an island in the Kern Valley. There were gifts and cakes. Ladies night at campfire."* And the following day: *"Fished down river with* George Putnam. *Bully trout lunch on a pine isle. Arrived late at Coyote Creek where ten of us camped overnight. Two rattlesnakes."*

Returning home to Connecticut for the rest of the summer, she boasted to her family and friends about the "swell fella" she had met. Coincidentally, she had learned that the Putnam home in Rye, New York, was a few miles from where she had been raised. But George was bent on a life in California and Dorothy was still two years shy of graduation. Young Putnam managed to court his new lady friend by returning east whenever he could, and during the Christmas holidays he joined the family at their North Carolina retreat. George was a skilled marksman, which impressed Dorothy. *"Up at dawn. George and me for 'blind' in Cocklebends Marsh. Shot my first duck, a redhead! After lunch over to ocean with George all afternoon. . . ."*

Returning to college, Dorothy continued to date other men while faithfully corresponding with George. *"Letters almost every day from G.P.P. History for quiz, a whopper."* Almost as frequent as his letters were the red roses delivered to her dormitory. *"My picture in Boston paper, as 'Star in Wellesley Jr. Play.' Exciting day, everyone congratulating me. Flowers and letter from G.P. . . ."*

A high profile on campus prompted a glowing article in her hometown newspaper. "Miss Dorothy Binney, of Sound

Beach, Excels in Swimming, as Vocalist and Has Histrionic Ability":

> Miss Binney is a versatile girl. She excels in outdoor sports, is accomplished in music and the more homely arts. Among the treasures she carried to Wellesley with her were medals won during the summer in swimming races at the water sports of the Stamford Yacht Club and the Riverside Yacht Club. She rows admirably, plays basketball well enough to be twice center on the college team, holds her own at tennis and golf and drives and rides skillfully.
>
> She has taken up music seriously and her strong contralto voice is heard frequently in solo parts in the college chapel. She was elected leader of the Glee Club for the year 1909–1910. Last season she was a great success as John Hale in the dramatization of "The Trail of the Lonesome Pine" made by members of the junior class. In the annual Shakespearian production of commencement week last June Miss Binney appeared as Ferdinand in "The Tempest."

Dorothy pushed her body to greater extremes and adopted an almost masculine sense for competition. *"In p.m. won cup first prize in Ladies 50 yd. Dash at Rye Yacht Club after cheering of a big crowd. Yesterday rescued a drowning man—stranger."* Music had become her soul's companion and she had an extraordinary talent for whistling while she played piano. Not only could she whistle the latest show tunes, but Dorothy possessed an unusual gift: People remarked that she whistled like a bird. She was not shy about it, often drawing stares when she could be heard across campus whistling the precise notes of her favorite songbirds. *"Glorious warm day to make anyone happy! Saw 2 orioles and a grosbeak on the hill behind the house. A Whistling Quartet."* She had also developed an early fascination with airplanes: already flying meant freedom and escape. *"Off to aviation meet. Had a splendid day—saw 2 Wright biplanes go 1,500 feet up and Latham in his monoplane."* In my grandmother's scrapbook, there is a photograph of Orville Wright flying overhead in his simple, almost toylike airplane, the *Flyer*.

Yet despite all her activities, personal relationships were very much on her mind. In 1909, during Dorothy's junior year in college, her younger sister Helen married Allan Kitchel. For several months after her sister's marriage, Dorothy pondered her own future, and painfully described her deepest insecurity. *"I wish someone would love me."*

Dorothy was aware of George's undemonstrative persona, but hoped that with her influence, he would loosen up a bit. There was an element of suitability about George Putnam, and the two families saw their relationship as a convenient social merger. Not surprisingly, the two-year courtship resulted in his proposal of marriage. In truth, George was desperately in love with the accomplished young college student, though she was not a total believer in the engagement. *"A strenuous letter from George, and two apologies in next mail. So, do I love him enough to wear his ring? Oh, heavens. Why this?"* At this early stage in their relationship, my grandmother had already begun to question her love for George. Perhaps her eagerness to leave home was in part responsible for her willingness to marry.

2

A PRELUDE TO DOROTHY

JANUARY 8, 1910 *Chapel. Letters from George and Mother. Senior play trials and with my accustomed nerve I tried leading man! Wrote George I would be <u>engaged</u> to him! Symphony. Mischa Elman played violin.*

JUNE 21, 1910 *Commencement Day! And I'm a "B.A." at last! Class supper at Somerset Hotel. Serenade. Dead tired, bed!*

*D*OROTHY ANNOUNCED HER UPCOMING marriage to her family and friends, and shared one last Christmas holiday with George in North Carolina as Miss Binney: *"George off alone, quiet day in house. Glorious moon. Wrote many letters announcing my engagement. Ahem!"* The following day, she had another bout of uncertainty: *"Feeling bumsky! Discouraged and scared, so stayed at camp. . . ."* Dorothy still could not believe, given her mother's cruel edict and the power it held over her, that she was worthy of becoming anyone's bride, let alone the wife of a famous publishing heir.

On December 21, the young couple made the announcement of their engagement to George's parents. *"Stamford in a.m. to hairdressers. Ahem! After lunch Mr. and Mrs. Putnam called to see their new daughter-in-law elect. Quiet evening. They are extremely cordial."*

For Christmas Eve, the Binneys, their financial and social position much enhanced thanks to the success of Crayola crayons, held a dinner dance in their daughter's honor at Rocklyn: *"Hairdressers. Town with George, to lunch with his nice Dad and brother, Bob at National Arts Club. Theatre, saw 'Concert,' then home and big dance to <u>announce engagement!</u>"* On December 29, 1910, a feature story appeared on the front page of the Stamford newspaper tracing the history of the intrepid romantics:

Cupid Shot Arrows at Mountain Climbers. Result is Engagement of Miss Binney of Sound Beach to Mr. Putnam of Oregon.—Linking as it will two substantial families of social prominence, the announcement is of wide interest. A pretty bit of romance gives an added interest. The engagement is the culmination of a romance that began in 1908 in distant California on the slopes of Mount Whitney, perhaps the loftiest mountain in the United States. Miss Binney and Mr. Putnam first met as members of a mountain climbing party there. While they toiled up the lofty mountain, Cupid was busy.

During the ten-month engagement period, George was living in Bend, Oregon, where he had purchased the weekly newspaper, the *Bend Bulletin*. He was its editor, publisher, and regular columnist on environmental and political issues. Aside from his work, his thoughts were occupied by his bride-to-be. Local residents remember that the "boy" editor kept a life-size photograph of his Mount Whitney girlfriend thumbtacked to the back of his closet door.

His father and his uncle (known as "the Major" of the Putnam clan) had urged him to return to New York and join the family publishing business. But George, somewhat of a rebel, was determined to succeed on his own, and no amount of family pressure could pull him back.

Though Dorothy and her fiancé were miles apart, they managed to design their first house and buy furniture to be shipped out west later by train. The task, however thrilling, left Dorothy rather overwhelmed: *"Shopped, Oh, how I want George to see some of the beautiful rugs and furniture. Wrote long letter to George about our house plans, etc. Plumb scared!"*

While waiting for George to return to New York, Dorothy was becoming better acquainted with his parents: *"I went thro' Knickerbocker Press with Mr. Putnam. Very interesting despite rain, etc."* A lengthy honeymoon was planned—to Central America—and she prepared eagerly for both the trip and her wedding: *"Cut rag carpet strips, etc. Saw Mother, Mary and Helen. Bought material for my wedding dress! Hand embroidered crepe de chine, Japanese. Wrote George, am crazy about him!"*

As the date for the wedding neared and Dorothy's dreams of an independent life came closer to reality, she was clearly now enjoying the prospect of becoming Mrs. George Putnam.

OCTOBER 9, 1911 *George and Helen to city with Mary in auto. Mother to Equal Suffrage Meeting in Rye. Hairdresser. After quiet dinner, Mother, Bub, George and I planned wedding, caterers. Money, etc.*

The ceremony was held on October 26, 1911, at Dorothy's family home in Sound Beach. The elaborate affair was catered by the legendary Delmonico's, with four hundred and fifty guests seated beneath a white canvas tent anchored to the sloping lawn beside Long Island Sound. Dorothy had chosen her youngest sister as maid of honor. *"7:19 p.m. wedding with red-red roses. Mary as Maid of Honor. A clean 'get away.' "*

After the wedding, crates of silver, Dorothy's delicate trousseau, winter clothes, odd pieces of furniture, and the essential grand piano were all packed and loaded onto a train for the cross-country journey to their remote destination in Oregon, a world removed from the elite enclaves of Sound Beach, Connecticut, and Rye, New York.

On November 18, Mr. and Mrs. George Palmer Putnam sailed out of New York Harbor for Panama. The honeymoon to remote villages of Central America would reflect their unconventional lifestyle, and would also launch George's career as an author and newspaper correspondent. Their mutual sense of curiosity was a powerful bond.

My grandmother was as much in her element, embarking on an unfamiliar journey, as her adventurous husband. How ecstatic she must have felt, for at last she was on her own. *"Sailed for Panama. Eight of us to lunch at Flemish Room. Then the ship with many there to say goodbye. Our deck cabin full of fruit and candy and my red roses. Cold and clear."*

The extended honeymoon was an opportunity for George to visit Panama, Costa Rica, and Guatemala, and it provided the material for his first book, *The Southland of North America*. His new wife was an enthusiastic collaborator. She insisted upon reading and typing her husband's daily pages while he studied the Panama Canal project, taking notes and photos. He and Dorothy were shown Panama's dense interior by its president, Don Pablo Arosemena. They met other political leaders on the trip, thanks to George's family connections, for the Putnam name was a passport around the world.

NOVEMBER 18, 1911 *Sat in Cathedral Plaza all a.m. while George had interviews with Arosemena and the leader of the "Outs." Read a book and studied Spanish. Dinner at Club—Bailey, Close and Arosemena. Walk in Plaza.*

DECEMBER 2, 1911 *On tug at 9 a.m. for 22 mile rough voyage to Porto Bello where we rambled thro' old Spanish ruins of forts, cloister, etc.—cemetery. Saw Black Christ in church. At 4 went out in President's coach with Bailey and Arosemena.*

In p.m. a picnic—lovely ride in moonlight to Tobago. Read copy for George.

The unconventional couple celebrated their marriage again in Guatemala by toasting each other from the misty summit of Mount Acatenango. Though the climb represented a physical accomplishment for both, it was also a sentimental reminder of their first days on Mount Whitney. *"Awfully stiff and aching in every joint from that terrific climb down 6,000 feet yesterday. By 12:30 p.m. were again in our saddles on 18 mile ride down to Antigua. A glorious day, with sunlight on orchids and flowers. George rubbed my stiff body, supper, bath, bed."*

In studying my grandmother's diaries, I find there is little mention of intimacies in contrast to the detailed accounts of endless meetings with various dignitaries. In many ways the honeymoon appears to have been more of an extended business trip than a passionate interlude.

On February 25, 1912, the Putnams steamed into San Francisco, boarded a train for Portland, and finally arrived at the western settlement of Bend, Oregon. *"Took 11 a.m. train for home. Delayed two hours landslide. All day sky rather cloudy but glorious country. Bend 10 p.m. 'Pinelyn'! Oh, Oh, our home!"* The newly built brown-shingled bungalow, Pinelyn, was filled with George's friends and neighbors, who had provided an extravagant feast for the exhausted couple's first night in town. The next day came very quickly. *"Up early and plowed right into mountains of crates and furniture. Morris Lara helped all afternoon—with Steinway grand piano! Finally got bed, bath and kitchen rooms habitable then had tea. To dinner at Lara's. Home by 10. Chill."*

Dorothy was never far from her piano, despite the tedious task of unpacking. *"Busy with 'pots and pans' for most of day. Wrote Grandma Faulkner. Played my beautiful grand piano for half an hour."* She quickly established Pinelyn as a social center. Her dinner parties were soon the talk of the small town, where she orchestrated her soirées with musical acts and dancing. In typical Binney fashion, the Putnam parties required costumes and often prepared skits were attached to the invitations. Away from her parents, Dorothy had come into her own. For the time being she was completely fulfilled.

The *Bend Bulletin* was thriving mainly because George Putnam, too, had found his calling. As publisher and editor, he thrust himself into the center of every issue, such as town expansion, county division, irrigation, and the coming of the railroad. Almost overnight he transformed the newspaper into an independent forum for the progressive voices of central Oregon. Even as a young man, he was recognized for his outspoken opinions, and by the end of the couple's first year in Bend he was appointed mayor of the frontier town. (The mayor-elect had fallen from a second-story window to his death, and George was chosen as his replacement by the town's councilmen.)

In *Wide Margins*, George's autobiography, he characteristically downplayed the obstacles he faced in order to bring Bend (a town of six hundred residents) into a post-frontier life of civility:

> The little community, for the moment, was in my lap. I tried to do right by it. A reasonably thorough housecleaning was had. We presented a shining face to the outer world, though perhaps the back of the civic neck hasn't been scrubbed too thoroughly. Mostly, the dubious ladies went, what gambling remained became orderly and unobtrusive. The saloons found wisdom in keeping strict hours and discouraging drunkenness. Rough stuff was frowned upon. Toughs who wanted to fight were beaten up and sent on their way.

Dorothy was deliriously happy. Her husband was a far more tender and affectionate man than she had imagined on the honeymoon. This was clearly one of the happiest cycles of my grandmother's life. Her diary is alive with passion and excitement. And she described her contentment openly in one letter to her mother:

> Dear Mother . . . my mighty big thin husband seems to love me more all the time. As a matter of fact he's much sillier over me now than when we were first married. And does any number of dear thoughtful things for me. . . . Yes, next summer, I hope we can both go unencumbered! Then too, I want you to know him *married*. Oh, Mother, I'm glad he was decent and good always! And each day I am prouder of my own insistence on that matter. To think that *I* mean all to *him*, that he does to *me*. It's truly wonderful, and makes me so happy. He's good to me in every way, too. And indeed it is *he* "who has controlled the situation" thus far, even more than I. Of that, though I've told you before. No, I want a little more play and then my babies. If one comes however, I shan't brood and worry! D.

Dorothy's reputation as a socially prominent young heiress had preceded her to Bend. She was quickly anointed the town's civic and cultural leader, and began raising funds for cancer—an unusual activity for 1912, when the disease was barely known. *"Benefit, Moving Picture show for a ranch woman with cancer."* In a scrapbook photograph she is pictured among a group of volunteers dressed in white uniforms, sewing bandages for Red Cross hospitals.

By now, Oregon was debating whether to give women the vote. Dorothy took it upon herself to champion the fight, recruiting a prominent spokeswoman from the East to make the arduous journey to Bend to speak to the local women. *"Went to train to meet Mrs. Ehrgott, prominent woman suffrage speaker who is to lecture here."* And a day later: *"Another meeting in a.m., the question is a <u>moral</u> one from religious point of view. 18 guests for 'tea' in afternoon to meet Mrs. Ehrgott. Won 'em all over!"*

The two most important men in Dorothy's life, her father and her husband, were both outspoken supporters of women's rights. George's mother in fact was a leading suffragette. The *Rye Chronicle* recalled Frances Putnam's fight for suffrage in 1911: "A branch of the Equal Franchise League embracing the whole town of Rye was formed here with Mrs. John B. Putnam as president." The editor commented somewhat smugly, "Frankly, this paper has not taken the movement seriously yet . . ." He little knew what was to come.

On December 3, 1912, Dorothy claimed the honor of being the second woman to cast her vote in Oregon's historic election. (The wife of the governor had voted first.) A newspaper clipping reported that Dorothy rushed across the continent from Connecticut, where she was visiting her family, to vote in the election. She was equally thrilled by the news that George had been reelected mayor of Bend by such a large margin: *"Election Day! And Oregon Women voted! 360+ votes altogether, at Bend, and 112 were women. George re-elected by big majority!!"*

On the national level, Woodrow Wilson defeated William Howard Taft for the presidency. George was unimpressed. The mayor and publisher of Bend wrote: "National politics is a diversion, a duty, and a nuisance. In its acute form and triple character it is now behind us for another four years. . . ."

The couple's first child was born at their house on May 20, 1913: David Binney Putnam arrived at 1:15 A.M., a strapping nine pounds eight ounces. Attending was Dr. U. C. Coe, the local physician. There was also present a close friend of Dorothy's, who was a concert pianist. Going into labor, Dorothy asked her to play music from Beethoven's "Fifth Symphony" at full volume to drown out her cries. The proud father later noted: "The lad himself was spanked by Doc's huge hand and washed up on the dining table and then, nestled in blankets, set to toast before the open fire."

David would eventually become a constant source of love and support for his mother, who adored him. He was doted on by both parents and never out of their sight. A curly headed, infectiously cheerful infant, he was carried into the mountains on horseback, and it was not unusual to see the Putnams camping and canoeing with their small son tucked beside them.

After their son's birth, a young artist and poet named Donald Blanding arrived at the house bearing a garden shovel filled with freshly uprooted wood violets. He carried them directly to Dorothy's bedside. This talented and eccentric friend, who was working at the local bank, would in later years play an even greater role in her life. *"George had long council meeting so I went to Picture Show with Donald then we talked late in front of open fire till George returned. Read aloud."*

In 1914, George decided not to seek reelection as mayor and instead was tapped by the state governor to be his secretary. *"George in Portland, appointed Secretary to Governor Withycombe!!"* With the latest career change, the three Putnams packed up and moved north to Salem, the state capital.

Reluctant to lose control of the *Bulletin*, George traveled between Bend and Salem, performing both full-time jobs at once. Although he did not particularly covet a spot in state politics, he accepted the appointment enthusiastically, primarily because it had come from a man he considered a political maverick.

For recreation, the Putnams spent their weekends in the backcountry, on horseback camping trips to the upper glades of the Cascade Mountains. As always, Dorothy thrilled at the abundance of bird life: *"Red winged blackbirds, robins, bluebirds and juncos are here for good now."* She continued to swim as she had back home, and impressed even the athletic westerners. News stories summarizing her achievements were pasted in her album full of other Oregon memorabilia:

Mrs. George Palmer Putnam is receiving the congratulations of her friends today over the victory in the 50 yard swimming race at the Women's National Championships meet Saturday night at the Multnomah Athletic Club in Portland. Mrs. Putnam is an unusually fine swimmer and won the race easily, using the Australian crawl, which is one of the most difficult strokes known.

My grandmother was a champion swimmer. Over her lifetime she taught hundreds of children to swim and always rewarded them with prizes. Today, I treasure the small copper trophy for first prize in watersports she won in 1911.

In 1916, a restless and patriotic George Putnam found another opportunity to go where the action was. In his thesis, Jim Crowell described Governor Withycombe as "a man who preached military preparedness, and when the time came during World War I for the state to do its duty, Oregon led the nation with a volunteer enlistment of 92% of its manpower quota."

Sharing the governor's enthusiasm for his country's need for enlistees, George left for Mexico's border that June, as a member of Oregon's National Guard. And in September, just before the troops returned home, an article by G. P. Putnam appeared in the *Bend Bulletin*: "It's a long way from Bend to the Mexican border and a big change from newspapering to packing a rifle in the federalized national guard. . . . We were hurried down here on the jump, our battalion, the Third, going directly across a little valley into Mexico and hear the bugles playing in the quartrell of the Mex garrison."

By the end of the year, George had turned his small weekly newspaper into a daily publication. For this new expansion, he signed a contract with a young man to provide a five hundred–word telegraph pony service. His name was Hugh Baillie, and his agreement with George was the first contract for the United Press. Baillie would eventually become president of U.P.

With a taste of military service under his belt and the threat of war casting uncertainty over the nation, George enlisted in the army. The three Putnams moved to Washington, D.C. He was appointed to the Department of Justice for a year and a half, after which he received his field artillery officer's training at Camp Zachary Taylor, Kentucky. Dorothy was also engaged in wartime employment, as she wrote in a letter to a college friend:

> I found myself president of a group of college women taking the special war course at Mt. Holyoke College. Instead of going to one of the big munition plants (for which I was preparing) I was called to Washington as head of our group there and became Head of the Inspection Division Department of Civilian Workers branch of Ordnance—that title by the way almost made me a divorced woman! But suddenly there was bedlam among my nine hundred girls in Ordnance all crowding to the streets to cheer for Armistice Day.

George had found the time to write his second book, *In the Oregon Country*, filled with glowing descriptions of the state's wild and uncharted interior. This parting gift spoke eloquently for a land with no voice, making his initial decision to go west all the more understandable—"On the river's western flank, between it and the Cascade Range, is a playland of beautiful pine timber, crystal lakes, and mountained meadows, bounded on one hand by snow-capped peaks and on the other by the broad plains that sweep eastward to Idaho."

If his father, John Bishop Putnam, and his brother, Robert, had not recently died, George would have taken his family and returned to Oregon after the war. But at the insistence of his uncle, George Haven Putnam, then president of G. P. Putnam's Sons, George and his family returned to New York in 1919, where he joined the illustrious publishing house, whose authors included Washington Irving, James Fenimore Cooper, Ralph Waldo Emerson, Edgar Allan Poe, Nathaniel Hawthorne, and William Cullen Bryant.

George's first assignment was to travel to Warsaw, Poland, to convince the premier, Ignace Jan Paderewski, that G. P. Putnam's Sons should be chosen to publish his memoirs. Aside from his political career, Paderewski had been widely acclaimed as the world's foremost pianist. This noteworthy talent was particularly appealing to my grandmother. With the Putnams on the go again, her diaries contain cryptic notations reminiscent of their honeymoon. There was the usual assortment of fascinating characters on board the steamer *France*, and once in Paris she took the opportunity to visit the Binney & Smith office.

SEPTEMBER 26, 1919 *Paris. A good long sleep and I woke to "first impressions"—the low buildings of four and five stories and the knee high skirts of women on the streets and oh, the hundreds and hundreds of women in deep mourning! Every man has a service ribbon in his coat lapel and many are decorated with several medals.*

The couple left Paris by train, traveling through Switzerland, Austria, Czechoslovakia, and then into Poland. They finally reached Warsaw. *"Off for Poland thro' <u>Germany</u>. Risky but thrilling. Took a couple of 'snaps.' Thro' a maze of streets to Poliski Consulat. We must first have a letter of recommendation from the police!"* Enduring the often frightening train ride, George wrote of the war atrocities, the teeming hordes of starving families, and of the scorched farmlands. Dorothy was hurriedly typing, trying to keep up with him. At the same time she recorded her own impressions of the battle-scarred countryside.

On October 26, 1919, the Putnams marked their eighth wedding anniversary. Dorothy wrote in her diary that they *"were almost too busy to speak of it!"* Departing for home, the weary couple cleared customs again, and then collapsed in the dark safety of the ship's inner cabin. Often seasick, she was determined to be a part of the assignment. Dorothy's contribution to George's work continued until his stories about Paderewski were published on the front page of the *New York Tribune.*

DECEMBER 5, 1919   *Oh, we'll never get there at this rate! And I'm so impatient. Furious with myself, too, because my tummy is too unreliable to do any typewriting and I do want to help George get his stories ready. Our sixth day and we're still in mid-ocean. Finally—Good luck at typewriting—I finished one of George's four stories.*

Settling down in New York after Poland, Washington, Central America, and eight years in Oregon were two young travelers enriched by worldwide experiences. They had spent their years away from home making their reputations in a high-powered, sophisticated world. They were moving in circles usually reserved for older, more accomplished adults.

I have found little documentation to describe my grandparents' marriage prior to their return to New York. However, based on the collection of letters, my conversations with Dofry, and the memories and impressions my father passed on to me, I suspect that she valued her work as George's assistant far more than she did her dutiful role as his wife.

The couple purchased a comfortable four-bedroom house in the center of town in Rye, New York. The Studio House was a working sanctuary rather than a residence and was only a short distance from the Rye Country Day School, which David attended. In this same home on Orchard Avenue, on May 9, 1921, the Putnams welcomed a second son to the family. George Palmer Putnam, Jr. ("Junie"), became his mother's newest traveling companion. Dorothy's addiction to adventure had been ingrained since childhood, and she had every intention of passing it on to her two sons, even if it meant taking them out of school for extended periods of time.

By 1922, at the age of thirty-five, George had become a visible spokesman for G. P. Putnam's Sons. His regular stories in the New York newspapers about Poland and its famous premier had thrust him into the limelight of the printed world. He had also become involved with several other concerned publishers on the issue of censorship of the press. In an article in *The New York Times* opposing censorship on August 5, 1922, George was quoted as saying:

> "It is my opinion that a supreme authority of censorship for publishers is unworkable, unnecessary and unwise. The publishers are, or at least should be, capable of judging the decency of their own output. The proposition of submitting manuscripts in advance of publication to any committee whose advance OK must be secured is to me preposterous. . . . I'm afraid I agree with Heywood Broun who says that a censor is a man who has read about Joshua and forgotten about Canuete."

With her husband's rise to success, Dorothy realized that he no longer needed her to assist him any more. He had emerged as a noted journalist, his byline appearing regularly in newspapers. Dorothy was relegated to the home, and she was not particularly suited to this new suburban domesticity. She adored Junie and David, her garden, and friends; but it was not enough. Travel would soon become her escape. *"Oh to be transported here and there in the world on the 'magic carpet' of the printed page. The people who travel only thro' books! No, I want to go myself, always."*

With George spending so much time in New York, and on frequent trips to London, Dorothy grew restless and decided to accompany her parents and two sons to Fort Pierce, Florida.

While cruising on the family yacht *Dohema* in 1911, Edwin Binney had been struck by the unpretentious beauty of this sun-washed ocean and river town, and in 1913 he built a clapboard farmhouse, which he called Florindia. Before long, the small fishing and citrus village with a population of four thousand also captivated Dorothy. *"Quite lovely little creeks and bays all thro' the mangrove islets with marine gardens at every turn, corals, sponges, angelfish and other colorful varieties. Lovely trip."*

As a child, chasing my own dreams along the same creeks and mangroves, I never pictured my grandmother as a young woman doing the same thing. In retrospect, I can't imagine a nook or cranny along the Indian River that she did not explore.

By 1924, the Putnams' Studio House was too small for the expanding family. Dorothy and George had begun to reminisce about their days in Bend, when, sitting on the banks of the Deschutes River, they had fantasized about their dream castle. After several months exploring Westchester County's outer woods in search of a site, they discovered and purchased a piece of land just off the Old Boston Post Road in Rye. The rolling fifteen acres were dense with enormous hemlocks and elms and wild dogwoods cascading down the hillside. Taking care not to destroy the deciduous landscape with its massive boulders, Dorothy roped off an oddly shaped piece of ground that lay on the top of the knoll. She then drew an outline of the house to fit into the irregular clearing. Without an architect, she and George finished the plans and selected a building contractor. They didn't expect to begin construction on Rocknoll, as it would be called, until the end of the year, so Dorothy was free to continue traveling.

Her parents had planned a three-month cruise around the world on the steamship *Resolute*, and they invited their daughter to come along. She and George had discussed the idea of her bringing back tiles and silk fabrics from China for their new home, and he hoped that the project would be a stimulating diversion for his wife. As Dorothy herself observed: *"Women grow old prematurely because our badly organized civilization gives them so little to do except talk and dress."* Having lost her role as George's typist and editor, Dorothy was finding fewer ways to share his demanding but exciting career.

The day before sailing, Dorothy met George at his New York office on Forty-fifth Street, where he was directing a myriad of publishing projects. His small desk was covered with papers and books, pens and telephones. Bookcases lined the walls, except for one that held pictures of friends, airplanes, and dogs that George had clipped from various magazines. It was their standard meeting place before dinner and the theater, but George had planned this evening as a special sendoff for his wife. As it happened, the more he talked of business, the more Dorothy withdrew, and what was planned as an evening of celebration became one of hostility. *"Two kinds of people I loathe. Men who see only their business, women who really care terrifically what's being 'done' this year, and who must be invited to so and so's party!"* Years later, as her circle of friends broadened, she would write: *"I find myself differentiating people. The ones I like: The highly decorative male and female. And people with keen tongues and brains, and not ashamed to really use them, with minds and tastes (and bodies!), highly sophisticated."*

Her trip was to provide plenty of touches for their home. The discovery of green Chinese tiles for her entrance hall, ornate Oriental rugs, and silk wall hangings embroidered with multicolored majestic birds, added distinction to the new house in Rye. In Tahiti, the final stop on the way back, Dorothy borrowed an old dugout canoe from a native islander and left the ship alone for ten carefree hours. She preferred to discover local beads or stones rather than cultured pearls for herself, and returned laden down with unusual local wares.

G. P. Putnam's Sons had recently published a book by a noted explorer and naturalist, William ("Will") C. Beebe, entitled *Jungle Days*. George and Will had become friends and were equally supportive of each other's professions. Will valued George's interests in scientific exploration and was aware of his financial assistance to other scientists over the years. Dr. Beebe was preparing a six-month oceanographic expedition for the New York Zoological Society in the spring of 1925. As director of the Department of Tropical Research, he had selected eighteen other scientists to join him on a trip to the Sargasso Sea, and the Cocos and Galapagos Islands in the Pacific.

Just back from her voyage around the world, Dorothy learned of Dr. Beebe's project and asked George if he would speak to his friend about the possibility that she and David could join Beebe's expedition for two months as unpaid assistants aboard the *Arcturus*. They both went. In typical Putnam fashion, twelve-year-old David Binney Putnam wrote his first book, *David Goes Voyaging*, to describe the trip:

> Mr. Beebe lets me call him Uncle Will, even if he is the head of this big expedition. He was awfully nice to let me go on part of it. I had my twelfth birthday on the "Arcturus" down on the equator, and I know how lucky I was to be taken along. It was great fun and I think I learned a lot, though perhaps it will hurt my school work, being away and everything. Anyway, Mother and I joined the Arcturus—Uncle Will's ship—at Pan-

ama. I spent nearly three months in the Pacific Ocean, studying sea life and visiting seven uninhabited desert islands. And I promised Dad to write a little story about it all.

Not since her trip to Poland had Dorothy been so enthralled by a challenging adventure. When the first phase of the scientific project ended, she volunteered to remain for an additional six weeks, despite the fact that she had a husband and four-year-old son at home. Her cable to George, advising him of her decision, elicited a somewhat forlorn and envious response:

Thursday, May 7, 1925

Dearest:

. . . This morning at the office came your cable from Panama. Tonight you are there. Probably having a grand time. Lord, how I wish I were there, too! (Hell, it's disheartening to realize this won't reach you for six weeks or so, anyway, you'll be glad to find accumulated mail when you get back to Panama. And how glad I'll be to have you starting north and home to me! You'll get the most comprehensive loving of your career.)

I never before was quite so lonely. Likely because you are doing things just as I want to do, and love doing. You and I certainly will go next Winter, on a trip together. A grand trip. Then the following summer I want to have that cherished outing out West with Carl Dunrud and David, and I hope you will relent and go, too. . . .

What a house! Hon, it is <u>enormous</u>. I am plumb terror stricken at it. Not costs, they are all right—but size. We should have cut down all around twenty percent. I realize, more and more, that for the rest of my life I will look back at the comparative quiet, and guestlessness of this old house, with occasional yearning. Inevitably, we will have a hotel all the time. That's alright. Only, dear girl, once in a while just pretend you like me better than anyone else, and that you prefer being with me all alone, to being with a giddy crowd. . . . You bet, yes, I urged you to go and you were sportingly willing to exchange places with me. I miss you more than ever.

. . . A little while ago I phoned your mother about your cable an-
nouncing you'd stay another six weeks. She was pretty surprised and
critical. "Can't see how she can do it. Leave you that long. Leave
her new house. Leave the baby. It's not fair." Ho, hum! Lordy, I
miss you.

   Good night, Your lover, George

Twelve-year-old David faithfully jotted down his scribbled anecdotes in the leather notebook supplied by his dad.
Every evening after supper and kitchen duty, he found a
quiet place out of the tropical breezes and recorded his observations, as well as wild tales of pirates and the South Seas.
By the end of the voyage, the nearly shredded, weather-
stained log would be transformed into a neat manuscript for
young readers, and his first published book.

   In Panama, a stack of mail awaited the weary seafarers.
There were cables and letters from George, who realized his
wife was not eager to return home any time soon.

Dearest,

This is Sun. evening, about ten o'clock—just back from supper.
Spent evening with the folks at Sound Beach—out on the sound in
the boat as the full moon rose—fine—but I was pretty low . . . I
want you to come back to love me ridiculously. There's an immense
amount of work that you must do, but that's the small part of it all.
The big job is to fuss over me, get that! I'm just played out playing
solitaire.
Now I'm all in and going to bed, and I need you so much. Look,
Hon, I didn't mean to make this note a wail.
   George

Kiss Dave—his letters to friends of his are treasured. I'm proud of
my boy—and coming up on the steamer, get out all his "book" ma-
terial. He must tutor during the summer!

On July 30, 1925, after ten weeks of travel, Dorothy and
David returned home.

   There was a grand celebration in New York Harbor, as
every ship from garbage scows to ocean liners sounded their

salutes. Dorothy was tanned and thin, appearing weathered by the sun and salt. Wearing her trademark full slacks and scarf fitted like a cap across her forehead, she was greeted by her husband, David's friends, and Junie, who could be seen peering shyly from behind Edwin Binney's trousered leg. Beebe and his group of scientists were jostled by the crowd, and they smiled wearily as photographers' flash bulbs popped.

Before dawn, Dorothy and George lay silent, each waiting for the other to speak. Familiar shadows fell across the room and the curtains pulled to the side made way for a breeze that never came that night. The reunion was hardly what George had envisioned. He felt his wife's cool detachment, and it seemed that the distance between them was greater than ever before.

The return to a home routine was not an easy one. On the voyage, far removed from the reality of familial ties, my grandmother had begun to question her "perfect" marriage. For the rest of her life she spoke proudly of her role as a scientist aboard the *Arcturus*. The expedition had jarred her out of the complacency of her domestic duties. Her new self-confidence had blossomed without George's support. She felt independent, self-sufficient not only physically, but emotionally.

In discovering her own self-worth, Dorothy would no longer be satisfied as Mrs. George Putnam—hostess, wife, and mother—and she could no longer disguise her growing detachment. She was cautious not to move too far emotionally at one time, and therefore, Dorothy used her house and garden as a stabilizing influence. There was a side to her that wanted to take flight, and there was another side of her that wanted to stay grounded in the earth of her house. *"I seem to have reached the exact spot in the general 'spottiness' of life, when I am undecided which road to take!"* At this point, my grandmother was feeling unraveled. This was the beginning of an ambivalence that would take four years to resolve.

3

TROUBLED WATERS

"Marriage is a stupid idea. It seems to me its main purpose is to keep together people who don't love each other. For people who do love each other are going to keep together anyway!"

*D*ESPITE HER CONCERNS, MY GRAND-mother threw herself back into domestic routine. Between July and Christmas of 1925, Rocknoll was nearly complete except for her finishing touches. She found the time to design and plant her new flower garden, arranging favorite springtime colors down the hill beneath an umbrella of green. From a curious child to the woman she had become, Dorothy's need to root in the earth had never died: She belonged outdoors.

She was pleased with her handiwork. The angular house, with jagged stones jutting out from the exterior wall, was impressive. Mammoth gray boulders lay half-covered in the leafy undergrowth, and just beyond the sloping lawn at the creek's edge were the towering clusters of ancient oaks. Viewed from a hillside nearby, the artistry of meandering paths and planned gardens could easily conjure up the deliberate casualness of an English country estate.

On December 24, an article in *Mid-Week Pictorial* glowingly described the interior of the house, accompanied by a portfolio of full-page photographs:

The main part of the rambling low, slate roofed Putnam house, is pink stucco with wings of unusually large native stone. The three interesting guest rooms are on the first floor, but two of them are highly unusual in their decoration. One is an undersea room, its walls representing an under surface sea elevation, gay with tropical fish, corals and seaweeds. It is the work of Donald Blanding of Honolulu. Its twin is a "jungle room" painted by Isabel Cooper, artist of the Beebe scientific expeditions. Its walls picture a vivid jungle scene, with trailing vines and plants and flowers and gay colored birds perched here and there and a huge python winding about the baseboard, partially hidden, fortunately, for "screamish" guests, by the bed.

David decorated his bedroom with nests, arrows, eggs, and snake skins, leaving plenty of room for sporting trophies and ships' lanterns. The surprise he had saved for his grandparents from the *Arcturus* voyage was this dedication: "To Grandma and Grandpa Bub." *David Goes Voyaging* was the title that appeared on the bright yellow cover of his book about his adventures in the South Seas.

While Dorothy was momentarily satisfied with her grand new home, George was busier than ever publishing books, particularly those by explorers. In 1926, he decided to organize an expedition himself. In his own words, "I practiced what I published. It seemed inappropriate to promote books about exploration without doing a bit of exploration myself. So, I did. And, in the natural course of events, from the vicious circle, books resulted. The whole technique just about approximated continuous motion."

His Greenland expedition would head north, skirting the barren shores east of Ellesmere Island in search of Arctic specimens for the Museum of Natural History in New York. The previous winter, George and Captain Bob Bartlett, the famous Arctic skipper from Brigus, Newfoundland, had walked on the Putnam estate discussing the possibility of such an expedition. (Captain Bartlett was in command of the *Roosevelt* in 1909 when Robert Peary reached the North Pole.) The weeks of sorting gear, gathering permits and equipment, refitting the one-hundred-foot *Morrissey*, charting, and weather-watching became the talk of the coastal town. Of course, David would accompany his father.

Shortly before their departure in June 1926, Dorothy and David had a final talk in the leafy woods behind the house. She needed this time alone with her son. In a few days he would sail with his father toward the Arctic Circle. As they talked of the high seas and frigid nights that lay ahead, Dorothy began to weep. Young David was seldom privy to his mother's vulnerable side; he leaned across to comfort her, holding her shaking arm. Her fear of losing him seemed unbearable.

My father vividly remembered that day. His mother normally carried an aura of calm about her, never appearing to worry. It was a hint of the stormy times that lay ahead.

During George and David's absence over the summer of 1926, Dorothy continued to entertain her husband's business associates. The gatherings usually included the most stimulating and celebrated adventurers of the day. On the morning of one such dinner party, an engraved note was delivered from the Putnam offices, listing the invitees. At the bottom of the card she had drawn a table and carefully placed the location of each guest. Dorothy was at the head of the table, and at the opposite end was Admiral Richard E. Byrd, who had just returned from England after successfully flying to the North Pole with his pilot, Floyd Bennett. Mrs. Robert Peary was seated at Admiral Byrd's left. Her son, Robert E. Peary, Jr., was currently the chief engineer aboard the *Morrissey* with George and David.

The Putnams were so well known for entertaining famous adventurers that Will Rogers joked you couldn't snare an invitation unless you had conquered some uncharted territory. "Dorothy's parties were memorable and beautifully done," recalls Nancy Bignell, whose mother was a close friend of the Putnams. "They were not exotic, but suited to the environment. Her table settings were a collection from around the world and the colors represented the colors of various countries. She was an imaginative hostess and insisted that her guests play games she had organized ahead of time. Her large shadow box in the living room would have the latest color-coordinated artistic arrangement. She always entertained with her piano music and sang songs." Adds Bignell, "She had a good voice, a lower-register contralto. She loved popular and romantic songs. Dorothy was a totally romantic woman."

Meanwhile, the Arctic sailing trip concluded without incident, and the *Morrissey* and crew returned with the species they had hoped to find. Two baby polar bears were captured alive and brought back for the Bronx Zoo in New York. Walrus, seal, a large white whale, and the fetus of a narwhal were preserved as specimens for the Museum of Natural History. Standing on the dock as the vessel came into view, Dorothy hoped the exuberant crowd would camouflage her growing despair. At the completion of David's second book, *David Goes to Greenland*, it was no surprise that it was dedicated: "To My Best Friend who really should have gone to Greenland, MOTHER."

The Putnams' Christmas card that year was a line drawing from Greenland at the top of the snow-covered world: George Putnam, with his son David wrapped in seal fur, making tracks across an arching globe. Baby Junie and Mother with a halo placed gently to one side of her head were depicted waiting at home to greet the Arctic travelers:

all greet you:

nagdliugfigssuarsiornekunekarpusigok

which in Eskimo means "Merry Christmas"

1926.

Yet the Christmas was not as merry as the card suggested. Fifteen years before, when my grandparents married, they each believed they had found the perfect mate. Both were young and highly motivated explorers, drawn to lively and intellectual personalities. But Dorothy had entered into marriage out of touch with her full womanly self. Nor had she experienced the whole range of her abilities. How could her husband not have suspected that she was becoming increasingly frustrated? Whatever purpose she had served at the start of their marriage had dramatically changed, and her need for fulfillment would never be satisfied by a mansion and garden as her husband had believed.

By 1927, my grandmother had begun to question whether her marriage could survive.

The Putnams were spending less time together, and Dorothy made no attempt to overcome the estrangement. The struggle to come to terms with her role as George's wife, while clinging to the aspirations she still held, was beginning to consume her. It was only a matter of time before she succumbed to the temptations of a more gratifying existence. The first diary entries for the year provide a window into her growing frustrations, and at times, into the depths of her despair:

JANUARY 3, 1927 *Married Couples—10 hrs. Out of 24—apart 8 hrs. Sleep 6 hrs. In each others company 6 hrs. x 7 days = 42 hour week. Soon we'll see each other by appointment only if this goes on. Well it suits me.*

JANUARY 11, 1927 *Death: These things I invariably thrill over and "sense" completely. Yet before God I am willing to die today—suddenly—"snuffed out"—and "cut off" forever! After a month or two I wonder who would still care!*

Yet Dorothy felt the familiar rush of anticipation as she planned another getaway, this time to South America. Among the many friends stopping by to wish her a safe journey was Annie Laurie Jaques. She had brought her beau, whom she had already written to Dorothy about. George Weymouth was a sophomore at Yale University and had been looking forward to meeting the celebrated Putnams for some time. At six feet, he was handsomely athletic and known affectionately as "King" by his brothers.

Weymouth had been raised in a small Pennsylvania town by loving parents, with four brothers and a sister. During the early twenties, the family had fallen on hard times and had gone from fancy cars and private schools to frugal ways and a public education. His mother had persuaded the headmaster of a private day school to accept her five children on scholarships. They had all been taught to appreciate the advantages of a fine education and strongly believed in the work ethic.

That January morning in 1927, Dorothy sat playing her

piano next to a towering arrangement of dried flowers with her back to the picture window. It must have appeared an illusion, as though she were playing outside on the wintry terrace. She was so engrossed in her music she did not notice the two visitors as they stood in the hall, listening. It was not unusual for her to continue playing if someone entered the room. But by the time she finished and had lowered her hands to her lap, George Weymouth stood motionless, transfixed by her elegant beauty.

A fire was burning. It suited the day that had begun quite innocently, cold and clear. As the two were formally introduced to each other, Dorothy explained that she was preparing for a trip around South America with her six-year-old son, Junie. Weymouth politely apologized for the interruption and walked toward the piano. Dorothy could feel his eyes on her and she flushed.

It was several days before he returned to New Haven, and he did so hoping he would see Dorothy again. They had enjoyed an instant rapport, and he had not felt like a student in the company of a married woman nineteen years his senior.

In a letter George Weymouth wrote many years later, he recalled that first meeting with Dorothy: "GTW is a sophomore at Yale in love with Annie Laurie Jaques from Lake Forest, Illinois. She was a guest of George Palmer Putnam, and wife, Dorothy, in Rye, New York. Two children: David and George, Jr. During the weekend GTW's love switched from Annie Laurie to Dorothy Binney Putnam. . . ."

Dorothy suspected as much.

She was concerned about her own feelings for the young man and whether they were inappropriate. Her passion was evident. *"Imagine in a crowd of rather sophisticated, over-busy, sallowish people—a boy, modest, good looking, well built, impressionable, adoring young barbarian. God, what a relief to jaded feelings."* From their first meeting, the young man occupied a constant place in Dorothy's thoughts and diaries.

Dorothy and George Palmer Putnam when they first met on Mt. Whitney (1908).

Putnam with me most of the time—
I like him!

Fished down river with G.P. Putnam. Bully trout lunch on a pine island.

Pioneer publisher and mayor of Bend, OR, (1912) on back of a stagecoach.

G.P.P., the consummate reporter, onboard the Binney Yacht *Dohema* (1913).

Dorothy and her beloved Steinway piano (1915).

Dorothy and David, age 3, visit Rocklyn (1916).

Dorothy and David (1916).

G.P.P. and George "Junie" Junior (1923).

David and Dorothy "always reading" during 1924 Tetons camping trip.

Dorothy and G.P.P.
on Yellowstone-Tetons
camping trip (1924).

The Temple of Heaven,
Peking, China (1924):
"Dorothy would rather
have discovered local
beads or stones than
cultured pearls about
her neck."

David and Junie in front of Rocknoll (1925).

The Putnams and Binneys sharing a wedding anniversary, October 26, 1925.

G.P.P. in booknook at Rocknoll (1925).

Capt. Bob Bartlett, David, and G.P.P. aboard the *Morrissey* prior to the Greenland expedition of 1926.

David with rabbits aboard the *Morrissey* (1926).

Rocknoll from the bottom of the hillside (1927): *A marvelous day— with a thrush singing in the woods.*

George Weymouth and Dorothy at Rocknoll, May 19, 1927!

Crew of the *Morrissey* with G.P.P. on left, Dorothy on right, and G.W. rear center, before the Baffin Land expedition of 1927.

G.W. on whale
boat prior to
Baffin Land
expedition (1927).

G.W. hanging
from rope on the
Morrissey (1927).

Amelia Earhart on the roof of
a Boston hotel before her
Atlantic flight on the
Friendship (1928).

Dorothy and Junie enroute to
Hawaii (1928).

Amelia wearing the wings
presented to her as honorary
major, 381st Observation
Squadron, U.S. Army Reserve
(1928).

Lou Gordon, Amelia, Wilmer Stultz, (unidentified woman), Ann Bruce, Dorothy, and G.P.P. (1928): *Take off for Boston in a trimotor Ford plane. George and I with Amelia.*

Amelia and Dorothy sign the guest book of G. H. Rand's trimotor Ford, the *Rem-Rand* (1928).

1928: *After dinner Amelia and I drove my new Chrysler '75 (actually, the very first one delivered) to see Sam Chapman at Stamford.*

Junie, David, Dorothy (wearing the fish necklace), Amelia, and Larry Gould at Rocknoll (1928).

Amelia and David at Rocknoll (1928).

Amelia and Junie at Rocknoll (1928).

Mary Binney Davey, Dorothy, Amelia, (Sam Chapman?), G.P.P., and Junie (1928).

David, Amelia, and Dorothy at Manursing Island Club (1928).

August 1928:
*Took my first
flight in a small
plane in
Amelia's "Avro
Avian."*

Amelia, G.P.P.,
and Clarence
Chamberlain at
Rocknoll cookout
(1928).

Dorothy, G.W., and
Amelia at Rocknoll
(1928).

TAT flight arrival in Los Angeles with Amelia, Dorothy, Dan Schaeffer, Betty Brainerd, Anne Lindbergh, and Col. Charles Lindbergh (1929): *10 hours of sheer beauty. Painted desert, sun, parched desert, wind-carved mountains, great rocks and ranges. 8,000 to 11,000 ft elevation.*

Dorothy and Amelia after TAT flight (1929): *Everyone thrilled, and tremendous crowd at arrival, L.A., photos, etc.*

The following week, after an early breakfast with several of George's business associates, Dorothy bundled up for a walk outside. The ground was covered with a blanket of snow—*"A light drift of snowflakes, and everything seems to be whispering."* There were no traces of leaves, but the sloping hill and the giant boulders kept her from view as she wandered out of sight. It was a crystal blue day, with layers of ice wrapping the branches, transparent in the sparkling sun. A spot nearest the creek facing the morning light was the place she loved to visit.

There came a sharp crack from above, as if a branch had been snapped in two. Startled, Dorothy turned around. Following in her footprints, George Weymouth had approached cautiously. They had both anticipated this reunion, and the mutual attraction was impossible to deny.

George had thought of nothing but Dorothy since that day in the house watching her play the piano, and he wasn't certain how she would respond to his returning so soon. At first, like two old friends who had nothing in particular to say, they tried to exchange polite greetings, masking their longing for one another. Later, in the midst of preparing to leave for South America, her diaries exposed her temptation: *"Love—Why is it there are so many men who consider love outside the bonds of matrimony the privilege of the male only? There are so many. And equally wrong are those who believe when you're away from husband you must crave some male indulgence. Rot! Vacation!"* Once again, she would turn to the sea to provide answers to her growing dilemma.

PART TWO

1927-1928

Love should have a
right of way thru the
universe — & never be
belittled or profaned.

We should like both men
& women, discriminatingly
& love very few

Love should have a right-of-way thro' the universe—and never be belittled or profaned. We should <u>like</u> both men & women, discriminatingly & <u>love</u> very few.

D.B.P.

4

THE PUBLISHER'S WIFE

"If a woman takes a lover, I understand it. If she's single. Or if she's married, has abundant vitality and finds her husband immodest, impotent or unsavory. But if she takes a lover lightly, then I loathe her. In other words then she is a light woman and soulless. It can be a marvelous experience, but not that way."

ON JANUARY 29, 1927, AS SHE WAVED good-bye to family and friends, Dorothy was evolving into a different woman. Her moods and her thoughts were consumed by the promise of a new passion. *"Junie and I start on the Laconia for a cruise around the whole of South America. We have a comfortable inside cabin on D deck opposite Frances. Daddy, David, George Chamberlain, to see us off. Wires from George Weymouth and many others."*

At any other time, she would probably have welcomed the escape. Now she must have had second thoughts about leaving home. *"There is no reasoning out people's conduct! For we are like the sea, and our movements are far too complicated to explain, and the depth may bring up God only knows what at any moment. Yet we seem to need that life rhythm."*

From the time she had waved good-bye to her family and

friends, she knew that this trip in particular was more significant than any she had taken before. During the lengthy
cruise, her mood grew more pensive as she examined her
choices, spending hours alone with few distractions. Dorothy realized that the three-month holiday, though filled
with exotic adventure, would not blur her memories nor di-
minish her thoughts of G.W. Her questions about the future
appeared to be growing more serious.

Highlights of the voyage were captured in her daily entries: "*Straits of Magellan. We're going more and more South.
We enter the Straits out of a terrific sea on the west coast. Alba-
trosses flying at the stern, 8 ft. from wing to wing. Junie and I
stay aft to watch them for hours. Mt. Sarmiento in the fog and
snow squalls, glacier flanked.*" But many of Dorothy's diary
entries suggest a restless heart as she questioned herself, and
her future.

Naturally active, Dorothy buried her emotions in ship-
board activities. She was most proud of winning first prize
in the costume competition. She always packed up and
brought along odds and ends from previous trips, clearly
expecting to win first place. This trip was no exception.

MARCH 10, 1927 *So far I have won all the "first prizes"
for costume parties, etc. Head costume. Fancy costume. Original party, etc. It undoubtedly annoys the other women on board
and that's funny. For each time I've been <u>grotesque</u>, ugly, comic;
really disguised!*

Yet there was no permanent relief from her heart. Nearing home, Dorothy stood on the forward deck leaning
against the railing as the flickering lights from shore came
into view. Those foreign ports with their marimba bands,
the verdant jungles and brown faces swathed in Incan colors, were left behind. The ship was silent except for the
swish against the cold gray hull. Junie and his grandmother
Frances wouldn't awaken and prepare to disembark for an-

other five hours, but Dorothy needed those final moments alone before daybreak: *"The sea—and delicious long idle days of watching a far horizon. Without sense of time or the relation of me to the universe. It's almost the unquestioned acceptance of childhood again. I seem to shed my encumbrances and responsibilities too easily."*

Running ahead of his mother on the gangplank across the narrow strip of black water, Junie jumped into the outstretched arms of his excited father. Clutching his son's hand, George dashed to greet his wife, reaching her before she had crossed the rickety walkway. There was the usual flutter of homecoming, and an almost childlike eagerness to share it with loved ones.

APRIL 1, 1927 *Such a delightful homecoming! All my family on the dock to see us. Mother's car waiting. Cold and wintry, but oh so good just to be here. . . . And everything so fresh and spacious and my own! A treat after the small quarters on the ship. And Junie telling everyone about Rio and Peru and llamas, etc. And the piano.*

For the moment, Dorothy was content; and the servants were anxious to have her back again. The estate had been silent too long. Passing through the dining room and into the grand studio where her piano waited, she was pleased by the sight of springtime flowers arranged throughout the house. The familiar faces and sensations gave her a much-needed sense of security. Still, there were nagging thoughts of G.W. She wondered if and when he would come.

Dorothy disappeared upstairs to the privacy of her bedroom. Sitting at the window, noting the forest of tiny spring buds, she thought of the young student. Her restlessness returning, she wandered through the upstairs rooms and out onto the screened loggia. The chatter of conversation rumbled up the back stairwell; she thought she recognized a familiar voice. Treading softly to the stairwell, she leaned over and listened to the group in the kitchen. Her heart jumped. She confirmed that it was George Weymouth, and then tip-toed back to her room. Suddenly, her exhilaration dissipated and insecurities returned. She felt exhausted, anxious about their reunion. She questioned whether she had mis-read his affection for her and whether she was foolish in believing that he cared. Had it been only a slight infatuation on his part?

G.W. and David were talking in the pantry as she came downstairs and pushed the swinging door open from the dining room, trying to act surprised. There in a single glance was her answer. David excitedly regaled his mom with the news of an upcoming trip to Baffin Land, but to Dorothy only one fact registered: Her lover's return was more perma-nent than she dared hope. George Weymouth had been hired by her husband as the ship's third engineer and her son's new tutor on board the *Morrissey*. *"Such a lovely wel-come and it is so nice to be home again. George Weymouth the nice Yale boy is here living in the house, tutoring David and doing a thousand other jobs."*

George Putnam was relieved to have found someone to help his worldly fourteen-year-old with his failing grades. A month earlier, during Dorothy's absence, David and his fa-ther had gone to dinner with their close friends the Ches-ters. George Weymouth had also been a guest. During the course of the evening, Putnam learned of the young man's love for sailing. He was also in need of a job, as his scholar-ship from the Yale Club of Philadelphia would probably ex-pire at the end of his sophomore year. In one evening, the deal was sealed. George made it clear that young Weymouth must quickly move into Rocknoll, for there was work to be done in preparation for the Arctic trip to Baffin Land that was only two months away.

In the past, my grandmother had responded to G.W.'s amusing and affectionate ways with open innocence. But now her feelings were becoming more serious. Early one spring morning, before the sun broke through the trees, Dorothy was up whistling and making lunch for an outing that she and George Weymouth had planned. The previous day they had walked to the top of Laddin's Rock, a nature sanctuary covered with hemlock trees where songbirds often nest. They had sat for hours, laughing and telling stories. It was on that first outing together that Dorothy began to use the name "G.W." in her diary.

Perhaps they had resisted giving in to temptation the day before, savoring the prospect of the picnic planned for the following day. After she dressed with deliberate simplicity, Dorothy rummaged nervously through the kitchen drawers wanting to choose the perfect napkins and dinnerware. Standing at the sink, she washed the fresh strawberries, packing them carefully in a basket beside the chocolate fudge she had made the night before.

Although at first both tried to make light of their excursion that morning, each understood the seriousness of their actions. When they first arrived at Laddin's Rock, G.W. teased Dorothy that she must have come over the week before, to plant the white violets throughout the meadow. The setting was romantic and Dorothy flushed at their easy intimacy. Placing a worn blanket on the ground, G.W. was careful trying not to disturb nature's own spring bouquet. But suddenly, they erupted in laughter when he accidentally slipped and stomped on several of the flowers, breaking the tension.

The following day Dorothy recalled those playful hours together:

APRIL 19, 1927 *Thank God for my humor and my sense of play! It's always there, even when I'm soaked with emotion. The most perfect lover is the one [who] even in his most passionate moments is never far from laughter. It distinguishes him from the beasts and endears him to his loved one.*

The days that followed evoked a stream of sensuous thoughts and feelings: *"Spring is full of love, all kinds. It may be just love of outdoors, of music, or birds, or of man and woman. And there is nothing so dead as an <u>old</u> love. God forbid I should ever blow on its embers. Oh, please let me stop first to avoid this ghastly thing. Rather suffer more."* Clearly, she was tortured by her new passion.

APRIL 29, 1927   *Apparently I can't do without men and yet my time of love has nearly gone and I can't wholly love one! Does one ever? Do they love us, wholly? To be wholly in love one should have no mental reservations. It's done every day, I'm sure. Yet why can't I? One's whole make-up should cry "Yes" without a qualm. The <u>positive</u> woman does: Ludovici says.*

One morning a few days later, she was awakened by birdsong deep in the woods, and lay quietly in bed. Her husband had risen earlier and gone downstairs to begin working on his maps. Slipping into her bath robe, Dorothy began the day with breakfast in the open air of the second-floor porch. Captivated by the distinct smells and noises, and the wind with its moody changes, she was at a momentary peace. Reaching for her small black diary, she wrote: *"It's funny, the less a woman gives and the more she exacts from a man, the more the world respects her, in marriage. But if she gives her self wholly, willingly and asking nothing, the world cries out in horror and scandal."*

As the date for his own expedition neared, George Putnam's daily life took on an added momentum. As publisher, he was already blessed with boundless energy. Now he wanted to clear up his business affairs before embarking on the Baffin Land trip. For the second year in a row, George had commissioned Captain Bob Bartlett and his schooner, the *Morrissey*. In an article for the *Geographical Review* written several months later, he explained the purpose of the trip and named its crew members:

> The main objective of the Expedition was a geographical exploration of this virgin territory of Baffin Island—work in the charge of Professor Laurence M. Gould of the University of Michigan, assisted by George Weymouth of Philadelphia, Monroe G. Barnard of New York, and John A. Pope of Detroit. The other general personnel of the party included Robert E. Peary and Wallace R. Hawkins, engineer and assistant; Dr. Peter Heinbecker, surgeon; Edward Manley, radio director, Maurice Kellerman, motion picture photographer; Junius B. Bird, botanist; and two junior members, David Binney Putnam and Deric Nusbaum.

On an early evening in May, the chauffeured automobile idled at the railroad tracks in Rye, waiting for George Putnam's commuter train to arrive. Manhattan was the pulse of his activities, and he was consumed by the desire to make G. P. Putnam's Sons the most powerful publishing house in the world. The first sound to announce his arrival home was the bang of manuscripts bound together, hitting the pantry floor. Between the office and home, he carried the drafts about like school papers waiting to be graded.

George called upstairs to ask Dorothy if she had had a chance to speak with G.W. about his dinner plans for the evening. She said she had, and that he had decided to return to Yale that afternoon, where he was busy at the fraternity house doing odd jobs before summer vacation. In fact, she added, he probably wouldn't be back until the following morning.

After dinner, George collected his weather maps and stood in front of the fireplace waiting to update Dorothy on the expedition's progress. Two twenty-four-foot whaling boats had been constructed especially for the trip north and were ready to be picked up in Cos Cob. He hoped that Weymouth and David might drive up with him the next day and run them back down to the American Yacht Club in Rye. George was oblivious to the relationship developing between his wife and the young tutor; he was far too consumed with his own interests to notice her change in attitude.

Weymouth's memories of his role within the Putnam household offer a guarded view of the relationship, as well as an explanation of his job. "Subsequent visits to the Putnam household led to more serious attention to Dorothy and an invitation to go on an expedition on the famous Arctic schooner, the *Morrissey*, to an undiscovered land, the East coast of Baffin Land. . . . In addition to my job as third engineer I was also charged with the care and direction and tutoring of *David Goes to Baffin Land.*" However casual the reference to my grandmother, I know how he must have suffered, keeping this secret from my grandfather and father.

One evening a few weeks later, Dorothy wandered through the huge house, grateful to be alone. With George in Washington, D.C., for two days and Junie at Rocklyn spending the weekend with the Binneys, the Putnam home was deserted. It was a perfect setting for a clandestine relationship to flourish. The only sound came from outdoors; the romantic trill of the wood thrush. My grandmother listened to its pleading call for love and sensed in her own heart a similar desire.

May 19, 1927, would be celebrated for the rest of Dorothy's life as the turning point when her willingness to accept a passionless marriage ended. She was reborn, and in that new womanly self found mounting strength and desire. Though she recorded the following two days on separate pages, the evening of May 19 and the morning of the

20th flowed into one, with Dorothy and G.W. clinging to a dreamlike reality. Sitting before the fading fire with a glass of red wine, they had stretched out before the warm hearth, their bodies intertwined.

> May 19, 1927　*A rainy day—with a gray drizzle. Yet there's an electric something in the air which makes me breathless and panicky. I have to go to town for an errand or two. And G.W. drove to New Haven for fraternity initiations. He returned late, and after dinner we sat in the studio before the fire. Before going to bed we opened a bottle of delicious old wine 1859—An evening never to be forgotten—music— wine—content!*

Beside the date, she drew a secret symbol to record her lovemaking. This private, romantic code has helped me interpret my grandmother's diaries with greater accuracy and understanding.

> MAY 20, 1927　*A marvelous dawn—with a thrush singing in the woods. And apparently the whole world has a new significance! At least a part of me long forgotten is here still, and awake in full force. A gay, intense, utterly pagan self. Ruthless perhaps and self willed. Yet, too very sweet and understanding. Contradictory.*

Once again, world events were conspiring to interrupt Dorothy's euphoria. She was forced to abandon her delirious state, for Lindbergh was preparing to fly across the Atlantic; and her own husband and home would become a part of the media event.

5

A SPIRIT OF ADVENTURING

MAY 21, 1927 *A mail pilot from St. Louis flew across Ocean from NY to Paris! Solo 33 hours. A world hero of course in a day's few hours and quite rightly too. Left night of May 19th, arrived May 20th—Charles A. Lindbergh!*

WHILE DOROTHY AND G.W. WERE transported by passion, Charles Lindbergh had made aviation history. George Putnam, preparing for his own Arctic trip, was immediately fascinated with the commercial possibilities of Lindbergh's flight.

Dorothy had just returned to Rocknoll from a quilting lesson when Junie raced out to greet her with the news. Although Dorothy had followed Lindbergh's flight plans, she could not understand her little boy's excitement about a man in an airplane who had almost fallen into the ocean. Dropping her basket, and spilling dozens of cotton flowered squares across the grass, she rushed inside to learn the true story.

George had called earlier and left word that a bulletin of Charles Lindbergh's flight had just come across the wire service from Paris. With all of the excitement, he didn't expect to be home until late, but hoped that she would take the train into town and join the spontaneous celebrations. All of New York, it seemed, was caught up in a jubilant display of patriotism. She hastily packed a light bag for the evening and reached the station in time for the early evening train.

George had not exaggerated; the city was wild. Strangers were hugging each other, horns were honking continuously, and in office buildings thousands of workers waved flags from the crowded windows. By the time Dorothy arrived at G. P. Putnam's Sons on Forty-fifth Street, the city was caught up in a frenzy of excitement over Lindbergh's amazing and daring feat. *"The whole world quite agog over this unknown youth's superb nerve and courage—An Envoy from U.S.A. to all of Europe. An International hero, truly, and the world's first of his kind and an American thro' and thro'. Tall and blond."*

George called his friend Fred Birchall at *The New York Times*, anxious to reach Lindbergh in Paris to make a substantial offer to publish his story:

> I went to Fred Birchall, then managing editor of *The New York Times* and a good friend of mine.
> "We'd like to get the Lindbergh book," I said. The stocky, bearded little Englishman's nearsighted eyes crinkled in a grin as he peered at me over his glasses. "Indeed," he chuckled, "you—and who else?" As to that, I suppose every publisher in America wanted the book. Anyway, Birchall did what he properly could to help. What I needed most was a lift in getting word promptly into the hands of the harassed flyer, and the Paris office of the *Times* could help with that.

Lindbergh had already asked an American newspaperman, Carlisle MacDonald, who was traveling with his party, to ghost-write the story for him. Lindbergh accepted Putnam's staggering offer. Snagging the rights was considered to be one of my grandfather's greatest publishing coups. He wrote an advance check for $100,000, certain the book would become an instant bestseller.

Within days, the project was under way. In George's own words: "MacDonald moved into my house at Rye. I reinforced him with secretaries and he went to ghosting in a big way, equipped with the flyer's own newspaper stories of the flight and the notes gleaned from Lindbergh on the return voyage from France."

Dorothy took on an active role as Rocknoll filled with writers and staff members. The normally bustling household became frenetic, but Dorothy was swept up by the challenge and excitement of another publishing event. Highly organized, it was her task to provide a comfortable and stimulating household, and she was uniquely qualified for the job, for she exuded intelligence, wit, and literary knowledge. As G. P. Putnam's charming spokesperson and hostess, Dorothy delighted in taking guests sightseeing or to the Manursing Island Club for a swim and picnic. Up at dawn, she prepared breakfast for those whose sleeping habits matched hers. The garden tours and gathering flowers for the house were her special way of introducing visitors to Rocknoll.

An emotionally riveted public eagerly awaited Lindy's personal account of the historic flight. Over a hundred thousand advance orders from booksellers poured in, thanks to George's personal visits to stores across the country, where he delighted in drumming up interest. The world-renowned geologist Laurence Gould would recall: "He was a stormy petrel who incited all kinds of reactions from people." A gifted promoter, my grandfather was universally recognized for his unfailing commercial instincts while giving his writers creative freedom.

His support of writers was legendary. "I believe that it might never have even occurred to me to think of myself as a writer except for George's insistence that I was," observed the artist and author Rockwell Kent. "Despite the habit of all publishers to assume the right to direct and edit their writers' work, George never even suggested the alteration of a comma in anything that I did."

By the time MacDonald finished the Lindbergh manuscript, however, the famous pilot had a change of heart. *"Fitz [G.P.'s assistant] is dog tired and very worried over the Lindbergh book. There is difficulty and Lindbergh doesn't want to accept it, now that it's written for him."* Lindbergh refused to sign the release form for publication and had decided after all to write the book himself.

My grandfather was beside himself. He imagined irate customers and empty bookshelves. Lindbergh assured him that he would be finished in several months.

Lindbergh retired to Harry Guggenheim's (sponsor and promoter of aeronautics) house on Long Island, agreeing to write 40,000 words. He wrote in longhand, and delivered the manuscript in time for a July publication. *We* would be published to great acclaim, and G. P. Putnam was once again the envy of his peers. His name was forever linked to the famous aviator, who earned an unprecedented (for the time) $200,000 in royalties. The two men would remain friends for years to come.

Amid the Lindbergh saga, the Baffin Land expedition was gathering steam in the Putnam household. Dorothy was keenly aware that it would mean the absence not only of her fourteen-year-old son and her husband but also of her new lover. Moreover, she recognized the loss of personal opportunities as she felt the familiar pull of being seduced into another publishing event for Putnam's. As the sailing date neared in June, Dorothy and G.W. attempted to steal a few moments alone, but ultimately they conceded to the demands of the trip. *"Delicious lunch and we ate it atop Laddin's*

Rock, on the cliff in the hemlocks, with a thrush singing in the oaks above us, and white violets in bloom!"

Most of G.W.'s days were spent filling orders for the crew as he traveled between Washington, D.C., and the *Morrissey*, now being loaded with supplies at the boatyard on West Seventy-ninth Street in New York. He also acquired permits for taking specimens for the Museum of Natural History, and in general made himself useful as a third engineer. *"G.W. left for Washington to see the Coastal Geodetic Survey people. He is the most beguiling person. So sweet and considerate in the little things. Active, tireless and unfailingly thoughtful of me. I shall miss him tremendously."*

The week before they were to sail was filled with giddy abandon, as Dorothy allowed herself to delight in the pleasure of her love affair. *"George in town on the* Morrissey. *To woods with G.W. for azalea and greens and lay on a sunny rock singing."*

JUNE 5, 1927   *Late this morning, G.W. and I paddled my yellow canoe from the yacht club to the Manursing. A soft grey day with not a ripple, a calm and exquisite morning and we talked and paddled leisurely "round to the beach." We lolled and laughed. We found Gill [Dorothy's college friend Agnes Gilson] and the two children waiting on the beach. Just as we came ashore, G.W. fell overboard! So funny, and soaked, although only in two feet of water.*

JUNE 6, 1927   *G.W. came back from Washington and I know Annie Laurie is anxious to see him. She can't believe he's not in love with her still. It was antagonistic infatuation and he has conquered it.*

JUNE 10, 1927   *All day back and forth—errands— trunks—phones—Phil Weymouth from Harvard and two younger brothers from Pennsylvania to see G.W. off. A huge dinner party and a wild kiddish evening with boys all over the house. A warm summer night.*

Two days later, at 3:00 A.M., the *Morrissey* set sail. The day and night before had been consumed by last-minute errands. Dorothy had attempted to transport her own duffel bag to the ship without being seen by the bevy of newspaper reporters, but she was spotted and written up in one story. She had agreed to go on board as far as Brigus, Newfoundland, but she had tried to keep her presence a secret and described her role as "insignificant." "*All day we are going back and forth to the ship at the Yacht Club. Lunch at the Club for some sixty people; Will Beebe, Coe, Green, etc. Meanwhile, ship moved from Yacht Club to Casino. Engine trouble and G.W. sent to city for new parts. Sneaked aboard after midnight, on lifeboat. Sailed at 3:00 a.m.!*"

My grandmother's personal descriptions flow from page to page, rhythmic and lilting. But in her heart, she resented the fact that within a week she would leave the ship while her husband and the others pursued the exotic life she so envied. Only the year before, George had been jealous of her adventure on board the *Arcturus*. It seemed the Putnams preferred separate challenges, as they both needed to be in control.

On the *Morrissey* for one week, she relished being the only woman with her "mob" of "dirty boys."

JUNE 12, SUNDAY *So pleased to find I don't object to the smells of the engine, the lack of privacy, the strange meals— nor the roll of the ocean! Soft, clear sunny first swells. Long Island Sound. Feel marvelous and like the whole gang.*

JUNE 15 WED. *Oh, heavenly day! Shark fins in night and many new birds and way off the horizon several whales disported themselves. Time goes swiftly and suddenly it's time for supper. Most of the boys, except G.W. and Bob Peary have felt a touch of sea-sickness.*

JUNE 16, THURS.   *A gray day, cold with a huge follow-ing ground swell and some fog. The boys shoot clay pigeons. Watched gorgeous full moon rise with G.W. out of bank of black clouds.*

JUNE 17, FRI.   *Gray swells, fog; drifted to fish for cod, 50 fathoms, caught 100 lbs. or more and G.W., Monroe and I went swimming off the deck. Water 48 degrees, air 50 degrees. Saw three schooners. Heard a big steamer whistle, sang late with J.P. and G.W.*

JUNE 18 SAT.   *In cabin all a.m. Cold and wanted to finish reading "The Immortal Marriage." G.P. insists upon David doing a bit of work on his book each day and he's reading up much good history.*

JUNE 19, SUN.   *Our meals are such fun. A mob of huge, hungry, dirty boys! I laugh to look down the table! Played brains after supper and finally got them all interested and ar-guing. G.W., David and I sat in "nest" on top of the cabin and read or sang or talked.*

JUNE 20, MON.   *Early last night at 2:00 a.m. I went on deck—full moon and fine breeze and full sail. Brigus, New-foundland at 8:00 a.m. Grand welcome and all the Bartletts so nice. To Bob's house and tub and shampoo. After dinner a heavenly climb with G.W., John Pope and Ed Manley way over the hills and cliffs.*

JUNE 21, TUES.   *George, David, Deric and J.P. off fishing all day. I climbed hill with G.W. and visited the house the Kents lived in 1915. Delightful and quaint and a heavenly setting. Everyone at junction to see me off.*

Dorothy was certainly qualified to be a member of the expedition, yet her role aboard the *Morrissey* was considered unusual, for Captain Bob Bartlett was adamant that women on his ship were bad luck. In his book *Sails Over Ice*, the captain later evaluated her presence and noted that Dorothy had been the exception:

> She fitted in perfectly with the ship's life aboard, and the best thing about her was that she minded her own business. She was no gossip—and a real gossip can make more trouble at sea than any ten jinxes you can think of—and whatever she saw and heard remained her own property. Not that much got by her. It didn't. She was like the wise old owl in the tree, who became more and more silent as he heard more and more that would make good telling. And for the logbook, let me add that we had the best of luck while she was onboard.

Her father, Edwin, and son Junie were waiting at Grand Central Station in New York to greet Dorothy upon her return. When Bub spotted her casual wave through the window of the slowing train, he and Junie walked quickly toward the door where she would appear. To a small son, she was only a mother returning home. But to a father who respected her need to push boundaries, he saw the spirit of an independent daughter he was proud to have nurtured. He handed her a bouquet of flowers. Somewhere beneath her adventuring eyes lay the mystery of a more mature woman. The flowers momentarily reduced her to a young girl, as she affectionately cradled her father's sweet gift.

Dorothy had returned with presents for her parents and Junie. They were not exactly the kind of mementos that one might consider souvenirs. From high above the snug little harbor overlooking Brigus, she had collected rock specimens to share with her family. Attached to each one was Dorothy's handwritten story describing the point of land and her adventure there.

At home, the dusk shadowed the dimly lit studio as Dorothy returned to her Steinway and sang "Blue Skies." Irving

Berlin must have had her in mind that year when he wrote these lyrics:

I was blue just as blue as I could be.
Ev'ry day was a cloudy day for me.
Then good luck came a-knocking at my door.
Skies were gray, but they're not gray any more.

Blue Skies smiling at me.
Nothing but blue skies do I see.
Blue birds singing a song—
Nothing but blue birds all day long.

Never saw the sun shining so bright.
Never saw things going so right.
Noticing the days hurrying by;
When you're in love my how they fly.

Blue days, all of them gone.
Nothing but blue skies from now on.

My grandmother's original sheet music with her name and address across the top still rests on our piano at Immokolee. The faded yellow and blue cover with two birds facing one another is a gentle reminder of the woman who played its romantic melody.

Between June 21 and October 1, when G.W. would return, Dorothy's summer was marked by long hours of despair. The same diary that had reflected such unadulterated happiness the month before now was filled with loneliness. *"To sleep on the loggia . . . I find myself full of thoughts of moonlight and Arctic and a ship load of young men very dear to me."* Her imagination swirled from alarming images to soft moonrises and psychic contact with "her boys."

JULY 25, 1927 *A depressing day with physical inertia and low feeling all day and around house.*

Filling the rooms with bunches of daisies, Dorothy tried to transform her moodiness with warm memories. She slept on the outside loggia, sharing the moon and stars with thoughts of G.W., feeling closer to him. She imagined his sunburned face, and the touch of his callused hands. *"Feel sad and worried and will be so relieved when I hear the boys are back again on the* Morrissey!*"*

She read over and over again the one batch of letters that was mailed back in June. But her diary reveals what was deep in her heart. Phrases like "heavenly moon," "homesick," and "so little word," jump out from the pages. And weeks later, *"Sat in swing in garden to watch moonrise. Special radio from G, Whaleboat back at* Morrissey! *Thank God!"*

Three months would pass without the talk of books and exotic trips, without David and his husky teenage pals or G.W.'s unpredictable antics. Somewhere, headed for Baffin Island's rocky coast, were her three men, living together in tight quarters, all of them missing her in their unique ways.

In his absence, George had provided Dorothy with a fortuitous bit of damaging evidence. Going through his clothes, she discovered that he too had found solace outside the marriage, and she welcomed it, believing for the first time that they both shared blame for the slow death of their love.

JUNE 30, 1927 *Today when putting away George's summer clothes, I found a letter from a woman, to him. A compromising affair and his penciled acceptance. A woman whose name he has never even mentioned to me, so undoubtedly a clandestine affair and about cocktails, etc. It's odd, but it just makes the separation between him and me more complete. And lightens my sense of fidelity.*

JULY 1, 1927 *I have bought a new Dodge roadster. Very snappy sports model. Ridiculously expensive and really unnecessary. But it's a funny reaction. And inexplicably, an antagonism against George.*

Filling her summer days with carefree projects was Dorothy's way of hurrying the season along; and on one July day, a heavy rain suggested its own kind of activity: *"Made 50 glasses of apple jelly. Rain and thunder in late afternoon again!"* For Dorothy, it was a day for writing letters or reading slowly from Walt Whitman's *Leaves of Grass*. It was also a day to reminisce, and she found herself opening the dresser where her secret mementos lay hidden.

G.W.'s first hand-picked daisies had died like the four-leaf clovers within her diary's pages. She had wound the stems together with a piece of yellow ribbon and hid them under her nighties in the bottom drawer. Now, she recalled his first visit, when he gave her the daisies that lay in the palm of her hand.

There were also more tangible connections to her new loved one. In his absence, G.W. encouraged his family to visit Rocknoll. Two of his brothers, Clarence and Tyler, and Mr. and Mrs. Weymouth arrived. Dorothy was thrilled: *"A strange Sunday, despite all the crowd here. I stroke Larry's [G.W.'s brother Clarence] head for an hour, thinking of G.W. And at six o'clock his mother, father, and 'Ty,' came quite unexpectedly."*

On July 20, Dorothy was alone and facing her thirty-ninth birthday. Reflecting on a life without sufficient achievement, she wrote emotionally of her failures:

> JULY 20, 1927 *My birthday. Seems too ridiculous and I hate to check the passing years. I drift along—busy, active, procrastinating, energetic, ambitious, slovenly, lazy and indifferent! And Oh, so slack! It's cheating life somehow and I hate myself for letting down, yet haven't character to spruce up more in my real efforts.*

A family celebration for her birthday was marred in part because Dorothy and the whole Binney family were worried about her brother, June, who had been stricken with the spinal disease amyotrophic lateral sclerosis (later named Lou Gehrig's disease). His illness had preoccupied everyone, and Dorothy was deeply concerned for her younger brother. *"Poor June is shockingly ill and I'm horrified at his appearance.*

He had been sick for over a year, first with threatened blindness and other illnesses and now, lame! But despite even that we did manage a gay evening with music and ridiculous jazz and then some brainy games."

Since the *Morrissey* sailed nearly six weeks before, Dorothy had found little to celebrate. Waiting for news from the crew was discouraging and stressful as she fretted over their safety. *"There is so little word of the boys this summer, they seem to be held in the ice—and for 20 days have made only two days progress."* At last, on August 5, she received letters from all three men: *"After all these weeks I suddenly get some adorable letters from the* Morrissey! *George, David and G.W. Mailed in North Labrador on June 30 and brought down by some little boat. All so dear and I'm so lonely for them. Yet so thrilled to hear these <u>personal</u> messages."* And on August 6 she was even more elated by the hand delivery of a cleverly masked radiogram that G.W. had wired to her directly from Baffin Land:

A second wireless from the *Morrissey* had been sent directly to *The New York Times*. She recorded in her diary on August 7:

Yesterday's "N.Y. Times" had long account of Arctic boys. George has gone off in the whale boat with Dave, G.W., Pope, Barnard, and an Eskimo hunter. So far, the boys have two polar bears. Eight weeks now, and in another eight they ought to be <u>home</u> here again.

She had gone so long without news that now she was filled with enormous relief and an almost psychic sense of G.W.'s presence: *"I have had a strange feeling of <u>nearness</u> to G.W. Either he is thinking <u>very</u> constantly of us and this house, or my thoughts are trying to get over to him."* Anticipating his return, Dorothy poured out her love: *"I am more contented, in a way, than ever in my life. Perhaps I'm in love—peacefully— and with no further stirrings for anyone else! To give oneself to an affair and burn out, to remember the glow and give oneself again!"*

For weeks she had planned to welcome the *Morrissey* back in Nova Scotia personally, though George had discouraged her from making the long trip. In mid-September she was on her way. *"Off on the early train to Nova Scotia. I'm so restless and under such a strain I wish I could 'let down.' At noon a follow-up wire from Fitz—relayed from G.P. He wants me to wait in New York! Little does he know <u>my</u> summer or what mental reactions I've had."*

Leaning back against the stiff maroon cushion of the northbound train, she visualized the vessel sailing toward home. Nova Scotia was three days to the north, and exactly when the *Morrissey* would arrive was still unknown. She vowed to be there at first sighting whatever the day.

On September 21 her journey ended on the island of Cape Breton in North Sydney, Nova Scotia. At Dorothy's request, a small, weather-battered inn made preparations to welcome the crew with clean rooms, baths, and fresh fruit and milk. *"The countryside is too gorgeous for any description, a riot of reds and deep greens with a flash of gold. I walk—read much—write letters—think over my past indiscretions and plan future sins! And yet, fundamentally, I'm good, really!"*

The separation between G.W. and Dorothy had been wrenching, but she hoped their love would be renewed. Each day she walked to the top of the highest hill, looking out to sea. Staring toward the horizon, she was prepared to hide her disappointment if G.W. showed no signs of affection, or if one hundred days at sea with the two Putnam men had altered his love for her. In her heart, she still had faith in him.

One morning there was a sharp rap against the door, which hung at an angle making a bright triangle of light beneath it. Impatient for news, Dorothy pulled it open quickly, only to find a young boy standing before her holding a piece of yellowed paper. A radio message had been sent to Dorothy from the previously unknown shores of Northern Fox Land to New York, and then had been re-wired back to her again in North Sydney. Pushing the door closed across the swollen floorboards and latching it this time, she read his words and recorded them in her diary:

SEPTEMBER 25, 1927 *"Even in Fox Land I found yellow daisies.—George W." Rather dear to remember and more, to send the little message.*

In the mention of the daisies was the answer that she had been yearning for. Relieved, now standing before the open window, Dorothy breathed in the misty air and listened to the cackling scream of hungry gulls. A second radio message arrived shortly after. The ship was due the next day. There was also some unwelcome news: G.W.'s hand was badly infected and required immediate medical attention. Dorothy fretted about this unsettling development: *"Why? Why, should he be the injured one?"*

The long-awaited morning finally dawned, and into the snug little harbor steamed the *Morrissey.*

OCTOBER 1, 1927 *Just after midnight the* Morrissey *arrived! I had lain awake early late worrying, then at last gone to sleep. And in walked George with a full, brown beard! Rather unpleasant and ugly. We talked oh, so many topics while he drank milk and ate fruit. Everyone has been sea sick lately, beastly rough weather.*

OCTOBER 2, 1927 *Big dinner party and again supper for the whole gang. Gay flowers and leaves. A fine talk in my room and magazines and candies and books, etc. Walked to hill, Pope, Ed, and G.W. afternoon. G.W. a bad thumb, very serious and has been his whole arm. Off to hospital and gas.*

The following day, Dorothy, along with the six members of the *Morrissey* crew, boarded the train for home. First, she had said another good-bye to G.W., for he was left behind, hospitalized with a severely infected arm and hand. *"On train to New York. Amusing. They're a great bunch. I fancy the other passengers aboard are wondering about us. Hated to leave G.W. in the hospital there. He's so cheerful and optimistic and dear, as ever."* Their love for one another was evident, but their true reunion would have to wait. Reluctantly, she joined David and other crew members for the long train ride back to reality.

After three days of raucous tale-telling, the bearded troop of adventurers, accompanied by an amused Dorothy, arrived in Rye. She had only two days to get David ready for boarding school at Hotchkiss. Sitting at the foot of her bed, with a pile of blue towels and folded white sheets beside her, she lifted the final piece of linen to sew the name "David Binney Putnam" across its tiny hem. The huge foot locker was filled with blankets and new underwear, socks that would soon become unmatched, and the oldest sweaters that David had chosen, not wanting to look too proper.

OCTOBER 5, 1927 *Took Dave to Mother's and then off to Hotchkiss to school. Heavenly clear lovely day and fine drive. All well and happy, pleasant room, etc. I believe he will adore it later on, and the discipline of crowds will be good for him.*

During this period, Dorothy's relationship with her sons was unusually close. David had grown as a fourteen-year-old well beyond his years and had become somewhat of a celebrity in his own right. His first two books for young readers became bestsellers and reflected the maturity encouraged by parents who had introduced him to the world at an early age.

David completed his book about the Arctic sailing adventure, *David Goes to Baffin Land*, and described the journey's end on the last page. The final paragraph is set apart, in a quiet tribute to his mother, Dorothy Binney Putnam:

> And that really about ended the expedition. Of course it was a long way home. About 1500 miles to Sydney, I guess—a long, long sail along the coast of Labrador. Much of it was very rough and pretty slow going. We were delayed a lot by head winds and heavy seas.
>
> But at last, on October first, we got to Sydney. And there the summer actually ended for me, as I took the train and hurried back to school. And at Sydney I found a fine surprise. It—that is, she—came all the way up to meet us, Dad and me. That was just like Mother.

6

THE TUTOR

"Loving changes you—according to whom you love you are different. True of all intimate companionships. How can one explain to anyone how you've once been to someone else?"

*D*OROTHY WAS IMPATIENT FOR G.W. TO be released from Sydney Hospital and transferred to Rye. It was early October 1927. She was distracted by a flurry of activity, making sure his favorite foods were stocked and that his cozy jungle room was cheerful and bright. A pitcher of ice water and a blue ceramic bowl filled with oranges and bananas waited beside the bed, and on the table in the sunlight were the yellow daisies she had picked that morning.

The following day, she received word that G.W. was on his way. She sat at the piano playing Brahms, some Irving Berlin, and a scattering of pieces she had written for herself over the years. G.W. was not afraid to interrupt her this time, as he appeared in the door and walked toward her. His one free arm lovingly circled her waist, and she turned her face upward to meet his. He was home.

OCTOBER 6, 1927 *Servants out. George in town and on a wild rush, G.W. arrived for overnight before going to the hospital. His hand is bad, his color frightful and he's haggard and worried. But determined not to complain. As sweet and thoughtful as ever. Such a charming personality, really remarkable for a youth. Like Spring.*

Feeling even further detached from her husband and family, and spending most of her time attending to G.W.'s needs, Dorothy began to consider the frightening prospect of separating from George. *"My brain is in such a whirl! Such an odd life I'm facing! And questioning oh so much! What is ahead of me?"* Her husband had become aware of his wife's growing discontent, yet he still believed that with all of her financial security and social standing, she should be satisfied. What he wasn't aware of, however, was Dorothy's boredom, and her determination to escape it. *"Lunch at Helen C.'s [an unidentified acquaintance of Dorothy's]. She has divorced, and is living alone in a small house. It is very odd, and yet oh so understandable! Why go on forever living with a person who bores one excessively! It's easier to be beaten."*

OCTOBER 10, 1927 *To town, primarily to see G. W. in the hospital. Took him a bath robe of gay blue and yellows and grays. He wanders around the halls, etc. or sits in his tiny room. Had a nice talk, but he is so utterly cheerful and determined not to have any sympathy.*

The antiseptic hospital room was stark when G.W. first arrived, but after a few days Dorothy had transformed the sterile space into a cheerful sanctuary with pots of plants and flowers. Despite the emergency medical attention he had received in Nova Scotia, G.W.'s left thumb had to be amputated in a New York hospital soon after he was admitted. He had taken the surgery with his usual nonchalance and did not want Dorothy to worry.

There are numerous diary references to moonrises from the woods and golden sunrises from the shore that symbolize their moments together. During George's speaking engagements away from home, these brief interludes were all they had. The full moon in October 1927 would hold a sentimental meaning forever. *"Cold and crisp and clear. A heavenly day, and my instincts <u>singing</u>. I long for the tropics. Met G.W. at train. He has a short leave from the hospital. We talked late and <u>adored</u> the lovely night. <u>Moon</u>."*

In the span of Dorothy's diaries the most moving entries cover the next two years. As a conscientious diarist, Dorothy often sought guidance and approval from outside sources, which would help her understand and accept her own behavior:

> OCTOBER 23, 1927 *There's a new novel about "George Sand." Hers was not a search for love, but appeasement of a primordial urge. She had one great desire in life, to be loved as she loved. And to love when she liked. A profound inconstancy and a thing rarely granted to a mere woman and yet a Goethe-like, Wagner-like passion.*

G.W. spent most of November and December commuting between the hospital and Rocknoll, where he wrote stories and speeches describing his trip to Baffin Land. His own words in the third person cryptically recalled events following the expedition. "GTW got an infection and had his thumb amputated which necessitated him spending two or three months in the Putnam household in Rye. . . . A lot of publicity followed that enabled me to earn my way through the last two years of college lecturing on 'My Trip to Baffin Land.' "

Dorothy continued to find odd jobs for him around the house to help him earn his keep, something he had insisted upon until his hand healed and he could return to Yale. *"G.W. doing some painting jobs, etc. A gay lunch—G.W., Hub [Hubbard Hutchinson, friend and Putnam's author] and myself and a charming afternoon and music and naps and hours to-*

gether full of enchantment and gaiety. Hub playing in inspiring notes. The beloved Pagan appears in jungle costume!—and sleeps and roughhouses divinely."

As the year drew to a close there were fewer opportunities for them to be alone, and she dreaded the upcoming separation. They both recognized the significance of his move back to Yale; it was the end of the romantic idyll they had shared.

After his lengthy recuperation, G.W. wrote a private letter to Dorothy revealing his dependence on and affection for her. He expressed an obvious gratitude for my grandfather as well:

NOVEMBER 15, 1927

Dearest Dorothy:

Nothing to do—an excellent opportunity to attempt the impossible—thank you, Dorothy dear, for the past, the present, the future incomparable happiness which is mine and for which you and G.P. are 99% responsible.

You must have realized how I dreaded the prospect of and my actual confinement in the hospital. To be home and yet not home at all was dreadful, but for a physically ambitious animal like myself to be pushed into a stuffy, coldly plain room after a summer of healthy, exciting exercise was ghastly. How vastly you alleviated and brightened my state of mind. I can never tell you mere words would not only be superficial, but absurd as well. I also learned that it takes the meagerest kind of sickness to bring bubbling to the surface G.P.'s thoughtfulness and altruism which is so latent that, frankly, I have often questioned its existence. Rather a rotten admission, but all the more condemning to me in the recognition—if I know what I mean. If I ever should succeed in accomplishing something worthwhile in life—you and G.P. must feel responsible to no small degree for you have broadened me inside and out, and given me things so delicate, and sweet and dignified that, although I cannot describe them, they are an integral part of me. Just to be always a part of your house I should gladly take a job as a gardener or chauffeur or nurse at no salary—so just yell when!

In 25 minutes—the hospital again and then if possible the two o'clock for Philadelphia and my devoted, really wonderful family once more. They mean a great deal to me as you know and I do want them happy. They are happy, but foolish people, they are allowing a few paltry financial worries to darken their horizon away out of proportion to their importance.

You were such a brick at the game Saturday. Know—although you deny it—that you were bored to exhaustion, but you made a brave attempt at seeking pleasure where there was none to be found and I love you for it. Hope Junie is better. Will be over sometime this week for a dressing. Will—if O.K.—come out to house.

My love always,

George

The following day G.W. arrived at Rocknoll, and he and Dorothy seemed delirious in their passion.

NOVEMBER 17, 1927   *G.W. came out from Philadelphia, just before supper arriving in a violent rainstorm. A thundershower, vivid lightning and wild wind. A weird night altogether, and apropos to unusual exotic dreams of unbelievable things for hours and hours. Theatrical—all night!*

It is clear that Dorothy was experiencing a passion she had not known before, and was overcome with emotion. I can sense a gradual transition in her life, as if she were finally willing to pay the price for such abandon. *"Would I rather be dull, apathetic, unawakened or a hot-blooded lover of life who willingly meets things halfway? Then suffers!"*

With George away again on a three-day speaking engagement, Dorothy and G.W. had the opportunity to spend most of their time together. During this period their love affair grew more intense, and my grandmother's elation over finding such a powerful lover is repeatedly recorded:

DECEMBER 1, 1927   *We may love to "baby" our lovers, but when they love us, we demand to be dominated and con-*

trolled. And so soon as we can control and direct them in that process, so soon then we cease to consider them our lovers. Perhaps the elemental pagan woman in us wishes to be <u>mastered.</u> I do.

DECEMBER 13, 1927 *There must always be turned-down pages in everyone's life, I suppose. For some of us can't <u>ever</u> have a confessional or a confidante. I realize, now, how utterly far I've ever been from having one. So much is bottled up. With just the most evasive surface touching of facts. I've <u>never</u> confided in anyone! And do they consider me the matronly turnip I seem?*

In truth, Dorothy was an exotic, intoxicating woman. G.W. later wrote that she had introduced him "to a lot of very intimate things, such as wine is better than liquor, Jack and Charlie's [now the "21" Club], which was the best speakeasy in town, not to smoke is a worthwhile attribute, and champagne bubbles helped lovemaking a lot, etc.!"

She also wrote out a list of favorite senses, and experiences, many of which no doubt were influenced by their deep love for one another.

These are things I love and really care about:

1) My two boys with an aliveness and intensity that sometimes scares me.

2) The look of transparent deep water.

3) Ragged mountain peaks against distant skyline.

4) Rising tide lapping edge of beach.

5) Yellow; all shades from pale cream to burnt orange.

6) Any physical feat well done—long strong muscles.

7) Smell of ferns and earth.

8) Salt sweet smell of sea.

9) *Smell of pine needles in the sun.*

10) *Hot desert, noon day smell of sagebrush.*

11) *Perfumes, sachet.*

12) *Blossoming orange grove in moonlight.*

13) *Feel of satin against my skin.*

14) *Crunch of fresh snow.*

15) *Feel of hot summer sun against my body.*

16) *Smooth muscles in a man's back.*

17) *Bundle of tiny baby at my breast.*

18) *Man's clean strong hands, power.*

19) *Man's wide throat muscles where they lead in to the shoulder.*

20) *Man's instep and turn of the foot.*

21) *Low voice.*

22) *Natural laugh (rare).*

23) *Thrush's dawn note.*

24) *Whistling softly.*

25) *Perfect orchestra.*

26) *Certain clean sweet utterly masculine scent.*

27) *Same of women——these are very unlike.*

"*Sailing into the morning of another glorious year,*" was Dorothy's tribute to January 1928. With George on a mountain climbing trip with his boy author Bradford Washburn, Dorothy and G.W. drove David and his suitcase full of Christmas gifts back to the Hotchkiss School: "*G.W., David and I had a picnic lunch. Left David and we started for home. Stopped for awhile near the bridge at the old marble quarry. A really perfectly adorable day. It's awful to feel oneself torn between conflicting emotions, yet isn't that the penalty of intellect?*"

At this point, travel did not hold the same appeal as before. But Junie had been plagued by a series of illnesses since the beginning of summer, and doctors suspected he had infantile paralysis. Her concerns for his health prompted the suggestion of a trip to Hawaii, with George agreeing that the warm Pacific air would have a restorative effect on them both. Dorothy saw an opportunity to ease the growing tension with George. At this point, she could not bring herself to share even the slightest intimacy with him. Making love was impossible. *"An unhappy evening. I refuse because I mentally don't enjoy it. He can't believe my attitude is _real_; possibly because it hurts his conceit. But it seems immoral to me when two people are _not_ mutually in love and desirous, and I can't go thro' with it."*

Two days later she was in G.W.'s arms and deliriously happy:

JANUARY 11, 1928 *All day a singing in my head and really on the crest! Drove to town in Chrysler with G.W. when he went to hospital for finger dressing and then out again just in time for a delicious dinner. In a white dress and blue crystals, etc! And a bottle of 1913 wine and gay spring flowers and an adorable evening in every way! We read poetry, we had some good music for an hour. There are days occasionally when one walks on air, and the world seems all sunshine and joy! And this has been one!*

The following day Dorothy came down with a fever, and typically blamed herself. *"Yesterday was the last fling before a fall! For today I'm sick in bed with vile throat, fever and chills and no food. Maybe this is a punishment for me, for being so happy!"* And after another day in bed with tonsillitis: *"G.W. came and talked to me late and was so sweet and considerate. I feel just ill enough and miserable enough to love his little attentions and favors. I believe he has the most perfect carriage I've ever seen."*

Even in illness, she was at peace with herself:

JANUARY 14, 1928 *G.P. lectured Boston, 11th; Rye, 12th; Summit, N.J., 13th; and Phila on 14th. Despite being ill and in bed and just dragging around, I'm happy in my mind and between doses I lie and think and enjoy the world. I feel <u>old</u> and already know more poignantly what a tragedy it must be for a beauty to grow old. For God knows I'm not that, yet I regret the years.*

Prior to Dorothy's departure for Hawaii, George realized that he would miss her, despite her belief that he did not need her any more. *"George home very early and dog tired after his many lectures. He is growing a bit lonely at the thought of my going away and is pretty sweet to me every minute."* The man she had married sixteen years earlier had changed, and his success was not without a price. His long absences only exacerbated her need for attention. And as a result, her most precious moments were those spent with G.W.

JANUARY 17, 1928 *My last day at home for a long time—packed and did some final house accounts, bills, etc. and all day G.W. helped or sat in a big chair nearby and chatted. Then just before sunset we went for a perfectly adorable drive high in the hills and then stopped in a little cove to see a gorgeous sunset over the lake. I had a tiny sip of apricot brandy and a cracker and suddenly the sun has gone, the year's at an end, and my trunks and bags are all ready for departure.*

Don Blanding, the Putnams' artist/poet friend from their early days in Bend, Oregon, was now living in Hawaii. During a visit to Rye in 1926, while painting a fish mural on their guest-room wall, Don had extended an invitation to

George and Dorothy to visit him in Honolulu. Now, two years later, as the SS *Malolo* eased up against the crowded dock, Don stood waiting, his arms piled high with fragrant leis. *"The pier at 4:30 and immediately leis of temple flowers for Junie and me. And reporters galore! Don on the dock with huge and very lovely wreaths for us, and a car. Stopped in town and at his studio, then on to the most lovely Royal Hawaiian Hotel on Waikiki Beach."*

Dorothy's uncertainty over her marital status and her feelings for G.W. plagued her two-month stay: *"Gorgeous sunset above the clouds. Supper and then that most marvelous grandeur, full moon over volcanic peaks of crater!! Oh, some thing one can't write of, all night in little cots in the resthouse. Cold, but clear as day. I want him here."*

Despite her passion, she felt guilty over her indiscretions and questioned her judgment. Away from her lover, she saw more clearly the potential for disaster, dreading the scandal if the truth were known. She seemed contemplative, reflecting on her future as she and Junie sat on the beach for days at a time, watching the passing parade of bathers.

FEBRUARY 19, 1928 *Waikiki. My conscience—long dormant or atrophied is suddenly coming to life and I loathe myself as never before! I'm useless, senseless and wrong. Absolutely a mess. Ah, God, may the present determination to turn over a new leaf really take hold and accomplish a change in me!*

MARCH 9, 1928 *Women grow old prematurely because our badly organized civilization gives them so little to do except talk and dress when their children are grown! Oh, this place is too full of useless old people! Yet that is harsh to say. What should they do, and do they deserve no rest for what they have already done in the world? But the majority of them are huge and pulpy and shapeless, mentally as well as physically, and* *repulsive to see. The pity, the tragedy of age! And the joy when one sees an <u>artist</u> at the game of life, and old!*

MARCH 23, 1928   *I wonder, is chastity an overrated virtue? Apparently it's only for women, and men seem to regard their own lapses so casually. We, alas, feel ours as too burdensome for words! And suffer remorse in silence. Is it different? Can it be so <u>much</u> worse? Certainly, one strives for it and controls unruly desires for years. And I do believe in it fundamentally for all. Yet, what of this quite unchaste habit of married couples who most of the while loathe each other, yet continue to indulge!*

She and Junie returned home to Rye that spring, and George was relieved to see his son fully recovered. The weeks away and Dorothy's countless hours of soul-searching had made the once-dreaded return to her husband a relief. With G.W. back at Yale, the Putnams attempted to resume their marital duties, at least for the time being.

Dorothy responded to her husband's joy in her presence again: *"Life is very full and very sweet. Perhaps I'm all wrong, but I'm happy."* For the time being she was safe.

APRIL 17, 1928   *Last night my husband said: "Your reticence and innate modesty about certain personal things is one of your greatest charms. I have never known you to fail this in any tiny respect in the eighteen years I have known you. And I think I love you more as the years go on because I see how rare a quality it is!" This is a comforting tribute, I hope it is true.*

PART THREE

1928-1929

A phone from ~~St~~. I go to Boston ~~tomorrow~~. I shall see her depart. I trust. What nerve, courage, intelligence — & faith . . . .! As perhaps its fatalism. If I go my rep is made forever; if I'm lost, I'm always a mystery... or what do I care ? —

A phone [call] from George. I go to Boston tomorrow. I shall see her [Amelia] depart. I trust. <u>What</u> nerve, courage, intelligence—& <u>faith</u> . . . ! Or perhaps it's <u>fatalism.</u> If I go, my reputation is made forever; if I'm lost, I'm always a mystery . . . or what do I care!

D.B.P.

7

THE FLYER

"Illusions, not realities make life bearable. This dangerous age? When is it? Surely 38 is the age when women most desire an attractive man's admiration. It probably comforts one to think we are still attractive, but more than that we want to feel power."

$\mathcal{M}$Y GRANDMOTHER MUST HAVE KNOWN that the affair with G.W. was ultimately hopeless, and that the possibility of admitting adultery might cost her custody of her sons. She continued to play the role of Mrs. Putnam.

Calling downstairs to George one morning in early May, she announced that she would take him to the train. Harold, the Putnams' chauffeur, had already started the motor when she tapped from inside the bedroom window and motioned that she would drive Mr. Putnam.

Bounding down the stairs, she found George sitting with his open newspaper, more preoccupied than usual. As always, he looked studious and neatly dressed for the city. His still damp hair was meticulously combed straight back in the fashion of the day, and his white collar stood up stiffly inside the dark, tailored suit. His wife's presence caused him to look up, collect his papers, and stride out to the car beside her.

Speeding over to the station, George hurriedly began to tell her about a secret project he was involved in—something that had come up quite by accident and had the potential to become another sensational book along the lines of Lindbergh's *We*. He did not have time to elaborate, except to say that it involved a top-secret trans-Atlantic flight. *"A wild scrabble to get G.P. off. Missed the very early train by 2 minutes. A futile rush—but it turned out all right."* She would not hear anything more for several days.

Returning home, Dorothy anticipated G.W.'s arrival. But the day so filled with promise would turn sour when her young lover showed up with an attractive young companion, Darcy Kellogg. Dorothy was stunned by the attention that G.W. paid to Darcy. *"They stayed late into the evening."* She recorded her underlying disappointment and hurt: *"An odd business. Darcy is most attractive, intelligent and talented (cello) and I believe G.W. is very fond of her."* After the cordial good-byes, Dorothy sought comfort at her piano, but even the soft music could not soothe her. The old insecurity had surfaced. Could G.W. really love her, so much older than the girls he knew? How could she possibly compete?

Meanwhile daily life at Rocknoll kept her distracted, and later in the week, after a visit with G.W., she decided to continue the affair despite her doubts, although the emotional confusion left her exhausted.

MAY 7, 1928 *Oh, Oh—Thank God! For strangely, unexpectedly and happily I am suddenly freed from a wretched indecision of mind. A misery hanging over me many months—a compelling force of desire has ceased to function. I am free, free of it and recognize it in a certain sense of rapture, in myself. Floating, with a mind and body at length unpossessed by any thought of another!*

But the next day she appears to have regretted her decision:

MAY 8, 1928   *Even sin is to be made as difficult as possible. And I had imagined it so easy! Will God ever forgive me for not committing the sins intended for me! Well, I have committed some perhaps, very mild ones. But, often my conscience hurts me and I'm full of remorse. We're such ridiculous chicken-hearted souls at best!*

Dorothy broke down and wrote a farewell note. She was heartsick and more alone than she had ever felt. She sought solace in the multivolume history of civilization by Will Durant, seeming to need that moral justification for her decision. *"Wrote a 'goodbye' note today! Durant says Christ was a great moralist, not necessarily a great thinker. Confucius, Plato, Aristotle, Spinoza, Copernicus (Earth round), Francis Bacon, Kant, Newton, Voltaire (Emancipator of Mind), Darwin (Evolution). Oh, there's Spring in my nostrils and the orioles are here again."*

Amidst Dorothy's turbulent odyssey, George Putnam was on the verge of helping to make aviation history.

He arrived home one evening in mid-May bursting with pride over the mysterious project he had alluded to a few days before. Once again, he enlisted his wife as partner. They sank back on the sofa in the living room with their legs propped on a huge storage trunk that served as a coffee table. Dorothy sat motionless as she listened to his story unfold. A wonderful promoter, George reveled in the role of publisher and adventurer as he unveiled his plans, describing the series of interviews and discussions he had held over the past few days. As he would later recall, "Just then my career as a publisher of exploration and adventure books was in full cry. And here I had stumbled on an adventure-in-the-making which, once completed, certainly should provide a good book." By the end of the evening Dorothy was convinced that her husband was about to embark on the most ambitious project of his career.

Over the years he had given financial support to many unknown young adventurers, and now was enlisted to find the first woman to fly across the Atlantic Ocean. He was convinced that the story would be another bestseller for G. P. Putnam's Sons and that he would find just the right candidate. In George's own words, "I was commissioned to find an American girl who would measure up to adequate standards of American womanhood."

George had heard quite by accident that a wealthy social-ite from Pittsburgh, Mrs. Frederick Guest, was searching for a suitable candidate to be the first woman to cross the Atlan-tic Ocean in an airplane. Mrs. Guest, an amateur pilot her-self, had originally planned to make the flight but had been dissuaded by her family for safety reasons. Already, six women had risked their lives attempting to set other flying records. The dangers were real, and Mrs. Guest's family were adamant in their decision. Nevertheless, Mrs. Guest had leased a tri-motored Fokker floatplane built originally for Richard E. Byrd's Antarctic expedition and now renamed the *Friendship*. Two accomplished male aviators had been selected as well. Wilmer ("Bill") Stultz would serve as pilot and Lou ("Slim") Gordon as the plane's flight mechanic. Be-fore Mrs. Guest bowed out, she stipulated that her replace-ment be a well-educated "lady pilot." The candidate was required to be physically attractive and—like Mrs. Guest— possess all the social graces that reflected the appropriate image of a modern American woman.

Through the Putnams' friend Hilton Railey, George had heard of a potential candidate named Amelia Earhart, who was living in Boston. Railey had met with the young flyer on April 25 and described her as a "female Lindbergh." My grandfather was intrigued by the comparison.

George's initial interview with Amelia Earhart in early May 1928 had been brief and not entirely positive. Her first reaction to him was somewhat harsh, as he had kept her waiting. He noted later: she was "sore as a wet hen!" and Amelia had not disguised her annoyance with him.

Nonetheless, she was instantly intrigued. "Unquestionably, George was enormously attractive to women," recalled his friend, the playwright Robert E. Lee. "A trim but husky hulk of a man, handsome, irascible, sly, opinionated, a total stranger to fear, gifted (or cursed) with a vinegar wit, the champion of raw charm."

A settlement worker at the Denison House in Boston (where Dorothy and her Glee Club had once performed), thirty-year-old Amelia Mary Earhart was an experienced flyer. She was the first woman to be granted an air license by the National Aeronautic Association, receiving her certificate as a pilot in 1923. She was also deeply committed to the advancement of aviation, and particularly concerned with introducing women to the daring and exhilarating freedom of flight. Amelia's qualifications perfectly matched Mrs. Guest's requirements. She was intelligent, tall, and poised, and she became George Putnam's immediate choice for the secret crossing.

Only three weeks would pass between Amelia's first meeting with Hilton Railey, her interview with George Putnam in New York, and the scheduled date for the *Friendship*'s departure. My grandfather was determined to invest his considerable reputation on the risky flight and immediately left for Boston, where the crew was waiting.

Dorothy enjoyed having the house to herself. Gardening, reading, music—and of course sharing it all with G.W.— seemed a fair exchange for George's involvement with the project.

Though her role with the flight's backers was strictly social, at a luncheon Dorothy appeared fascinated by the company.

MAY 15, 1928   *Hated leaving the garden and out of doors to go to town. New maid, Swiss-German with no English! Dined with multi-millionaires, Mr. and Mrs. Phipps, their pretty daughter, Peggy, and nephew, Tony Guest and Lord Elgin at Colony Restaurant. It's Mrs. Guest (English sister of Phipps) who bought their big plane soon to go to London with American girl flyer!*

George was infatuated with Amelia and spoke freely to his wife about the young woman's intelligence and friendly manner. He also noted her graceful hands, her gray eyes, and quick laughter, describing the aviatrix as someone Dorothy would enjoy knowing.

May 19 was the one-year anniversary of Dorothy and G.W.'s love affair. *"A delicious soft rain just saturating my lovely ferns and garden! I watched two thrushes building in the dogwood on the terrace. And it made me a little <u>breathless</u> for various reasons."*

As much as she had wanted to be a part of her husband's venture in those first few weeks of May, she could think only of G.W., and had even devised a code name for him and their affair: the "child."

MAY 19, 1928   *The child is one year old, the darling and I adore it! Occasionally he seems almost intelligent enough to understand. He recognizes colors of sunrise, songs of birds, and once he thrilled over the moon. He can't talk, he is fat and strong, but his appetite is normal. The rain, the woods, ferns, azaleas and new dogwood trees. All day outdoors and loving every minute of it, every drop of rain.*

With George acting as Amelia's agent in Boston, my grandmother and G.W. celebrated their anniversary together. In spite of all the difficulties, this improbable union had lasted an entire year. Both decided not to question the future.

MAY 20, 1928 *Still a bit damp and off to the woods again. George in Boston expecting his girl flyer to leave at any dawn, great excitement and <u>very secret</u>. Buffet supper at Sound Beach and afterwards the Arctic movies and G.W. gave a very easy and good talk, substituting for George still in Boston. Slept on loggia and it seems so completely heavenly and in the woods. Deliciously sleepy.*

MAY 21, 1928 *Awake with the thrushes' song at dawn and lay listening for an hour all warm and sleepy. Then drove to the beach. The stillest kind of soft, gray day, rippleless and the sandpipers scurrying ahead of the incoming tide. But I doubt if she [Amelia] flies. Transplanting, garden, birds, letters, music.*

On May 22, after George had been in Boston for four days, he called Dorothy and asked her to join him. He was responsible for Amelia during the waiting period and decided she needed the support of a female companion who knew the specifics of the secret flight. Dorothy was the ideal choice, and she was pleased to be among the private group of supporters. With uncanny intuition, she wrote of the dilemma facing Amelia: *"A phone [call] from George. I go to Boston tomorrow. I shall see her depart. I trust. <u>What</u> nerve, courage, intelligence and <u>faith</u>! Or perhaps it's <u>fatalism</u>. If I go my reputation is made forever, if I'm lost, I'm always a mystery, or what do I care!"*

Dorothy became a witness to history, and her diary is a firsthand account of that frustrating period in Boston waiting day after day for a break in the weather.

MAY 23, 1928 *To town early and then took 1 o'clock train for Boston. G.W. came to see me for the minute or two I was in New Haven, and he's quite all thrilled, thinking there's a chance either for G.P. or me to fly the Atlantic. God, I wish I were! How utterly spectacular for "nobody me" to get all that sudden reputation if I made it and just quietly disappear into oblivion if I didn't. And I'm ready for it, really. And don't mind in the least.*

MAY 24, 1928 *Boston—Thurs. Amelia Earhart of Kansas, College Graduate—engineer, mechanic, writer, settlement house director and social worker and air pilot. Tall, blond and very slim is to fly the Atlantic in Byrds' Amphibian Plane "Friendship" with 3 pontoons and 71 ft. wing spread. Mrs. Guest is financing it. Bill Stultz is to be navigator, with assistant, Lou Gower, and mechanic Slim Gordon. Visited Denison House in a.m. Mildred Towle [official at Denison House], Amelia, etc. Dinner in our room.*

MAY 25, 1928 *Boston—Fri. Out to Wellesley with George and Amelia in a.m. Saw Bobby Kitchel [Dorothy's niece] and took her big box of candy. Back for lunch. Dick Byrd's for lunch at 9 Brimmer Street. A strange old fashioned house with many rooms and sombre furniture. Dickie, Jr. is 8, blonde and healthy and there are three younger sisters. I like the nice intelligent wife; and Dick, of course, is a charmer for all time! Tall, strong, flatteringly attentive and utterly beguiling. Amelia Earhart here at hotel with us: registered as Dorothy Binney—how odd.*

MAY 26, 1928 *Boston—Sat. George and Amelia talked nearly all night long last p.m. I did get some naps between times. But they didn't know till almost midnight that the plane wouldn't hop off this dawn. Rain, cloudy, bad. Keith's in after-*

noon with Gowers, Stultz's, Slim and his girl, then tea dance. These flyer people are an odd fatalistic lot. Stultzs married 9 years, and has only 3 trunks of belongings! The Gowers 4 years and have one magazine rack, 2 trunks and a suit case! And Mrs. Gower is also a flyer and a mechanic pilot.

MAY 27, 1928 Boston—Sun. Slept late—breakfast in room. First fine day of actual sun shine. Amelia drove us to Cohasset for a lobster dinner at the famous "Kimball's"—then a heavenly drive way down to the shore all afternoon. All back in time for supper. Planned on going tomorrow at dawn. Weather forecast pretty good outside and beyond and Stultz, Slim and Gower all "set" and packed. Golly, how do they keep so cool and collected.

Even George did not anticipate how well the two women would get along. During the six days that Dorothy remained in Boston, she and Amelia were constant companions. My grandmother admired Amelia's courage and self-composure, but at the same time envied her luck in having been chosen for the flight. Amelia for her part appreciated her older friend's genuine gestures of friendship.

On May 28, the two women left the hotel at three-thirty in the morning and drove through the silent streets to T Wharf, a setting that already had established itself in American history. *"Boston—Mon. To the restaurant with the crowd. All 'set,' all tense with excitement, at 4 a.m, then to the old 'Boston Tea Party Dock' in the harbor."*

The plane was moored off the Jeffrey Yacht Club in East Boston, but bad weather kept them in the car, talking and wishing the cool spring rain would stop. By this time the repeated delays had begun to wear on everyone's nerves. *"How does this astonishing girl stand the strain??"* Instead of winging their way into history, the crew remained grounded by the fog and drizzle that appeared as if out of spite every morning before dawn. For days, Amelia and the two-man crew could only gaze out at the Atlantic Ocean in hopes of liberation.

Amelia and Dorothy parked their car near the dock and sat huddled in the front seat. Condensation collected inside the car windows and Dorothy watched Amelia wipe the glass with the palm of her graceful hand, revealing a view of the waiting harbor. The *Friendship* rocked gently as the swelling and rolling water pushed against the enormous pontoons that held the floatplane high above the waves. *"She went down with me and sat all that time in the car, cuddled up in my coat, talking and grinning."*

Amelia and Dorothy exchanged stories about their child-hoods, families, and dreams. Though both women had developed a love for literature and theater, they also shared a passion for outdoor activities, such as gardening, horseback riding, and fishing.

Dorothy was thirty-nine years old, but their difference in age was of no consequence. The young flyer discovered in her friend a kindred soul as daring and as open to the world as she was. During those hours in the car, Amelia also learned that Dorothy had visited the Denison House with her Glee Club in 1908 while attending Wellesley College, and she had never forgotten the faces of the little children her group had entertained.

Their conversation ended early in the morning with the news that the flight would be postponed once again. But the hours had not been wasted; the bond between the two women would change their lives forever. *"Waiting for dawn in a thick soft fog and drizzle, had to give up at 8 a.m.—no 'hop off' today."*

This was Dorothy's last morning in Boston. She and George had made previous plans to give a dinner party at Rye; and since he couldn't leave Boston, she would host the party alone. *"Many errands and chores to attend for tomorrow's party."* On the morning of May 28, Dorothy left her husband and hurried to the train station and into the waiting Pullman car. *"Nine a.m. train back to Rye, exhausted."*

8

THE *FRIENDSHIP*

MAY 30, 1928 *Fine clear morning. Beefsteak Grill. Sen. Walcott and Bryn . . . George Chamberlain, Anna Case . . . Muriel Pollock (piano shark), Dorothy Speare (novelist and opera star), Scotty Allen . . . Dennisons, three Godleys, Greens. . . . A gurrand party, and gorgeous music, fine crowd, too. . . . So sorry G.W. was not here. He loved it last year.*

*T*HE *FRIENDSHIP* FLIGHT HAD NOW BE-come a major media event, and Dorothy secretly longed for her own adventure. *"Oh I'd give much to be far away, on an island with a cabin and the tides and sun and fishing and an occasional climb, etc. I don't want suburbs and cities. Rather loneliness and the sea!"*

Bogged down by poor weather, George and the frustrated crew continued to wait another three days. When the giant seaplane finally lifted from Boston Harbor, Dorothy recorded the eventful day:

JUNE 3, 1928 *Hooray! Sun. The "Friendship" hopped off from Boston at dawn. All kinds of excitement all day. . . . All p.m. newspaper men calling for George, and it's rather fun to sense their excitement trying to get dope on this trans-Atlantic flight. God, I hope that girl makes it!*

Instead of flying on to Trepassey Bay in Newfoundland, the plane was forced to land in Halifax, Nova Scotia, because of poor weather. At last, on June 4, Bill Stultz, Lou Gordon, and Amelia Earhart were given the clear skies they needed and flew on to Trepassey Bay, the starting point for the trans-Atlantic flight: *"Mon. The plane had to land in Halifax because of fog—then on, again, to Trepassey by 3 p.m. today. Every newspaper in the country full of it and many comments about George's connection with it. All day the phone rings constantly. I'm too emotionalized and upset to do anything all day. . . ."*

During the waiting period in Boston, Amelia had pieced together a loosely constructed will. George Putnam saved these "popping off" letters, one written to each parent, to be delivered in the event that she did not return. They are among his treasured papers.

May 20, 1928

Dear Mammy,

I am sorry I had to pass out of the picture in such a way. I am considerable and dislike leaving you with a burden, or rather without an income.

I have put down carefully all my affairs. Please destroy all my writings without examination and do what you will with personal effects. Even tho' I have lost, the adventure was worthwhile. Our family tends to be too secure. My life has really been very happy and I didn't mind contemplating its end in the midst of that.

Mildred Towle can perhaps tell you the circumstances surrounding my departure, etc. If you wish.

Affectionately, your doter,

A.E.

May 20, 1928

Dearest Dad,

Hooray for the last grand adventure! I wish I had won, but it was worthwhile anyway. You know that.

I have no faith we'll meet anywhere again, but I wish we might. Anyway, goodbye, and good luck to you.

Affectionately, your doter,

Mill

Amid the frenzy awaiting Amelia's departure, Dorothy felt a keen loss of privacy. However, on the last day of May, while George remained in Boston, she and G.W. spent a delightful day outdoors.

MAY 31, 1928   *The garden, some notes and two full hours at the piano. G.W. had cuts from class unexpectedly and came down here for lunch. We shot over to the beach, put on bathing suits and paddled canoe for four hours. And such fun. We each acquired a pink coating of sunburn. A lovely ride way back in the hills and down in the garden later to see the full moon. Some music, a cool drink, and oh, so sleepy, to bed!*

The following day, her words resound with the joy only G.W. could inspire. *"The flute and singing almost from dawn on another heavenly day. Roses, roses, yellow roses! And perfume and a conversation such as one has twice in a life-time perhaps."* A year ago, G.W. had brought daisies, a symbol of their innocent love. Now he brought yellow roses, which marked a new sophistication on his part. Dorothy placed the long-stemmed blooms on the bookcase beneath the window facing the front and more formal side of the house. They seemed to belong there, rather than on the bedroom tea table where the daisies once rested.

In early June, George returned home to await news of the *Friendship* flight. As always the house was filled with flowers from the garden to welcome him back and Dorothy still found it comforting at times to slip into the routine and security of her marriage. *"Worked in garden while George and the children burned off the orchard field. And it seemed quite like old times to be out exercising and pulling briars, transplanting, etc. I do love it and it keeps me sane when I might so easily go off the handle."*

The children were staying with their grandparents, where George's father was giving his two grandsons a picnic supper and another lesson in fly-casting. At home, Rocknoll was silent except for George's voice on the other end of the telephone, reporting updated weather reports. He decided it was easier to spend his nights in the city so that he could remain in constant touch with Amelia. *The New York Times* provided their wire service for communicating weather reports between Trepassey and the flight's backers.

Dorothy took the train to Manhattan every evening to meet George for dinner. On June 6 she noted: *"Still thrilled about the Atlantic. In town overnight to hear more intimate news. Dinner, Ritz with G.P. and Fitz. Hippodrome alone for an hour, while men at 'Times' office. Mabel Bolls [another flyer], the night club, fast, mistress of Lerne, girl now plans to hop, too. . . . Excitement of the flyers has somewhat subsided as bad weather holds 'em back. The Bolls woman had to return to Curtis Field—fog! Whoopie!"*

By now, the newspapers were breathlessly playing up a new angle: a potential race across the Atlantic between two rival pilots—one a demure Boston social worker, and the other a beauty queen. By the time Mabel Boll's plane made it to Harbor Grace, Newfoundland, both camps were waiting for the weather to clear. Amelia later denied any competition between them.

Trying to juggle the demands of family and Amelia's

flight left Dorothy wishing for an escape from it all. In her
June 11 entry, she describes her confusion:

> *The new wall in the garden has started. Iris are lovely and the*
> *fields embroidered with daisies! All the world seems happy and*
> *fruitful! Why should I be sad and inwardly so <u>hurt</u>? I want*
> *to go far away, alone and <u>work</u> to get myself straightened out.*
> *For here we have luxury, beauty, comforts and <u>discord</u>., a fric-*
> *tion no amount of ignoring on my part is able to conceal from*
> *me. All my fault perhaps, but nonetheless, here!*

Dorothy was never far from her beloved birds. Thinking
of G.W., she savored the melodic notes of the thrush's song.
*"Thank God for thrushes and ferns! They help one thro' a mental
hiatus as nothing else can do. Yes, seriously, thank God."* On
the 13th, her thoughts returned to Amelia. *"Still the Earhart
girl doesn't fly: can't get her plane up from the water with its
necessary load. And Mabel Boll on her second attempt has
reached N.F. [Newfoundland]."*

Much to her delight, Dorothy was interviewed by a reporter for
The New York Times. The story appeared on June 17, alongside news accounts and photos of Amelia.

MRS. PUTNAM, WIFE OF BACKER OF FLIGHT, GIVES WORD PICTURE OF GIRL
AVIATOR . . .

"I have seldom encountered a more thoroughly delightful
person," said Mrs. Putnam in speaking of Miss Earhart. "She is
most extraordinarily cool and self-possessed. Although I saw
her during the trying time when the hop was being delayed
from day to day, her poise was remarkable."

. . . A possession of Miss Earhart's which particularly ap-
peals to the residents of Tyler Street, headquarters of her social
work, is her battered Kissel roadster. Countless children of
slums crawling over it while parked in the street, have nearly
demolished the windshield. Its color is bright yellow.

"Mr. Putnam dubbed it the 'Yellow Peril,' " the publisher's
wife explained, "and Miss Earhart certainly drives the 'Peril'

remarkably well. Fast, too. But that's to be expected with a one hundred mile an hour air woman who herself has a woman's altitude record of 14,000 feet.

"... It will be a joy to have America and our own sex represented in England by such an altogether fine person as Amelia," Mrs. Putnam continued. "She is a lady in the very best sense of the word, an educated and cultivated person with a fine, healthy sense of humor. And a girl easy to look at, too. Her resemblance to Lindbergh is almost uncanny. She is a feminine counterpart of the 'Flying Colonel.' We certainly will be delighted to welcome her home to America, and eagerly look forward to having her as our guest at Rye."

Finally, on June 17, despite warnings from the U.S. Weather Bureau, the *Friendship* took off as a crowd of onlookers cheered from the shore. "I am going today in spite of everything," a determined Amelia told newsmen.

JUNE 17, 1928 *Earhart off for Atlantic flight at 11:21 a.m. from Trepassey N.F. and great excitement in the household. A phone from Mrs. Stultz, and a radio from Amelia herself and newspapers, etc. all day! I feel as tho' I were suddenly splitting the sides of my personality! . . . Hectic upset afternoon, phones and wires, etc.*

Mabel Boll and her crew were still grounded with mechanical problems on the morning of June 18, when Amelia Mary Earhart became the first woman to cross the Atlantic by air. The following day, newspaper headlines boldly proclaimed Amelia as " 'LADY LINDY' AIR QUEEN." Photographs of Earhart with her gap-toothed smile and her leather flying helmet appeared on every front page in America. Her feat was considered a daring accomplishment and she earned worldwide fame and respect.

Strangely, my grandmother made no mention of the aviatrix in her diaries until Amelia finally returned on July 5. Dorothy writes of George's involvement in the flight, but her life appears normal again, though her celebrated friend was the topic of conversations around the world.

> JUNE 18, 1928   *Dinner at a little place on B'way, then while George went to Times office to hear any news of the flight, I went to see Billie Burke in "Happy Husband," an amusing and very modern frivolity about husbands and wives and their infidelities. . . .*

The following diary entries lead me to believe that in fact my grandmother was thinking much more about her friend's new fame than she wanted to admit, even to herself.

> JUNE 20, 1928   *I wish I were way off, alone somewhere with the salty smell of the sea, the soft sound of the tide and a chance to swim naked when I really wanted to be luxurious and self indulgent. Perhaps it's just utter boredom of a daily routine which only satisfies in episodes and short periods. I'm neither young, nor old. I'm tremendously vital still, and full of a spirit of comedy and "play" which gets small opportunity and outlet.*

> JUNE 26, 1928   *Oh, why, why do I get such depressed and utterly disgusted days! When really I adore out of doors, and woods, and the sea and music and my two grand sons! Yet, there are whole days on end when I wish it were all over and done for. When I'd like to "finish my job" and crack off. Oh, I must go away this winter and by myself!*

Though technically only a passenger, Amelia was a very active one. Seated between the fuel tanks, she recorded her observations in the logbook as best she could with little light. From the moment the pontoons of the *Friendship* touched down onto the chilly water near the fishing village of Burry Port, in southern Wales, Amelia Earhart became an instant heroine, an almost mythical figure for women of her generation who only fantasized about escaping their domestic routines.

Back home, my grandfather was orchestrating her every move. He had already sent his associate Hilton Railey to England to help Mrs. Guest prepare for the plane's arrival, and together they engineered a public relations dream.

Before Amelia returned to the United States, she and George had communicated daily over the wire service. In several of their messages, they had both used the nickname "Simpkin," a name she had given him shortly after they first met. In observing George during the early days of their relationship, Amelia had remembered a favorite Beatrix Potter story from her childhood, *The Tailor of Gloucester*, about a tailor who lived alone with his cat, Simpkin. George later described the nickname's origin in his autobiography, *Wide Margins:*

> Simpkin was a cat who believed that if holding one mouse in reserve against the danger of having time idle on one's hand—or paws—was wisdom, then holding a good number of mice in reserve against such a likelihood was even better. So Simpkin kept a flock—or whatever the grouping of mice is— always available by the neat expedient of housing them, one by one, under inverted teacups. Somehow or other AE had hit on the resemblance in me to Simpkin's way of doing things, for she early perceived that, important as the project of which she was the center became, it was really just then one of the group of enterprises in which I was engaged.
>
> Seemingly, one mouse at a time was not enough. And so privately called me Simpkin.

Amelia arrived in London with very little money but almost immediately acquired an Avro Avian Moth sport plane from Lady Mary Heath, in which the latter had made a record flight from Cape Town, South Africa, to Croydon. Mary had inscribed into the fuselage a message for Amelia: "To

Amelia Earhart from Mary Heath. Always think with your stick forward."

She was also furnished with Parisian gowns and shoes, courtesy of Mrs. Guest, and was honored with dinners and luncheons. At a private affair at the exclusive Embassy Club, Amelia and the Prince of Wales were the center of attention. (He was an avid flyer.)

Amelia's victorious face appeared on the front page of every newspaper, and moviegoers thrilled to the newsreels of her stepping onto British soil. She was greeted by crowds everywhere she went, sipped tea with the Prime Minister and Lady Astor, and chatted with Winston Churchill. Ever the enterprising publisher, my grandfather had arranged for Amelia to write dispatches from London that were eagerly devoured by newspaper readers back home.

The English reception was only the start of what would be an extended celebration. On June 28, ten days after reaching the coast of Wales, Amelia Earhart and the crew of the *Friendship,* along with Hilton Railey, boarded the SS *Roosevelt* for the eight-day voyage back to waiting throngs of Americans. Dorothy could not have predicted how dramatically her life would change with the return of her famous friend, who was planning to take up residence at Rocknoll for the summer while she wrote her book. George was now officially Amelia's business manager, and with that came an enormous loss of privacy. *"Phone rang all night!"* Newsmen regularly perched on her front lawn.

George was swept up in the media attention, and Dorothy felt abandoned. She was still the same woman, and her friend's sudden fame had done nothing to improve her spirits or her marriage. On June 29, Dorothy experienced a premonition: *". . . Killed snake on way home and had curious feeling of something uncanny about it. Have I an unknown enemy? A back biter? And a slanderer? Sometimes I fear so. Is there a 'snake' I ought to be more aware of?"* The next evening, her relationship with George had ruptured once more.

JUNE 30, 1928 *Again a wretched long argument, all night. The same old story . . . my indifference and why and wherefore? And his <u>insistence</u>. Impersonally, I'm regretful and sorry, and yet personally I can't seem to <u>force</u> myself to another point of trying to begin all over again—as tho' one ever brought back romance—or could order it. . . .*

Yet life went on. Two days before the crew of the *Friendship* arrived in New York, the annual Binney family Fourth of July celebration took place at Rocklyn. All of the Putnams and Binneys, the neighbors, and the pals of Junie and David's donned their bibbed aprons and chef's hats for the traditional barbecue. *"A swim, late, then five Putnams to Sound Beach for a grill. But bad storm and only the lobsters were broiled. But a nice party. And <u>fireworks</u> later, to which the neighbors all came."* The group was buzzing with excitement over Amelia's record flight and her anticipated arrival. They were ecstatic at the prospect of having the flyer in their midst for a time, even if it meant that the rest of the summer would become a circus of photographers and reporters.

As the fireworks burst over the blinking lighthouse, Dorothy slipped away from the crowd and found her way up to her childhood room. It was quite some time before George realized his wife was missing. Walking around to the side entrance of the house, he climbed to the third floor and discovered her sitting on the edge of a table in front of a small window. Gazing out at the display, she seemed more interested in the man-made shooting stars than in her husband watching her from the doorway.

After an edgy night, filled with constant chatter about aviation and heroism, Dorothy awoke and began packing for the several days that she and George would spend in New York for the official welcome-home ceremonies. Dorothy wondered how her relationship with Amelia would change. She had missed her friend's vitality and the confidences they had shared in Boston only a few short weeks earlier.

Her diaries over the following days describe in detail Amelia's triumphant return. For a period of time her life was consumed by this Cinderella story, and she was even mistaken for the flyer by bodyguards hired to protect Amelia.

JULY 5, 1928 *Thurs. Many reporters, reviewers, etc. already waiting in the "Friendship Flyer's Suite" at 1717 in the Biltmore. Four bedrooms a dining room and reception room and it gives one quite a thrill of anticipation. Read Walpole's "Wintersmoon," a delicately done picture of aristocratic, conventional English life. The marriage of two people* not *in love and finally he falls in love with her and he loves their little son! The hopeless circle of it.*

JULY 6, 1928 *Up at dawn and then early down the bay on the little reception tug, Macom, to meet S.S. President Roosevelt, Dick Byrd, Laymans and Phipps, etc. on board and really quite a thrill. It pleased me for I knew nearly everyone and could really help a lot. Was tickled, really, to have Amelia throw her arms around me and kiss me, her only kiss, when she stepped aboard! Dick Byrd delightful lunch at Biltmore after Mayor's reception and parade up Fifth Avenue. Wilkins, Wilsen, Chamberlain, Fokker, etc. there, many notables. Paramount Theatre p.m. Special Earhart films, late.*

JULY 7, 1928 *After Paramount last night we went to special benefit performance for Olympic Teams at Palace. A great show where I was mistaken for Amelia and rushed into the theatre by guards, etc.! Very amusing, but embarrassing. Women's City Club lunch—22 Park Avenue—Good speeches and intelligent women. Amelia made excellent talk and fine impression. George a good speech. "Showboat" later. Fliers party. Capt. Manning, Mr. Woodhouse, and David, Helen and Mother joined us. David drove back to Rye with us, quite thrilled at motor cop escort and clearance of traffic!?*

JULY 8, 1928 *Amelia, George and I had to drive to town for Denison House Reception after dinner. The girl very tired and I fear I offended the committee by taking her away early. Again, motor cycle cops as escorts, clearing all traffic for us, and tooting siren every minute. It seems tremendously impressive to go against traffic signals!*

Dorothy, George, and Amelia were relieved to escape the pressures of New York City and retreat to their country home.

Briefly out of the limelight, Amelia was comfortably surrounded by the mossy silhouettes of Don Blanding's undersea mural in the guest room. That evening, she presented a silver fish pendant to her hostess and friend Dorothy Binney Putnam. The fish is etched with tiny scales and a flat fin lies against its small side. There is a ring in its mouth that originally held a thin satin purple ribbon. On the reverse side the inscription reads: "A.E.—6–18–28—D.B.P." The significance of the fish comes from a play that Amelia and the Putnams had seen in Boston just before her departure. The title was *The Good Hope.* Amelia would later write in her book *20 hrs. 40 min: Our Flight in the Friendship* that "The story is a tragedy; all the hopeful characters drown while the most tragic one survives to carry out a cold lamb chop in the last act. A recurring line is 'The fish are dearly paid for,' and our crew adopted that as a heraldic motto, emblazoned under a goldfish rampant."

The following morning, the three returned to Boston, where the official pageantry continued. Amelia was beginning to enjoy the nonstop parades and dinner parties, and charmed admirers with her "wonderful sense of humor," as Anne Morrow Lindbergh later wrote. "In a crowd in which we were all present, she reported hearing some stranger exclaim, 'the poor girl *does* look like Lindbergh!' " Dorothy's casual sophistication and natural understanding of celebrity had become invaluable to her friend, and she was delighted to help.

> JULY 9, 1928 *Left hotel at 7:15 for Curtis Field. Take off for Boston in a trimotor Ford plane. George and I with Amelia. Stultz and Gordons in a Fokker. My greatest thrill and joy of all new sensations. Hot, sultry, golden day, 2 to 3,000 ft. altitude, going at 85 to 110 miles per hour. Yellow daisies in field below looked like golden dust and no hills at all! And we watch our own shadow below. The other plane seems to glide, motionless and we feel no sense of moving, just hear the sound of motors! Boston in 2 hrs. Parade—Reception—Governor's house—Capitol—Parade—Boston Common, etc. A celebration out doing that for Lindbergh. We had Colonel Lindbergh Suite!*

Dorothy later recalled that "Dennison Airport was shouting and cheering; great ships in the harbor shrilled their whistles; on every roof handkerchiefs waved; and everywhere showers of gay papers made a snowstorm of welcome. . . ."

Amelia's fiancé, Sam Chapman, was waiting at the hotel in Boston when they arrived. On July 10, feeling excluded from the formal ceremonies, he gravitated toward Dorothy:

> *Almost before we woke, phone began ringing again and reporters and news photo men, etc. were waiting for interviews. Sam Chapman was sneaked up to her room to see her, and reporters immediately knew of it. There's a penalty to being famous and*

one pays the price by having no privacy whatever! Medford noontime parade and reception. While Sam Chapman and I stayed behind and had a fine talk. Such an insight in to a human being as I've only seen a few times before. I like him, but Lordy what a problem he is facing. Back to Rye on Private Car. Gilt Edge special.

Soon after the parades ended, Amelia moved into Rocknoll, where she began writing what would become *20 hrs. 40 min.* Though she continued to make personal appearances, she would essentially live in the Putnam home until the manuscript was completed. *"George and Amelia in town for a radio talk at night. When Dick Byrd introduced Amelia in Boston he said: 'A very gallant lady, at home in the universe and unafraid.' A fine tribute."*

Dorothy understood that the aggressive publishing entourage that had followed them back to Rye was a necessary part of book promotion. *"Secretaries and extras and neighbors, and relatives all crowding around. And an enormous mob for meals. All very hectic and upsetting, but it's all in the game."* She was swept up by the activity, but privately wrote of her longing for and frustration over G.W.'s absence.

JULY 12, 1928 *Busy all day around the house trying to get things caught up. Out to see the outboard motor boat races and the navy seagull races off Playland Beach. A flat ideal day, and returned in time to meet George, Amelia and Capt. Manning [of the SS Roosevelt] for dinner.*

JULY 13, 1928 *To town, Capt. Manning returned with me, many errands. Amelia worked all day. After dinner Amelia and I drove my new Chrysler "75" (actually, the very first one delivered!) to meet Sam Chapman at Stamford. Home—a cold drink and a little music and to bed in the loggia. Oh, sometimes it would be easier not to know so much about other people's intimate affairs. One suffers for it, often. I'm curiously apathetic. I don't understand myself—Why? What? Who?*

JULY 14, 1928   *Try to arrange fresh flowers, but the fields are so wet from constant rains that I'm drenched. Swim in a.m. altho' water cold and unappetizing, but we must have exercise. Amelia and I really swam, but Chapman and George quit as soon as they were wet. Damn the constant rain! Sam and Amelia out for drive after dinner, then cool drink and very soon a quiet house.*

The historic month had not altered her fundamental situation. Once again, Dorothy seemed to be moving toward a breakup of the marriage.

JULY 15, 1928   *The only man I desire, I can't have. The one who has a "right" (to hell with conjugal rights!) to me, I am utterly indifferent to, and anyway he's far too occupied with affairs of business to give time to any emotional life. But I don't really care any more. There's only one man I can think of loving.*

9

G.W. AND A.E.

JULY 20, 1928 *My birthday! And how utterly old and finished I feel. All the thrills and joy of life seem to be behind me. And yet I see a few older women who remain vital, keen and amusing and loveable. I wonder have I those qualities too? . . . Dinner, a very special one, with Junie, Dave, France. My child called on phone for my birthday—so happy.*

NEARING HER FORTIETH BIRTHDAY, MY grandmother became increasingly philosophic. *"No woman knows anything about a man till he has kissed her at least twice. . . . I would rather be loved for five minutes than be admired for an hour."* Diary excerpts like this one make me wish I had known her in her younger and more passionate years.

It may not have been her birthday that prompted the pensiveness, rather the painful fact that she was growing old without a plan or purpose, and that the only man she had ever loved was unavailable. She had just received a letter from G.W. saying he could not join her at the Double Dee Ranch in Meteetsee, Wyoming, later that summer. From her diaries, it's clear my grandmother was deeply disappointed, but understood that he was working in Pennsylvania. *"A long letter from G.W. which says he's hard at work with his Dad, on a mill in Danville. And I fear the Dude Ranch chance has fallen by the wayside. Too bad, and yet I know what it means to his family to have him home with the gang."*

On July 24, George and Amelia returned to Rye. Dorothy did not greet them outside on the drive, preferring to appear less eager than the rest of the household. By now, the two women respectfully acknowledged their dual relationship to the publisher. Amelia was sensitive to Dorothy's role as wife and mother, and appreciated her need to be in control of the domestic scene, just as Amelia was beginning to develop her own career under George's watchful direction.

The friendship between the two women continued, despite the tight book deadline that found Amelia at her writing desk for most of the day. Still, there were welcome excursions. *"Amelia and I spent all afternoon searching for a new dance frock for her in Port Chester and Greenwich."* They seldom missed their afternoon swim together, and Amelia particularly enjoyed visiting the Binneys' home, where she was afforded an unusual hour or two of privacy. *"Drove to Sound Beach to see my dad—took Amelia and Junie. Nice visit."* There was a spirit of free will and determination in both women, and oddly enough at this point, not a trace of jealousy over the man who had brought them together.

JULY 25, 1928 *The house seems so terrifically crowded and full of people. 4 in family, 4 guests, and 4 servants! I don't like it, really, and long for a quiet tete a tete with a congenial soul, or some satisfying music. Oh, for a quiet cool house, full of fresh flowers and <u>one</u> person such as Hub or G.W. to talk with and listen to good voice or piano or flute by the hour! Amelia working on her book with Fitz.*

In the waning days of July, Amelia became a familiar figure at social functions in Rye, accompanied by the Putnams.

Dorothy enjoyed introducing the young flyer to her circle of friends, who were taken by Amelia's modest charm.

JULY 26, 1928 *Home just in time for George's train and Hilton and a newspaper woman came with him. Club sandwiches and tea and then we six left for town and the big fight to see Heeney and Tunney. Dave, Amelia, George and I, a box, and a great fight to watch. A K.O. in the 10th round, but the bell saved Heeney. And the referee stopped the fight in the 11th—Tunney still champion heavyweight and not even gooey or bruised! Drove home—soft warm night.*

JULY 27, 1928 *To town early for hair trim and a few errands for Amelia. Cocktails at house, and a fine party at Casino. Shore dinner and dance. 15 of us. Rainy night, but no one cared. Every one really an exceptional dancer. All men left for N.Y. and Marty and Laurie took midnight train for Boston to see Hub at Martha's Vineyard. Good party all around.*

JULY 28, 1928 *Amelia, Dave, George and I drove to Ogden Reid's home to a bathing suit party. Perhaps 40 guests, young and old in bathing suits, plus a fancy costume. Dinner on the terrace, moonlight and an orchestra, then afterwards a delicious swim in heavenly pool 75' x 30' and flooded with lights under the water.*

JULY 29, 1928 *After a minute or two at piano George and I walked to Manursing just for exercise. Home and dressed and off to a buffet lunch at the Bernhard Gimbels to meet Gene Tunney. A lovely day, a hundred or so guests, a beautiful big country estate. And our Amelia and Tunney were the cynosure of all eyes. Both, too, more than charming in their way—easy, agreeable and good looking. Except for a very slight purple stain under one eye, Tunney scarcely shows his affair [the fight against Heeney] of Thursday.*

My grandmother must have had some reservations several days later, when she and Amelia risked their lives by riding as passengers in a small plane piloted by an unsavory character. Despite Wilmer Stultz's refusal to go along, the two women leaped at the opportunity, eagerly climbing aboard.

AUGUST 2, 1928   *Off in a.m. to Teterboro Field with Amelia, by car. Flew from there with her and two men to Sea Girt, Military Review, etc., by Governor Moore. Big lunch and party. Stultz received Mayor's Commission. Had a lesson in courage; the pilot of our plane, Caperton, had a bad reputation—crashed two planes recently. The Stultzes refused to fly with him. Amelia walked over and climbed in. She and I went with him. Hot day—Small plane—Thrill.*

On August 4, Dorothy impatiently awaited the beginning of a long-planned weekend with G.W. It was to take place on Martha's Vineyard at the home of a mutual friend (and Putnam author) Hubbard ("Hub") Hutchinson. But G.W. had fallen off a scaffold earlier that summer and my grandmother was worried that he would not be able to leave after all. Waiting for him to arrive, she concentrated on the piano keys. *"All morning I did music and filled the house with blossoms."* She fussed over her appearance, even wearing a touch of rouge on her cheeks, which she once said was *"the second greatest boon to womanhood—the first being economic independence."*

Finally, the excursion moved into high gear.

AUGUST 4, 1928   *A poor start, with a three hour delay waiting for G.W. But it didn't really make any difference. A very scorching day and off in our gay blue Chrysler we started for 260 miles to Woods Hole! And oh, such delectable gaiety and fooling and jokes and good nature! We missed the last boat, then thro' a chance friend of George's went over in a private boat. Hub overjoyed to have us! Dunes, moonlight, swim, fooling, happiness, wit, joy.*

The reunion of old friends, the childlike frivolity, and the electricity between Dorothy and G.W.—despite Hub's presence—is obvious. She dubbed their gang "the Three Musketeers."

AUGUST 5, 1928 *Heavenly sunny day and off fairly early for an ocean beach with superb rollers and a positively inviting look. Sand dunes again and an inner lagoon, or shallow pond. After lunch the Three Musketeers lay on the hillside under a huge scrub oak tree and Hub read aloud his new story then with a picnic supper we started off for another beach, driving over hills and thro' deep ruts bordered with sweet bay and "brakes." But a brief thunderstorm chased us back to the car. Out to the first beach for an hour and back to our beds on tip toe.*

AUGUST 6, 1928 *Breakfast 7:15—then down the island 15 miles over rolling English moor-like country to catch the boat for Woods Hole. An occasional spatter of rain, but not enough to dampen or even distantly affect our ribald mirth and good nature. At noon we stopped for a lobster sandwich, delicious, then on thro' great country to Westerly and somewhat of a scramble to let G.W. off at New Haven where he just caught the train. Dined at "7 Gables Inn" leisurely, then on down Post Road to home at 10 p.m. David came in with three boys. Fruit, cake, cold drinks and to bed at midnight. Oh, what a delicious, ecstatic weekend!!!*

Dorothy describes her shameless love, along with her uniquely candid opinion of the aging process.

AUGUST 18, 1928   *I could take a rose in my teeth, and come skating into the picnic on one wheel! I am so mad about him that every other man in the world looks like my great aunt to me! Why the Greek dance! With its abandon of youth and the invariable abdomen of age! The people we know today who are hot tempered, witty, unconventional determined and passionate. Subtract the fire which is their motive force and in 30 years these same people will be irritable, silly, untidy, pig headed, and lewd! Nothing is in the ashes that was not in the log save the perfectly negative qualities of pallor, impotence and chill.*

While Dorothy was away for the weekend, Amelia finished her manuscript. The flyer cryptically recalled her impressions of the previous seven weeks, from takeoff in Boston through the completion of her book in the Putnam home:

Preparations . . . the flight . . . England . . . our return . . . the first receptions . . . photographs, interviews . . . New York, Boston, Chicago . . . the many invitations not accepted because of lack of time . . . mayors, celebrities, governors . . . splendid flyers; Wilkins, Byrd, Chamberlain, Thea Rasche, Balchen, Ruth Nichols, Reed Landis . . . speeches, lunches, radio microphones . . . acres of clippings (unread) . . . editors, promoters . . . settlement houses, aldermen's office . . . gracious hostesses, camera-wise politicians . . . private cars, palatial planes . . . and then my book . . . hours of writing piled up in the contented isolation (stoically maintained) of a hospitable Rye home . . . friends, a few parties . . . swimming, riding, dancing, in tantalizing driblets . . . brief recesses from work . . . Tunney vs. Heeney, my first fight (a boxer's career is measured by minutes in the ring; an aviator's by hours in the air) . . . more writing—much more.

I was sixteen when I first read *20 hrs. 40 min.* I found the thick black book with red letters in my father's library; it was inscribed to him by the author. I turned the pages and studied the photographs first. Here was this woman who had taught my father to fly. At the time, I didn't realize the book was dedicated to my grandmother. Growing up, I was unaware of their strong emotional connection. Now I know how much they influenced each other's lives. And I'm aware that had it not been for my grandparents, Amelia would not have moved in the circles she did. Dofry invited Amelia into her world, introduced her to a glittering array of celebrities, artists, adventurers, and socialites. To the unsophisticated young flyer, the Putnams represented a lifestyle she had only dreamed of. How ironic that Dorothy seemed to be Amelia's heroine, at least for a short time.

10

"LIGHT LOVE"

"George is absorbed in Amelia and admires and likes her. Maybe he's in love with her."

BY THIS TIME, MY GRANDFATHER AND Amelia were thrown together constantly. Their working relationship had certainly been a remarkable one, and now that the book was finished, they made plans for an extended speaking tour to promote it.

"George was a workaholic," recalled his former business associate, Charles ("Cap") Palmer. "His wife didn't have to worry about other women. She had to worry about the job." Now, Amelia had become George's job.

AUGUST 20, 1928

A perfect day and Amelia flew her "silver bug" for an hour, early. Home by 3 o'clock, then all balled up about going to S.B. to see my family. Very disagreeable altogether. G.P. had a date to swim with A.E. and I upset their plans by being home— and he tried to be sentimental. Followed me up because he was furious. When I came home he and Amelia were busy working.

George and Amelia had tried to keep their affection for one another secret, but gossip among the aviation set was circulating about a love affair between the famous flyer and her powerful business manager. At first, Dorothy could not believe that Amelia would disrupt her marriage, because of their friendship. Still, she was unprepared for the ugly speculation, and welcomed the chance to leave Rye for her long-planned western trip.

For George, there was no doubt that his wife had lost interest in their physical relationship, and by now he suspected she was involved with another man, as her diaries reflect his sudden jealousy.

AUGUST 21, 1928   *Packed—Drove to town with A.E. in time to have tea with George. Then took 6:30 train for Chicago. A sad and wearisome unpleasant "scene" with George at dawn. The same old thing, plus suspicions and accusations. Sick headache all day. Bed as soon as train left. Oh, Lord, such a stupid mess is my life.*

George and Amelia accompanied Dorothy to the train station and stood watching for a moment as she waved her two outstretched arms before disappearing into the dim compartment of the passenger car. *"Train . . . Dead tired, rather weary at heart and very unsettled in my personal affairs. Can one ever 'Patch up' the disillusionments and make a 'go of things' again?"*

Even on that steamy August day, Dorothy wore a long-sleeved dress and pinned a pale lavender orchid to her lapel. The corsage was an unlikely romantic gesture from George, and Dorothy questioned its significance. Around her neck hung the silver fish pendant. Through the train window she caught a glimpse of her husband with Amelia making their way through the crowd, and for the first time she saw what others had already begun to notice: They were a couple.

AUGUST 23, 1928   *Train. Through flat uninviting coun-*
try where women are fat and with poor complexions and wear
magenta or short sleeves on the train! And the backs of mens
necks are shaved! Read and dozed all day, pretty worried about
leaving when my whole personal "household" is unsettled!

Arriving in Wyoming, Dorothy stepped down from the
train and into the husky embrace of Carl Dunrud, the
Putnams' rough-weathered, Arctic explorer friend. She
squinted girlishly into the hot sun as he placed his huge
cowboy hat on her head.

An even greater delight awaited her: G.W. had managed
to make the trip after all, though his presence would prove
unsettling.

AUGUST 25, 1928   *Cody. Arrived early and Carl, with*
his ten gallon hat, etc. to meet me! Breakfast at the cafe then
off across rolling flat country, oil wells, 55 miles south to the
"Double Dee." Stopped in Meteetsee for vegetables, etc. and
a hobo on an oil truck came grinning over to us! G.W.; he'd
hitchhiked from Jackson Hole ranch (where he visited Darcy).
A great surprise and jolly time all round!! Much fun. Ranch
for a fine dinner. Sat around and visited all afternoon. Mr.
and Mrs. Charles Belden and Mrs. Gene Phelps to call. All
hands tired and happy. Big open fire, then bed early.

The next day, after a visit from other prominent cattle
ranchers, Dorothy, G.W., Carl, and his partner Cactus,
headed up Fork Canyon for an afternoon horseback ride.

The group set up camp and my grandmother requested
that her tepee be placed near the stream, but far enough
from the commotion of the cook tent and the boisterous
male voices. *"The boys have a fine tent outfit. Three boys in the
big cook tent and my tepee on the river edge, 150 ft. away. The
nights are cold, but my sleeping bag is fine and warm, and the*

sound of the stream is heavenly." Resting alone before supper, she ached with sadness. G.W. was still attracted to Darcy and had traveled to Wyoming to see her as well. Dorothy knew she would eventually lose him, and began to face the truth: They would never live together as man and wife.

The camp was quiet and G.W. hesitated before breaking the silence. The day had been long, and he knew that Dorothy was tired. After speaking her name, he reached his arm inside the tent and handed her a poem, written on a single piece of paper. She was not a diarist to neglect even the slightest event in her life, and if the entry was particularly significant, she turned to the last pages and recorded it under "Memoranda." Such is the case with this poem; its yellowed original still exists among her papers.

Light Love   25 August 1928

It will not last, this little love of ours,
But does that matter? Really not a bit,
We will have had one moment exquisite,
And it will vanish like summer flowers,
Blest be our failure—flint in little showers.
Not the great pyrotechnical display of Abelard and Heloise.
One day of love for us beneath these amorous bowers.
Lighter than snow is love that men call light.
Lighter than butterflies swift vagrant wings.
The least snow can make the world more bright
And who refuses what the summer brings?
Blest be all kisses,
And blest be the love that dies before satiety.

—C. H. Towne

Dorothy held the poem in her hand, knowing the two had made the decision together. The time had finally come to let go of the dream. She responded, *". . . loving teaches us all, we know. . . . We pass from one phase to another, opening and closing doors on emotions that at the time you were sure were <u>eternal!</u>"*

Dorothy had left home unsure of their future, but certain of their everlasting love. When they parted in Wyoming, she believed the affair was over.

She traveled on from Wyoming to Seattle, Mount Rainier, and her old home in Bend, Oregon, before the last stop in Pasadena, California, to visit her ailing brother, June, his wife, and child.

Dorothy often lingered in the dining car with other travelers, and delighted in the company of the cheerful attendant, who continually refilled her water glass and chatted. Her enduring smile attracted strangers to her table and to her side. No one escaped her infectious warmth. She was just as apt to strike up a conversation with the porter as with a passenger in a first-class car.

When morning came, she was transfixed by the lofty Cascade Mountains. It was early autumn in the high country and her diary entries focus painfully on the changing seasons within her own life: *"Montana. The autumn flowers give me a little heartache. Why am I sad? The checking off of another year? Do my cycles run from autumn to autumn. The forests are burning here and there. Spokane by dinner time. I have much to think about."*

With the realization that G.W. would no longer be the main focus of her life, she seemed lost and insecure compared to her husband and sister. *"George's birthday—41— he's keen, successful, has a fine reputation for ingenuity and cleverness. And apparently has what he went after in life."* She envied others who had lived an apparently happier domestic life.

SEPTEMBER 9, 1928 *Oregon: Helen's birthday! And she's still so slim, pretty and youthful. She has been the ideal wife and mother, I guess, with never a failure all the years. Drove all over town, up top of Pilot butte! There are mowed lawns and flowers and foundations and pavements where I once pushed Dave in his baby carriage across dusty streets.*

Nearing Pasadena, she steeled herself for what lay ahead. Her tall, athletic brother was lying helpless in bed near death and her thoughts returned to their youth. A world-class swimmer, June Binney had shattered several records— and roaring cheers from onlookers echoed now in her head. She thought of the day they raced out to the lighthouse and back, and how sheepish he had felt when he won. She remembered his visit to her home in Oregon, when he had traveled west as a teenager on the same train she was now riding. She could not bear to see him ill, or imagine his three-year-old son, Edwin, without a father. Grateful for the privacy that her compartment offered, Dorothy wept, her eyes filling with sorrow as the train pulled to a stop and Betty and little Dwin raced toward it.

SEPTEMBER 12, 1928   *Pasadena. Dwin and Betty met me at Glendale. Betty's house is big and sunny and open with a lovely garden and lily pool. But my heart breaks when I try to describe my dear, sick brother. He's completely paralyzed, all except his left arm! His hair and mustache are black, his face and body, white and thin and colorless. And even his speech is thick and distorted. In bed since April and blind. Oh, God, why should it be!? And not yet 30.*

The following day, she and her sister-in-law attended the local air show, expecting to see Amelia. She would find out that Amelia and George had been involved in an airplane accident in Pittsburgh, which had been the cause of Amelia's late arrival in Los Angeles. *"Pasadena—Amelia not arrived in L.A. yet—her plane broken. Went to Air meet with Betty. Saw Lindbergh in some miraculous flying, backpacked and off to train bound East."*

When Dorothy returned from the air meet, there was a desperate telegram from George. He had just heard rumors that he and Amelia had become more than business partners and he was worried. *"Depressing wire from G.P.—'Come home, etc.' Very sad!"* For the first time in seventeen years of marriage, he recognized the frightening possibility that he could lose his wife. He pleaded with her to return home immediately, conscious of the fact that her absence only gave credence to the rumors.

And so she was homeward bound. Reclining in the window seat aboard the *Sunset Limited,* she reached into the bottom of her worn travel case to find the single orchid still pinned to the frayed ribbon. She lifted the wilted flower toward the light and wondered why she had saved his gift. Unfolding its petals, she saw it as a fragile reminder of her loveless marriage. *"When I left New York a month ago George gave the one and only orchid ever from him. Why now? Is it significant of our unreal and artificial life, his and mine? It's a pretense of the thing real married life could be."*

Back in the comfort of her home again, Dorothy's thoughts were a tangle of emotions.

SEPTEMBER 19, 1928 *Flowers, music, and the house. It's refreshing to be in my own lovely home again, with my own belongings! The robins are already flocking and great metal blue-black clouds of blackbirds drift across the meadows! The touches of scarlet maple are here. Autumn, the brilliant but sad end of my year "cycle." I'm depressed, yet passionate and elated.*

SEPTEMBER 22, 1928 *George is determined to have me give up the Africa trip. Just why? Does he want me home? Does he miss me? Are we any pleasure to each other? Scarcely even a "convenience" anymore!*

Amelia's absence from Rocknoll restored Dorothy to her rightful role, however temporarily. *"Town late, dinner at Divan Paris with George, then he and I went to opening of Al Jolson's new 'talkie' movie. Songs and some conversation. Senti-*

mental, bored me, maudlin. Great hit." Following her up the stairs after their night on the town, George explained why Amelia had not reached California in time for the National Air Races. He said that she had crashed her Avro Avian in Pittsburgh. He confessed that he had been with her at the time and had kept it out of the papers. Upon landing, the plane hit an unmarked ditch, spun wildly out of control, and ended up on its side. He added that he had returned to Rye the same day, leaving Amelia behind to repair the considerable damage and deal with the press.

George worried about Amelia's public image, and the speculation surrounding the two of them could be harmful. For this reason, he invited his wife to join him, Amelia, and David on an Arctic trip the following summer. Dorothy was furious. She knew her husband wanted her only as a chaperone. *"I don't want to go! Yet if I refuse it's given up and blamed on my temper."*

On September 24, G.W. and his brother Tyler drove down from Yale for an unexpected visit. What began as another lighthearted gathering of friends ended in tears. *"Late afternoon Tyler and G.W. drove down from Yale. Coffee in studio. Then the two Weymouths to dinner. A little music, a cold drink and suddenly it is midnight. <u>Yellow Roses from Child. Awfully tired, awfully sad and weary</u>. George in town all night."*

Dorothy was still mourning the change in that relationship as well. *"Why should one put oneself in a position of caring so much? Why therefore, be so deeply <u>hurt</u> by another? A farewell, a gesture (or worse a forgotten gesture), a careless word or phrase from one you adore. Oh, can <u>hurt</u>, hurt so acutely. Lordy, I'm a fool! One side of me independent and impervious, another, sensitive, shy, too keen and analytical for my pleasure. Oh, oh, I'm hurt."*

"Light Love" had become their eulogy. Just as Dorothy had transcribed the poem under "Memoranda" at the year's end of her diary, so had she recorded two indelible dates across the same page. The first is May 19, 1927, the date that represents the birth of her passion; the second memorializes the end of their affair. Carved together across a paper tombstone, the composition is an epitaph:

MAY 19, 1927   *A heaven on earth*

SEPTEMBER 24, 1928   *"To my darling L. from her C."
And oh, yellow roses!*

Dorothy revealed the stages of her suffering in the pages of her diary: anger, hurt, blame, and finally acceptance.

SEPTEMBER 26, 1928   *He thinks of himself as unhappy, but high minded. He is actually a passion-scalded pig. What does goodness matter? One is either happy or unhappy.*

SEPTEMBER 27, 1928   *I cannot, cannot readjust myself! No amount of exercise, no amount of music and even my worry and sadness over my brother June—nothing seems to divert my present absorption. I cannot for a minute stop my mind going round in its "circle." It is impossible, unbelievable, can't be true! Yet.*

11

DEAD RECKONING

"George's obsession for A.E. and his clamor to be with her every minute, all day, every day on one pretext or another will give me the very excuse I need for a separation—if not a divorce. 8 years ago, April, I asked for a break; anything as long as I didn't have to live with him. And he broke down and cried, and swore he couldn't imagine living without me . . . I wish almost, I cared."

*T*HIS MUST HAVE BEEN THE MOST DIF-
ficult time in my grandmother's life, to realize that her friend and her husband had fallen in love. From reading the diaries, however, I know she did not blame them. But how hard to face her family and friends when they heard the rumors that he had chosen another woman. She must have wanted to tell the world, "I also love, and have been loved too." At least if her secret had been known, she would not have been perceived as the victim. She was too proud to gain any pleasure from pity, and she was beyond jealousy.

Reading the diaries for the first time, it shocked me to learn that my grandmother's anguish over G.W. and her strained marriage had prompted thoughts of suicide: *"Feel depressed and sad, that ghastly futility, when even music and the garden fail to stifle the charm of suicide."*

An abiding sense of comfort was visiting her son David at Hotchkiss. *"A little music, a chat, and suddenly it's time to drive to Lakeville for David."* G.W. couldn't stay away from Dorothy, and despite their agreement, he called to say he also wanted to visit David at school. It had been a week since they had last spoken, and she knew that severing all ties would be impossible. Even if they were not lovers, they knew it would be foolish to believe their lives would not continue to be intertwined. *"G.W. brought a Yale crew man here yesterday. They drove to Hotchkiss in the old Chrysler. Returned here for supper, very late."*

By October 12, news of Amelia's impending solo transcontinental flight dominated the conversations at Rocknoll again. She was reported to be somewhere between California and New York, attempting to become the first woman to break this barrier. Dorothy anticipated George's extended absence from the house and family once again. *"Just heard Amelia's on the last lap of her flight across continent and return. I have a strange detached sort of feeling about things and perhaps it's just as well. As if nothing mattered particularly and that I must just take each day as it comes, without any question or longing for it or things to be otherwise."*

Within aviation circles, Amelia's prowess as a pilot was hotly debated. Some considered her inept, and among the hard-core flyers there was the usual jealousy: *"I dashed to dinner and dance in town at 'Heigh Ho.' . . . Cocktails at the Barclays, then met, primarily three aces—Lyons (Capt.), navigator of the* Southern Cross *and Capt. [Bill] Lancaster and Mrs. Miller, who flew to Australia. Too much drinking and poor dancers. . . . Gosh, how these three flyers loathe Amelia! It's a shame."*

On October 15, Amelia successfully completed the record flight. As she touched down on the grassy landing strip at Bowman Field, my grandmother recalled that giddy morning in August when the two had taken off in the Avro Avian. *"All morning phoning, etc. to and from Amelia. It's foggy in N.J., smokey. Finally at noon, she landed at Bowman Field. A month ago she flew from there across continent and return—some 7,000 miles solo! Great stuff!"*

Despite the growing tension between them, Dorothy still held Amelia in esteem and owed the flyer a debt of gratitude for breaking new barriers for women.

OCTOBER 20, 1928 *George and I drove to New Haven. Met Amelia for buffet lunch at G. W.'s fraternity hall and a mob of boys. Then to Brown Game. 32–7 favor Yale. Darcy Kellogg came unexpectedly. Then to Lawn Club for dinner. Air Conference. G.P., G.W., Amelia, Darcy and I. Amelia spoke, etc. Dull dinner tho', then drove home to Rye and sat before the fire drinking milk, till late.*

OCTOBER 21, 1928 *George and Amelia horseback all morning. G.W. returned from Yale in time for dinner. Then he, G.P. and I went to the shore to await the "Ireland" sea plane. (Amelia packed her stuff after 15 weeks here.) Had a short flight with Capt. Lyon and Capt. Lancaster (famous navigator of "Southern Cross" across Pacific, etc.) Big party at house in p.m. Showed Amelia's movies of "Friendship" flight. A frenzy of airplanes and excitement and turmoil inside me.*

The day following the dinner party was particularly unnerving for Dorothy, who writes that she suffered from nausea. She ran from the house, sickened by the fact that once again she had paraded her false life as Mrs. George Putnam before the crowd of ambitious aviators. She knelt on the brittle autumn leaves, alone and torn over whether to end this deceit, whatever the consequence.

Toward the end of October, after George and Amelia had spent several nights in Manhattan, Dorothy writes: *"George stayed in town last p.m. with Amelia. But I don't care."* By now, she was determined to gain her freedom. *"Apparently George and I face our final separation momentarily. Oh, it's all so very upsetting and hectic."* The following day in the early darkened hours, George came to her bedside. Overcome with emotion, both wept openly.

OCTOBER 22, 1928   *A quiet let down day which began when George came in to my bed at dawn and cried. I guess we're all wrong, both of us and we're messing up our two lives pretty thoro'ly for no special reason. But, oh for years, its been so antagonistic. . . . And yet I am passionate and demonstrative. Why, oh, why should I want another's touch and embrace!*

Dorothy blamed herself as well as George. Years later, she hinted that the divorce might have been a terrible mistake. But she was not the sort of woman who ever admitted making a wrong decision. There was no question, however, that her husband loved her and tried to win her back.

NOVEMBER 4, 1928   *Sun. The house is a display of red leaves and flowers and fruit—very charming. G.P. and G.W. off for a ride. . . . Dinner and more music and again, inroads of people. . . . Then supper and G.W. back to Yale . . . and suddenly it seems quiet and lovely again. . . . Life is odd. G.P. is determined to woo me and win me all over again and he's certainly concentrating. He's even breaking dates with A.E.!*

NOVEMBER 5, 1928   *Life is topsy turvy and now G.P. is apparently breaking off all his dates with A.E. as a sop to me! Funny—And I'm trying, rather stupidly I feel, to calm*

myself and quit worrying and settle down to the humdrum
existence of middle aged women! Men at this stage, just begin
to have their fling. And we usually go in heavily for politics or
bridge or movies! And meanwhile I'm just fool enough to be in
love!

Among the flyers who gathered at the Putnam home was
an intensely attractive young man who now began to pur-
sue Dorothy. Frank Monroe Upton, an acquaintance of the
family, had reappeared after two years at sea with the U.S.
Navy. *"Frank Upton arrived for all day and overnight, after two*
year silence and disappearance. He's as nice as ever. G.P. to town
to go over movies, etc. with Amelia. Frank and I drove to Sound
Beach to see Helen and Happy."
During World War I, Upton had received the Congres-
sional Medal of Honor for bravery. In 1917, he dove from
the deck of his destroyer near the French coast and swam
through burning debris to rescue sailors after their ship had
exploded. More recently, in 1926 aboard the SS *Roosevelt,* he
had participated in another heroic rescue by saving several
crew members from a sinking vessel. For four days into a
midocean storm, the *Roosevelt* anchored alongside the battered HMS *Antinoe,* which was rolling and shipping water
over her decks. For this exploit, Upton and Captain George
Fried were awarded medals and honored by a ticker-tape parade in New York City.
Though Dorothy regarded Frank as *"an odd duck, perfectly*
simple and single track," she was smitten by his celebrity
status and flattered by his attentions. *"Yet he somehow gives*
an impression of depth and contradictoriness which isn't there.
If he had better teeth, he'd be a very stunning man, very much a
'mere male' tho'." "Eff," as Dorothy was quick to call him,
was aware that his rough manliness appealed to her proper
upbringing and that her marriage to George was floun-
dering.

While Frank was a weekend guest at Rocknoll, Dorothy had asked him to leave the family to themselves for a few hours. For the very first time, though it was a dubious undertaking, all four Putnams were planning a two-week holiday together; and on November 13, Dorothy felt surprisingly optimistic: *"We've decided to go on a 16-day West Indies cruise—all four of us. And I feel sure it will be a great lark if we can just meet each other halfway!"* David was home from Hotchkiss, and George had actually broken a date with Amelia in order to join Dorothy and the boys in finalizing the details of their Christmas cruise. These hours would be remembered for their unprecedented closeness and good humor.

Two days later, George joined Amelia on a ten-day speaking tour. Dorothy typically had little to say about their trip: *"George and Amelia off to Pittsburgh for 10 days."* But the business relationship sparked further rumors and the story threatened to break into print. *"Hub has heard gossip and talk about G.P. and Amelia, and whispers of a 'Putnam break-up' and he's unhappy about that. He doesn't want us to separate, and feels we're both foolish to let things go too far."*

George was clearly ambivalent himself.

NOVEMBER 22, 1928 *Wire from George. He and Amelia flew from Columbus to Cleveland, just ahead of a snowstorm. Funny, but at last his behavior with her is making him very self conscious. He tells me in every wire, etc. of their being at separate homes, etc. And there's much comment and speculation he now recognizes. Yesterday a news agency called Hilton to ask if there's truth to the rumor of a "Putnam divorce"—for Earhart? And poor sentimental Hilton is very obviously worried! Ah well, I'll have to go on the West Indies trip just to save George from a nasty bit of "Earhart and Putnam" gossip.*

On November 23, 1928, Amelia publicly announced she had broken her engagement to Sam Chapman.

DECEMBER 2, 1928 *. . . altho' George had been back from his jaunt to Chicago over a week, we still have not slept together. I'm indifferent and apathetic. . . . Perhaps never again will we live together, except as rather antagonistic friends . . . free, and yet more bound than ever, because age and conventions have jailed one. . . .*

DECEMBER 11, 1928 *G. left long before I was even awake! Busy all day around house. Town at 5:30. Cocktails with Fitz and G.P. at Coffee House and then dinner and actual tête-à-tête theatre for George and me. It's almost astonishing for he's only been out in public socially with Amelia since early June! While I've been with 10 different ones. Corking play, "Holiday" which Ted declares is absolutely D.B.P. Rebellion of smart girl against money.*

Dorothy shifted her focus to her seven-year-old son Junie, who was seriously ill with pneumonia and bedridden for two weeks. It was not surprising that during her vigil, G.W. returned to Rocknoll to offer his comfort. *"Junie has pneumonia, dear little brick! And he's been awfully patient and good except one spasm today when he ordered the nurse out of the house! I was so worried and panicky because it has seemed as tho' my own <u>fear</u> was bringing this on."* G.W. stayed by Dorothy's side to help nurse her son. He couldn't completely break away.

DECEMBER 14, 1928 *Today's G.W.'s 24th birthday and he's such a kid. But good natured, cheerful, slow to anger and lovable. George as usual, can't resist his sarcastic references to my interest in kids and callow youths! It's easy to understand tho' for they are, in their 20's, and are what we married. Young, enthusiastic, happy, with no ulterior motives in every contact. God, no wonder one turns from the preoccupied, overworked, irritable, disillusioned man of 40! Thank Heavens, there are "callow youths" in the offing to make one forget!*

On the eve of their West Indies vacation, a blistering cold wind had forced their outdoor barbecue inside. Amelia Earhart, Don Blanding, George Weymouth, Frank Upton, and Hub Hutchinson, now writing music criticism, comprised the loyal entourage that gathered for the farewell. As always, the notion of adventure energized the house, and for once not a single family member would be left behind. It was a belated show of familial closeness.

"Don and Amelia overnight, left with G.P. early. Then Dave, Junie and I with all bags drove to ship. Frank, Betty, Mother and Bub to see us off. Sailed on S.S. Duchess of Bedford *for a 16 day cruise to West Indies. Dave, Junie, G.P. and I—our very first trip anywhere for all of us together!"*

Edwin Binney's shock of white hair stood out among the crowd as the *Duchess of Bedford* moved away from the dock. Dorothy and her father locked eyes. Bub was troubled over his daughter's future, yet he deeply admired her. He knew she was incapable of living life according to society's demands. This last Christmas vacation that the family would share was taking place at sea, a bittersweet reminder of George and Dorothy's honeymoon cruise seventeen years before. *"Christmas. Gifts and good day. Deck sports and swims. Santa Claus party for children. Horse races, gay, noisy, and drinks and dance."*

The merriment ended abruptly on New Year's Day when Dorothy received a cablegram in Havana with the shattering news of her brother's death: *"Folks arrive Sound Beach Saturday with June's body. Hope you can get home in time. Helen."*

Dorothy was at the mercy of the slow-moving cruise ship. For days she was sick, often bedridden. Despondent, she questioned whether her own behavior might have caused her brother's untimely passing.

JANUARY 3, 1929   *At sea. Unhappy and blue about my brother's death. Not yet 30, a Yale Ph.D. and Professor of Geology and holder of two world records in swimming. Why did he need to be taken so soon? What is this reasoning Power? And when does it ever prove its necessity or Rightness? He is to be buried in the old graveyard in Sound Beach where Mother bought a plot years ago, believing of course, she and Bub would lie there first!*

JANUARY 5, 1929   *Sick in bed, really, and just so ill I had no desire to get up all day. Dr. called twice and nurse attended to me, but felt miserable and unhappy. Perhaps all of this is payment for my sins: a just punishment the Bible says. Yet that can't be for why should my sins be visited also on my poor family. But sorrow and illness and oh, a cruel cold ache of rebellion way down deep in me.*

JANUARY 7, 1929   *Not off the ship till 10 and then customs! Harold to meet us, drove home with all the baggage. Drove to Sound Beach with David early afternoon. Mother sick in bed. Bub sad and Betty and Dwin and nurse there. Hub here and G.W. to see us when we came down.*

Walking upstairs, Dorothy knelt at her mother's bed. The tragedy was senseless. *"G.W. off for Yale very early and David back to Hotchkiss. My own mind and heart are clearing. I shall work hard on my music, help Junie with his school, and really turn over a new leaf and try to amount to something! Oh, help me! A visit with Mother who is still sick in bed."*

Dorothy and her father had rarely used her bedroom as a place to visit, but the adjoining sitting area with the cozy fireplace offered the privacy they needed. The death of a son and brother, along with Dorothy's revelations of a loveless marriage, brought them closer now. They discussed her buying or renting Mugo Court, the home just across the lane from Rocklyn that the Binneys also owned. Dorothy and her mother had already examined the vacant house with an eye to refurbishing it, and Edwin hoped that Mugo Court would become his daughter's refuge.

Edwin was planning a cruise to Florida on his remodeled yacht, now called the *Florindia,* with his wife scheduled to join him later by train. He invited Dorothy to come. It was an appropriate time to be with her parents, and in particular her grieving mother, who was still under a doctor's care. June's death was a crushing blow and the thought of a divorce was too painful for the Binneys to bear. *"Right now my own plans are shot. For Mother has already insinuated how much it will hurt her and Bub to have me separate or divorce! What strange unexpected things life does to us! And I was* sure *this was the time!"* Dorothy, relieved to get away, accepted her father's invitation to travel south for the remainder of the winter months. Once again her official separation from George would have to be delayed.

During the month prior to Dorothy's trip, her home had become a way station for adventuring celebrities. *"Capt. Bartlett, Jim Pond and Capt. C. S. Knight (English birdman) for dinner. A trained golden eagle. Newsmen and movie men. House crowded. Mobs, crowds, talk, and I slunk away to play the piano. Can't bear it!"*

Amelia had become George's main preoccupation, and Dorothy, formerly her greatest admirer, was beginning to note her failings: *"Amelia has never written me about my brother's death. She's spent the weekend here and not mentioned it although I'm in mourning. Nor has she spoken of my Christmas gift to her. Nor did she even speak to the three servants in the house although she spent 12 solid weeks here last summer! Is it bad manners . . . yet 'she certainly manages herself wonderfully,' says G.P."*

What's more, she was stung by the fact that people were whispering behind her back.

> JANUARY 19, 1929 *G.P. introduced Amelia at the Geographic Society in Washington last night. Still appearing with her publicly all over the country and apparently totally unaware of his ludicrousness in telling me whom I shall or shall not go around with! I'm bored, and soon must boil over! Fitz said, "It's a good thing she's coming up for the weekend; in a way it will squash some of the comments about her and G.P." Corey [Corey Ford, friend and author] said, "Well, Rye at least will know you don't care particularly whether G.P. and A.E. are going around together all over the country!" Queer!*

By now, my grandmother's words were harsh. For the first time she revealed her anger at and disappointment in both her husband and Amelia.

> JANUARY 24, 1929 *Evidently everything I say of A.E. he goes and blabs to her! It's clockwork and obvious and a little disgusting when he's so eager to convince me he never discusses me with anyone! He immediately calls her up, tells her, reminds her and like a brainless puppet she does whatever he advises! Lord, how she must loathe it if she stops to think! "You must write Dorothy about her brother, You must mention her Christmas gifts to you, etc. etc.!" Ugh*

12

A CONGRESSIONAL HERO

JANUARY 29, 1929 *It's shocking! I'm becoming a shrew, a nag, a scenemaker. I, who loathe all three. Would to God, I could suddenly become a neuter, sexless, brainless and like millions of others just occupy myself with clubs, politics, etc. etc. 4 p.m. he called up, mostly to rub my nose in things and be nasty. I'm not to see this person, not to write to that one, not to pay any money, etc. To that one! He has such a right to dictate. How we wrangle! Ugh. I must quit altogether. . . .*

*T*WO DAYS LATER, DOROTHY, G.W., AND her friend Betty Chester climbed into my grandmother's new blue Chrysler and drove south. Though Dorothy and G.W. had made a conscious decision to end their physical relationship, their emotional bond was still as strong as ever.

There was no promise of paradise in Fort Pierce, Florida, only hope. Dorothy had envisioned a scouting objective, such as the one she was about to undertake, for years, and G.W. was the only person in the world who could have escorted her there. *"Clear, lovely, sunny! Early dinner at mid day.*

G.W., Betty and I left at 1 p.m. for Florida in blue Chrysler. Philadelphia at 6. Dinner at a terrible 'joint' at 7. Overnight Country Club Inn. Quaint, old fashioned and frightfully amusing rooms. Great fun, good spirits."

The sun-drenched days buoyed her spirits and the next six weeks were a blur of activity. *"Off along the Indian River by nine o'clock. Lovely drive and the two kids chortling with joy over each new orange grove or magnolia or cypress. Spanish moss in many places enchanting. All of us watched the sunrise and no one would wake the others! Out to Farm."*

No one engaged Dorothy's innate playfulness more than G.W. The weeks sped by in a rapid succession of meeting cars and trains and waving good-byes again. It was like a revolving tropical stage setting, surrounded by citrus trees and canopied with purple clouds. *"Oh, it's heaps of fun just to be camping here and it all seems like 'playing house.' We have screamed with laughter at G.W.'s episode with the huge snake in his bathroom toilet. He took us up to see it and we found still another in the rafters!"*

Dorothy had planned her days to the minute. On the same afternoon that G.W. left for New York, Frank Upton arrived by car. He drove the final few miles down the new Dixie Highway, and made his last turn west on to Indrio Road where Dorothy was waiting.

FEBRUARY 6, 1929 *Still the feeling of "playing house" and we're all gay, happy and fooling all the time! Betty and G.W. drove into town early for tickets, mail, etc. I cleaned up and did a bit of housework. Frank Upton arrived! Great fun, the two kids back and all hands went up to see Bub's "320 acre grove." G.W. packed a crate full of fruit. Hurried to town. Six of us lunched at Hotel. Hurried to see G.W. off on north bound train, hating to go.*

Alice Binney, Mary Davey (Dorothy's youngest sister), Junie and his nanny, Mrs. Bergquist, also arrived by rail in

Fort Pierce, and when they appeared, Frank—who had beaten the train—stood beside Dorothy and greeted them. He had made a concerted effort to ingratiate himself with the Binney family and Edwin saw great potential in the celebrated young sailor.

In the three months since Frank and Dorothy had become close, she had become more and more intrigued by his unsophisticated ways. The fact that he was a member of an elite group of war heroes made him a novelty, but it was his naval background that appealed to Bub, who was currently involved in developing the harbor in Fort Pierce. Almost immediately he offered Frank a job. *"Frank is so nice around the place and he already has done a hundred little things to make housekeeping here easier—paints, oils, removes rust, etc. And he adores being here, I know."*

Frank and Dorothy spent the days fishing or exploring the unspoiled inland estuaries where few tourists dared to venture. They drove to Silver Springs, taking Junie along, and swam in the clear sulphur water caves. They collected wild orchids to be transplanted later, and played with baby alligators. It was paradise. *"Off for Ocala. A spirit of joy and adventure! To Silver Springs. Out in glass bottom boat till sunset; turtles, fish, caves, springs! A tame deer on the beach. Frank and I drove out to the lovely jungle setting in the moonlight. Such tranquility and peace."*

Both Dorothy and Frank reveled in the freedom and privacy of their days, however short-lived. George was planning a visit to Fort Pierce to spend time with Junie, and she was not looking forward to it.

George for his part had no idea that Upton was in Florida, and he was shocked by Frank's presence at the Daytona train station, not to mention his wife's brazenness in inviting him to drive her there. A fight ensued and an embarrassed Upton left the car and returned to Fort Pierce alone on a train, leaving Dorothy to deal with her husband's volatile reaction.

FEBRUARY 25, 1929 *Went to town to meet G.P. and found a wire telling me "missed train, meet me in Daytona." And I hustled off within 20 minutes for a drive of 120 miles. Asked Frank to go along and G.P. perfectly raging. Altogether ghastly rude and embarrassing and unpleasant all round. A dismal dinner and a wild row and I drove home in the pouring rain. Such a tropic downpour as I've seldom seen! Home at 11:30 and Frank on the train, and <u>walked</u> out to Farm. Everyone ill at ease.*

FEBRUARY 26, 1929 *A terrible day. Town, phones, etc. Mary and Jim—family. No pleasure—no joy—nothing suits him. Sullen, sulky, critical and rude. Why oh why should we continue to go on this way all our lives? Surely there's some pleasure, peace and joy for us <u>somewhere</u>. But not together.*

The Putnams left Frank in Fort Pierce and drove south to Miami to visit friends and attend a prize fight. The trip only exacerbated the hostility between them. While driving over to the west coast, both silently wished to be elsewhere. When they arrived at their hotel, a telegram was waiting for George. The message took the form of an ultimatum.

MARCH 1, 1929 *9 a.m. Off on the Tamaimi Trail north and westward to the Gulf. Gators and snakes and turtles. Sarasota by 4 pm . . . "El Verona" hotel. Ghastly scenes and the telegram episode! A personal wire from her telling him not to return because she wouldn't be home!*

George had already planned on leaving the following day, despite the telegram. "*G.P. and I had lunch at Hotel with Mother and Bub before going to his train. He had an unsatisfactory and exasperating visit here; hurried, unsettled, unhappy and a constant bickering. And he says, entirely due to me. Sorry. Frank and I drove to Vero.*"

Putting the embarrassing row behind them, Frank felt more at ease and back in control. He was drawn to Dorothy, who was unlike any woman he had ever known. Far from being intimidated by her academic superiority, he often joked about their differences, which dissolved once they were alone. Both realized that their mutual attraction was based on the fact that they were extreme opposites. Frank must have been in awe of her social status, wealth, and worldly ways. At the same time, Dorothy was intrigued by his untamed earthiness. She finally succumbed. *"The wind rustles with palm trees, there's a squally rain and strange night whisperings and a sound of crying in the night. Yet there's enchantment in it all, too.* <u>*Conquest.*</u>*"*

Frank was an overpowering figure and their lovemaking was in sharp contrast to the tender intimacies with G.W. She knew she had to look ahead, and she had found contentment here with Frank.

MARCH 11, 1929 *A strange day, confused yet full of beauty, an electric something of recognition. I must learn some new music, a powerful thing of big chords yet an under harmony of pianissm. Sat on swing till nine. Oh, the delicious content of it here, so quiet and simple and easy. I hate to think of leaving. Alas, why does time fly so quickly when we're content and drag so dismally when things go wrong?*

The following day, she and Frank left Fort Pierce for the long drive back to Rye. Unaware that Frank and Dorothy were lovers, G.W. was waiting to greet her. *"A red bird follows us north with his meaningful whistle! We're off for Mt. Vernon of Colonial fame. Through Washington and Baltimore and Philadelphia and a <u>heavy cold rain</u>. Home at 11:15. Betty and G.W. to meet us on the road. Great cheerful adorable welcome!"*

Back home, Dorothy and George stubbornly continued to blame one another for their marital problems.

APRIL 18, 1929   *What's it all about anyway! Why couldn't it have been I that died last January, and who now was lying coldly content and at peace in a country churchyard! I try to think of a way out, and only succeed in going round and round. He wants this; I demand that. And probably each of us is 99% unfair to the other. And I hate it all.*

APRIL 25, 1929   *George decided to stay in town; he feels the house not worthwhile without a good cook! I would like to be the kind of person [whom] servants are fond of. They are all too few. The opposite is the kind of woman a man makes love to, but would never care to marry.*

Frank and Dorothy continued their affair, despite the fact that she was uncomfortable with his domineering personality, which frightened her at times. His behavior became increasingly irrational. He insisted, *"I'll go thro' hell for you."* He was pressuring her into a permanent relationship too quickly, she felt, and his attacks on her young son were unfair weapons: *" 'He doesn't love you anyway and if you don't discipline him he won't even respect you. He already considers you some kind of a convenient hack horse to wait on him.' Frank about Junie. That sounds harsh and it has hurt me a lot. Yes, perhaps he's right after all. . . ."* Once again, Dorothy was plagued by indecision.

MAY 6, 1929   *What an errant coward I am for I know what I want—and where—and why. Yes it seems as tho' I can't make the definite decision. It's just a matter of once making up my mind. Yet I'm stunned and flabby. And it is not just now, no seven years ago I tried to decide the same thing. Only now I see life and my own intimate personal happiness flitting by. Soon all my youth, my absorbent years will have fled. . . . And I shall be empty in my heart. . . .*

With Frank away for several weeks working on a cruise ship bound for San Francisco, Dorothy accepted a present from her parents: Mugo Court. The cheerful gray stone and stucco cottage had previously housed a garage and squash court before the Binneys renovated it in 1927. It was much smaller than Rocklyn, but would provide a temporary home, for she had begun to sort through and pack up those items that were small enough to be carried out by hand.

George and Amelia spent most of May traveling together on speaking engagements while Dorothy contemplated her future. *"To Sound Beach with Mother and went thro' 'Mugo Court.' The house has possibilities, but Oh, how I shall long for my lovely garden, here. Sorted books, putting all my special ones aside in my own bookcase. I'm sad, its like an amputation without anesthetic. Dinner entirely alone."*

Dorothy simply could not bring herself to tell G.W. about Frank Upton. He would certainly have been hurt and she did not want to lose him completely. In her diaries, she wrote continually about the trill of the thrush, whose song was a constant reminder of her true love.

MAY 11, 1929 *I slept on the loggia last night. And it's my place. I love it. . . . And have lived on it happily 2 years! A pheasant called—quail—phoebe—ovenbird—jay— wren and Oh, the luscious alto call of the dashing old thrush of so many memories! The dogwood is too lovely! Lordy, how I shall miss it! Each hour now I try to drink it in to keep, saying "Soon I shan't have this lovely garden of my very own soul!" For I am giving it up. And it's all my own fashioning—each bulb, each fern, each plant!*

A week later, on their May 19 anniversary, G.W. arrived and the two stood at the wood's edge listening to the flute-like notes before slowly walking away. It was the last time they would be together at Rocknoll, the scene of so many blissful memories. *"Drove to Hotchkiss with G.W. A lovely day and charming. Lunch at lakeside with David. Drove home with G.W. and a laughing, happy trip. Dinner. A moment on the terrace to revel in the thrushes' evening love song. G.P. returned from Washington—flying."*

Dorothy shifted her focus from G.W. to moving out of her house as quickly as possible. She drove to Mugo Court with flowers on the seat beside her, parked the car, and walked through the back door. She placed the yellow roses on the mantle of the empty room; then, sitting alone in the corner, she stared at the blackened stone hearth. She missed her son David, back at school, and feared that the divorce would have a devastating effect on him; more so than on Junie, who was too young to comprehend their actions. And besides, he would no doubt live with his mother, while David would remain in school. *"David's birthday. He's 16 and such a dear. Up to Sound Beach with a car load of things to put in 'Mugo Court.' Dinner with Mother and Bub. A long heart to heart solemn talk with the two of them. The first of all my life, I really think. And I cried all evening. Weak!"*

Returning to Rocknoll in the rain, Dorothy walked directly to her piano. But she had lost the will to play. She retreated to her salon and stared out into the misty night.

MAY 21, 1929 *A tear stained face and aching eyes and no sleep and exhaustion. . . . George sent Capt. Bill Lancaster (English RAFC) flyer. He crashed in Trinidad two months ago and is just out of the hospital. We talked quietly all evening, and had a mild highball late, and then to bed. Dog tired and more uncertain than ever of my future behavior. I can't feel for a minute that I'm not right. Yet my inclinations are all piling ahead. It's useless: hopeless.*

The following morning, George drove to Mugo Court and surveyed the grim scene: a vase of flowers, and books neatly packed in cardboard boxes were stacked against the walls. Floor lamps, curtains, towels, and other familiar belongings were also locked inside. He walked across the private lane and knocked on the Binneys' door. Although he feared the worst, there was still hope that his wife was behaving irrationally. He stood before his in-laws and waited to learn the truth; their resigned faces led George to break down, weeping. *"G.P. to Sound Beach where he had a bad time. Everyone apparently all upset and he developed a difficult situation."*

In the three months that follow, Dorothy's diaries reflect a wide range of emotions as she and George prepared to part forever.

JUNE 12, 1929 *A disgusting dawn when I couldn't resist making a pointed remark about his lady love! God knows he's often made beastly insinuations about all the men I like! Row, the first in weeks. For both of us are being icily polite and "careful." . . . David home from school! Hooray!*

JUNE 13, 1929 *What do I want? What is there in life of permanent value? What really counts? Am I resenting age and change, or am I meeting it becomingly? A year ago I had to go to dances every week or felt wretchingly sulky and "lost." So far I've not been this summer, don't even know when they are! Always, too, after dancing late, I'm wakeful and miserable and on edge with resentment. Why? Sex? Passion? I don't know!*

JUNE 24, 1929 *I suspect G.P. occasionally looks into this diary! He must have done so to say the things he did this morning! He's fed up, cured, isn't in love with me anymore and is eager, now, for me to go ahead and get a divorce. Odd. He's got over being in love with me as he called it in about two weeks.*

13

THE PASSENGER

"All day in a daze trying to gather myself together and do the necessary chores. I'm morbid and actually seeking this flight because 2000 miles by air seems dangerous and hazardous. Ah, well, who knows? They say when you <u>invite</u> disaster nothing ever happens to snuff one out. Drove to City—Penn Station at 5 and two hours of christening and talk, etc."

ON JULY 1, AMELIA WAS APPOINTED assistant to the general traffic manager of the Transcontinental Air Transport (TAT), which would offer to take passengers cross-country by air and rail. The TAT was banking on Amelia's image to convince more women to travel by air. Flying was still considered a risk, and she was committed to educating women in particular about air travel.

Since childhood, Dorothy had been passionate about aviation. For this reason she was Amelia's choice to become the first female passenger to fly coast-to-coast round trip in a commercial airplane. Amelia would join her for the flight to Los Angeles.

Ironically, my grandmother had written just the week be-

fore that she wanted to *"do something dangerous and rash."*
Now Amelia would give her the chance.

There was a time when the two women were inseparable,
but now their friendship was strained. Still, Dorothy was
grateful for the chance to accompany her friend on the
flight, and she writes a detailed account of the record-
making crossing.

JULY 8, 1929 *Overhead Trail—New York to Los
Angeles. City of Columbus plane No. 1, Seat 6. I am a
passenger on first passenger T.A.T. plane from Atlantic to
Pacific. 10 hours from Columbus, Ohio to Waynoka, Oklahoma. Over rich farms and fertile valleys, across Mississippi
River. Stopped: Indianapolis 9:13 a.m., St. Louis: 12:03, Kansas
City 2:47, Wichita 4:56 and Waynoka 6:24. Lunch in air—
delicious too, but weather very bumpy. Showers, sun, rain, lightning all day. But lovely effects. Read "Little Caesar," dozed
and looked. Terrible dinner at Waynoka with Amelia and
Mayor's wife. Bed, tired. A.E. looks like hell.*

JULY 9, 1929 *En Route—Clovis, New Mexico to Los
Angeles. Overhead Trail. Our Pullman train late. Breakfast
in depot. Drive to field. Stopped Albuquerque 10:17, Winslow
1:17, Kingman 2:31, Los Angeles 5:32. Lindbergh Piloted. Superb grandeur. Nothing ever like it before to thrill and excite
and enchant me. 10 hours of sheer beauty. Painted desert, sun
parched desert, winds carved mountains, great rocks and ranger.
8,000 to 11,000 ft. elevation. Head wind, too, some of the way.
Lunch served in sky. Everyone thrilled and tremendous crowd
at arrival Los Angeles, photos, etc.*

JULY 10, 1929 *Los Angeles. Tired but couldn't sleep
late. Breakfast in room. To Laskys* [Hollywood producer] *all*

afternoon and p.m. Mr. and Mrs. Arthur Weigall (English author and archeologist, wife, sister of Beatrice Lilly and musician.) Movie talkie in house, "Fashions in Love" Menjou ("Concert")

JULY 11, 1929 *Late breakfast, tub, letters, etc. To "Examiner" office for newspaper photo of self with renowned "Lindy." To Tycko to have photo taken (trial) 2 p.m. off to Lasky studios. Jean Le Meure (French Director), etc. Went all thro', etc. the "lot," the wardrobes, etc. and the new talkie works behind the scenes. Amelia here for a minute. Movie in hotel, theatre, bed.*

My grandfather was intimately familiar with Hollywood, having convinced Paramount Studios to film the war story *Wings*, for which he had the literary rights. The silent film—starring Clara Bow, and featuring spectacular stunt flying—won the first Academy Award for Best Picture in 1928. Early newsreels of attempted flights (and crashes) were a continued source of cinematic excitement.

Jesse Lasky, a famous producer, had befriended my grandfather, so Dorothy was treated royally on this visit. Lasky had tried to convince George that Amelia had star quality now that aviation in the twenties was such a popular and commercial theme. But George knew she was not interested in a career in show business.

JULY 12, 1929 *Los Angeles. A.E. here at 2 to take me for a flight in the Goodyear Blimp, one of the 4 in this country. Really very amusing and one feels like a "slow movie" after the roar and racing of the ordinary plane. Went over to the field where the Endurance fliers 246 (Mendell and Reinhart) hrs. had just come down. To Lasky's late to tea. Back late. Movie alone, dinner, bed. Sent off four telegrams and packed. I'm excited about tomorrow.*

JULY 13, 1929 *Los Angeles to Clovis, New Mexico. Left hotel at 8 with three men who fly all way across. Found Amelia and Mr. Clement in airport. "City of San Francisco" and off at 8:45, all 6 of us. It's very inspiring and something never to be forgotten. Within the hour we've had a terrifying thrill. Our radio burned out and the fire, smoke and smell at 10,000 ft. altitude, over mountains and canyons gave one to think! Lunch, afternoon tea, read Willa Cather and soon it is sunset a great rimrock mesa, purple against burnt orange sky. It is so utterly beautiful it saddens me. At Clovis I went to my compartment and hated the desert moon!*

JULY 14, 1929 *Waynoka, Oklahoma to Ohio. Off again, but as 4 times out of 6, our train is late. We're eager to be on the plane again. It is so much more beautiful, no heat, no dust. Oklahoma, Kansas, Missouri, Illinois, Indiana and Ohio. All day, we fly lower than over the mountains and desert of yesterday. Farms, grazing, ranches, etc. A.E. and Clement leave, much crowds to meet us. (Usually I am rushed and photoed and snapshotted instead of Amelia by mistake). Fine day thro' lightning storm. Late at Port Columbus. Rushed for train.*

JULY 15, 1929 *New York again. 8 nights across Continent and back. Four of them in Los Angeles. How different from the day when it took five nights to get to my Oregon home in 1912–16. Such a nice happy homecoming. Back to Rye. God forgive me for my shilly shallying, or strike me dead soon! How can I go ahead! I alone, know my problem and it is difficult! (No sleep, got up to write.)*

Four days after crossing the continent and back again in America's first commercial air carrier, my grandmother celebrated her forty-first birthday. On July 20, she wrote: *"Money doesn't help at all—it's simply pleasant to be able to help others."* Her health, she noted, was *"a thing to thrill over. But I'd be happier, poor—in a smaller, simpler menage—even a new baby. And work to do. This disgusting cloud of always bickering is corroding. . . . Lovely presents, yellow roses. Ghastly aftermath."* The end of her marriage was becoming closer to reality.

After the flight, George arranged a public relations event in which Amelia would attempt a deep-sea dive off Block Island. Once again, Dorothy was invited to join in. She had already completed similar dives near the Galapagos Islands with David four years earlier and was familiar with the risks. En route to Block Island, Dorothy and Amelia flew with Grover Loening in his revolutionary amphibian airplane, the *Air Yacht*.

JULY 21, 1929 *Senator Walcott and Bill Lancaster for dinner. Flew from Manursing to Block Island one and a half hours, in Amphibian with Grover Loening, the designer. Also Amelia and two pilots.*

JULY 22, 1929 *Up at 5:30 very soon off sound fishing. Amelia, G.P., Fred Walcott and I. Good fun and I had record catch, size and number. After lunch out to Falcon, the Mother ship for the submarines (which figured in salvaging the historic S. 51). A.E. put on diver's outfit, but didn't submerge. I swam alone. Lobster dinner and bed early. Was utterly disgusted with all the fuss over the "diving" performance.*

JULY 23, 1929 *Block Island. By 9 am on way out to Falcon and submarine, the Defender. But a leaky valve means no submerging. Meanwhile a snooty newspaper article about A.E. necessitates disproving a slur on her lack of nerve. So she dived all over "again" and went down 10 minutes in 25 ft. water. (Same helmet, etc. we used in Galapagos. David and I did this four years ago.) Had great diving out and up from the submerged sub air chamber. A.E., Loening, Ralph Chapman (inventor of underwater torch), and I. Quite a thrill. Only women in world. Flew back to Rye. I sat in cockpit.*

JULY 24, 1929 *. . . Amusing stories in all the papers about our having dived up to the surface out of the submarine. . . . Wrote (started) article "Air Minded and Sub Conscious." I hope I can live up to the title. My other remark about a future visit to a "submarine subrose" G.P. attributed to Amelia!!*

Dorothy had begun to abhor the public relations machine that drove George and Amelia. She was a deeply private person and never wanted the kind of fame that her husband sought. She appreciated a challenge, but she wanted a different life. Fame did not seduce her earthbound soul, and following the highly publicized weekend, she returned to Rocknoll more determined than ever to give George his freedom. "He doesn't need me anymore," she told one friend.

JULY 26, 1929 *Rye. Things are reaching a conclusion slowly, but surely. The end, now, is inevitable. It'd be far wiser to terminate everything now, to be poorer, but infinitely happier. To cease the jarring each other before it's too late. . . .*

In spite of Dorothy's continued indecision, she tried to stay close to her children and to deal with the personal and often awkward issues involved in raising sons.

JULY 28, 1929 *Today I've had a curious shock. When making beds and tidying up bedrooms, etc. I found some very illuminating evidence in David's suitcase! How sorry I am, how very very very sad that at 16 he knows all about sex and in a very sophisticated and unbeautiful way! Contraceptives inevitably detract from the beauty and completeness and spirituality of love. I never knew till marriage, nor G.P. at 23½.*

Two weeks after the inaugural cross-country TAT flight, David and his dad took the same trip to the West Coast for the start of the first Women's Los Angeles to Cleveland Air Race. (It was renamed the Powder Puff Derby by Will Rogers.)

Dorothy suspected that George wanted to be with Amelia when she took off for Cleveland. *"Of course, G.P. is going solely to see his Amelia start the Female Air Derby and will surely end with her at Cleveland."*

Frank Upton had badly injured his hand in a propeller, and he and his friend Bill Lancaster were still on the East Coast. *"Bill says it's the only case he's ever known that didn't take off a hand."* Upton, bandaged and sore, came to Rye to visit Dorothy. The following day, Bill and Frank left for the Cleveland Air Race. Later that day they wired her that they were forced to land in a pasture outside Syracuse waiting for the fog to lift. *"Frank from Cleveland, flew alone 600 miles in 7 hours—great stuff!"* A few days afterward came the cryptic conclusion:

AUGUST 28, 1929 *G.P. and David home from T.A.T. trip. And Amelia did not win the Women's Air Derby.*

By summer's end, G.W. had returned from Wyoming and came to see Dorothy at Mugo Court. The sun was still rising when she walked outside carrying the same iris bulbs that she and G.W. had first planted at Rocknoll and that she had dug up and carried to her new home. As a dark shadow fell across the upturned soil, she expected to hear either Mary or Helen. Suddenly she felt the tender grip of G.W.'s familiar hands on her shoulder blades. Without turning, she lowered her chin to her chest. Dorothy knew he would come. He fell to his knees and held her; she wept as they said goodbye. *"Mother's 'bus' took two loads to 'Mugo' and I went up, too. It's really happening and inside me is frozen and quiet and scared. George Weymouth here after a fine summer in Wyoming."*

Suspecting that my grandfather had begun to read her diary for evidence against her in a divorce suit, she stopped writing about G.W. Her future references to him would be cryptic, as would mentions of Frank Upton, who had made a calculated decision to stay away from her during this time. *"Frank has bought a plane and is flying alone now all the time."*

The idea of marrying a wealthy heiress was tantalizing to Upton, a man of little means and fewer social graces. He was pushing her to make a decision about the future and finally gave her an ultimatum. Flattered by his demands, she recorded his urgent promises: *" 'I want to devote the rest of my life to repaying your great generosity, and trying to be worthy of your love.' I wonder! Bless him anyway for thinking it. I wonder, could he be loyal and faithful for long years?"*

Dorothy had secretly purchased an Avro Avian, similar to Amelia's, for Upton, who had learned to fly at her urging. How could he avoid becoming a pilot? She was a vivacious member of the aviation clique and he, a war hero, would be the perfect mate. *"Before I departed for Rye, Frank had flown over from airport on Long Island and did some fine 'stunting' for the Kitchels and Binneys. Loops and barrel rolls and upside down. Surprisingly good! Astonishing after 19 days of flying. Very lonely, a little afraid."*

It wasn't long before Frank secured a job with the Cirrus Aviation Company in New Jersey, which kept him away from Rye and Sound Beach. His absence was welcome, since it helped preserve Dorothy's image of the wounded wife. Most of the Putnams' friends sympathized with my grandmother for her public humiliation over George and Amelia, and she was not about to surrender that position.

Using those rumors as an excuse to act, Dorothy decided to obtain a Reno divorce, and leased a house in the small, remote western town. *"Eff met me and off to order railroad tickets to Tahoe."* The dissolution of marriage—especially one as famous as the Putnams'—would be an embarrassing process. Divorce was still considered quite scandalous; but by taking up residency in Reno, a prominent figure like Dorothy Binney Putnam could simply walk into a courthouse after a few months, pay a modest fee, and be a free woman.

It would be the most expedient end to the marriage. Early in September, she and Junie packed for the trip.

SEPTEMBER 6, 1929 *Errands and train. Met George when he came on 5:00—short swim and dinner. A long talk while I sewed name tabs on David's school things, etc. Cried—both of us. Walked in the garden. It can't be true, yet it is. We're actually going through with a divorce after years.*

SEPTEMBER 7, 1929 *George's 42nd birthday and I gave him a monogrammed leather frame. He packed, etc. and stayed home till 2:19 and cried when Hub took him to the train. It is like death; it is utterly sad and wretched. And if we were quarreling heartily it might be easier. But this solemnness is too sad. We're both sunk. And yet I've not the slightest feeling of response to him and haven't had for years. I can't be his wife! God help me.*

Dorothy had arranged for George to take David on a camping trip to avoid an emotional parting. I can't help noticing how sad and hurt my grandfather appears in snapshots taken that day. The weight of their decision makes him appear suddenly older, and his gaze is vacant. Corey Ford, George's close friend, accompanied them. He was aware of George's depression over the divorce, and asked to be included. *"George and David and Corey Ford left last night on a fishing trip in Canada. Goodbye, Goodbye!"* On September 12, 1929, Dorothy and eight-year-old June left Sound Beach. Following the interim residency in Reno, she planned to move to Florida for good. *"Went to bank, etc. Baggage sent off. Busy. Frank met me. Mother, Mary, Bub, and Frank to see us off."*

Holding Junie's hand, Dorothy kissed her parents goodbye. As she turned to walk away, she was carrying G.W.'s yellow roses; she would arrive in Reno days later still holding the flowers.

SEPTEMBER 13, 1929 *Arrived Chicago 8:45. Rec'd 3 messages and if it weren't for them don't know how I'd go ahead with what's before me. I loathe it and wish I could be struck dead at any moment. God bless some one, anyone. And my adorable David—The idea of him, hurts most of all.*

SEPTEMBER 14, 1929 *Utah-Nevada-Cal. Train very hot and dusty and the same seems endless to Junie altho' he's being very patient and good. Sent wires and letters and rec'd two adorable messages. June is thrilled at the distant mountains and never tires of watching. I can't believe that what I'm doing is actually true or happening. Perhaps I'm mad—it's a nightmare of unreality.*

SEPTEMBER 19, 1929 *Reno. Oh, God—Moved into our own tiny house on 665 St. Laurence Street at 10 am. Paid rent, signed for phone, ordered groceries, and cooked lunch and supper. June, alas, considers it all a great lark. He adores our having no servants, etc. and thinks it fun to help with dishes, packing, etc. Brought my yellow roses along, and they help, somehow for I feel another presence here, too and not so utterly lonely and isolated. Bed early and read, but couldn't sleep. Nervous. Worried.*

To make sure that Junie would not fall behind in his schoolwork, Dorothy taught him at home. In a letter to her mother she discussed plans for her son's education in Florida: "Junie continues to thrive. I've ordered the third grade Calvert School Course for him. (To be sent to Florida in January.) And meanwhile, I'm teaching him to read his stories to me every night. Works like a charm, he's improving greatly. Oodles of love, and to Grandma P."

At the same time, she continued to receive urgent letters from G.P. He was relentless in his effort to dissuade Dorothy from her actions, as her diary reveals:

SEPTEMBER 22, 1929 *George's letter has upset me, he speaks of "having certain things in my possession for which I could prevent a divorce in any court." How strange! The very thing for which he would want to be separated and the reason why, for I 'spose he means those two, sweet, affectionate wires to L.A., which he, the dirty sneak, snooped thro' my personal underclothes to find! He'd do that and yet would try to keep me when he knows I don't love him! . . .*

SEPTEMBER 26, 1929 *Reno. One week today and already I'm breathing more deeply and walking more elastically! Saw the sunrise over the mountains. Up early, breakfast, cleaned up, swept house, had a bath and walked to mail and back before cooking lunch. (Alas, I fear newspaper reporters are on my trail.) Daily letters from George worry me. Evening Gazette carries paragraph "D.B.P.—wife, etc. here, presum-*

ably to establish a residence." Headed "Prominent Woman Here," etc. Alas!

Edwin Binney had devoted himself to making Fort Pierce the major seaport between Jacksonville and Miami. In 1919, he had helped organize the Fort Pierce Finance and Construction Company. Now Frank began working for Binney in Fort Pierce on his harbor project. Both Dorothy's parents were encouraging her to accept Frank's marriage proposal. They considered the young naval hero perfectly suited for their daughter.

OCTOBER 2, 1929 *A letter from Mother in which she says such awfully dear things about Eff. She trusts his instincts and love completely. "He has not George's brilliant mind, nor savoir faire, but oh, he has much more that is better and deeper and I believe he will be devotion itself to a woman he loves and who loves him." And Bub, in a letter, says "he'd be the last man in the world to marry for money."*

While Dorothy continued to receive letters from George begging her to reconsider, Bub was busy putting his daughter's financial matters in order in Fort Pierce. *"Blue, lonely, begging letters from G.P., in London. Bub has sold $6,986.00 rights for me! Whoops!"*

George was aware that Dorothy was considering marriage to Frank Upton once their divorce was final, and the prospect made him anxious about her financial vulnerability. He feared that Upton or some other man might take advantage of her philanthropic spirit, and he refused to agree to a divorce until she established unbreakable trust funds for their two sons. She followed his advice. *"Bank C.C. [Columbian Carbon] certificates. Endorsed and mailed east at 4 pm. 2,000 shares. To be put 'in trust' for my 2 sons, my husband's effort to prevent my leaving a fortune to any succeeding husband! Gorgeous chrysanthemums and sweet note from Eff!"*

Dorothy could not have foreseen the stock market crash of October 1929, which immediately cost her thousands of dollars.

OCTOBER 25, 1929 *N.Y. Stock Market undergoing worst panic since 1907. C.C. has dropped 100 pts! And "rights" sale will automatically dwindle to nothing. Everybody feeling the "pinch" and it certainly affects me, too, for it'll probably lose $20,000 cash sale for me.*

NOVEMBER 5, 1929 *C.C. has gone down to 119 and is now slowly going up again. Bub wires me he expects it to go to 200 soon. This recent (and continuing) stock panic is hitting many of my friends. G.P. has tangled himself up, too, and is worried. Mail and a little blue "broke" one from Eff. He's maybe flying to Florida soon, but he lacks funds and is impatient I know.*

There is no record of the extent of my grandmother's losses, but from her diaries it appears both she and my grandfather lost a great deal of money on paper. Fortunately, they were both in a position to hold on to their real estate and other assets until the crisis ended.

Eff secured passage on a freighter from Florida to Balboa, Panama, where he would meet up with Dorothy: "*Eff wired, 'S.S. Penn. Good if sure can make. Engage 4th Cuba, Key West absolute certain. Hearts love.' Music—A walk to see new Spanish house for sale. Absorbed several ideas for my own house in Florida!*"

Although determined to seek a better life, even now she still entertained the faint possibility of reconciliation—a result, no doubt, of feeling alone in a strange town. "*Wire from G. a long letter and a phone at night. It was grand to hear David's darling voice, he seems so far away from me and as if I were losing him for ever! What can I do? Go back, begin all over, stay there forever and relinquish all ideas of my pleasure in sex relations? God, I wish I knew."*

Unknown to Amelia, George continued to write a steady stream of emotionally charged letters to my grandmother. Letting go had not been easy for either of them, but I know of the two, the separation was harder on him. *"Mail, from George, a positively devastating long letter. He's sad and blue and miserable, and feels utterly 'lost' at not having me to come back to, etc. I'm sorry, sick at heart, but unchanged. Blue and depressed. Bed early and a book."* They had already agreed on joint custody of their two sons. Dorothy would receive $5,000 in cash, and George agreed to pay all of David's yearly expenses, and half of Junie's.

She was still moved by his unwillingness to let go, and continued to agonize over her decision to divorce.

> OCTOBER 16, 1929 *George writes me daily letters, always now very sweet and affectionate. He's suddenly realizing what it means to be without an "anchor," a somebody in the background who is responsible for making a "home" and its atmosphere. He is alternately furious at my "damn foolishness" and pleading with me to change my mind and come back. It makes it hard, awfully. It would be easier to fight and row! And yet why? Can't two intelligent people remain polite and considerate after they've gone thro' the years as we have? Oh, it's hard!*

Frank Upton was already in Fort Pierce waiting for her, and she wired him from Reno: "Dearest Heart, if I were in some enchantingly beautiful place I would be longing for you, too, to be there with me, to share it. And I am, and I do!" Despite her tender words, Dorothy had not yet decided to marry him. She wrote to her mother in Fort Pierce and reserved two apartments; one for herself and a separate one for him.

By the way, if there are still two apartments free, I'd better speak now for them and will begin paying rent on January 15th. I'd like one furnished one and the last unfurnished one to which you sent your odds and ends of furniture. Frank could sleep in that one, till later, and then we'd only need the one kitchen and ice box, etc. And I'd still have an extra bedroom for guests.

They spoke regularly by telephone, but the two-month separation was difficult, and Dorothy was simply not convinced that she and Upton would be happy. In his absence, their differences had somehow become magnified. For one thing, he was eight years younger. In the beginning this was appealing, but it now seemed to reflect his immaturity and financial insecurity.

NOVEMBER 7, 1929 *Oh, Eff was comforting and dear last night. His love for me I never question, but he's so totally unlike me mentally and socially, I fear sometimes. But he's younger too. And poor. God, can we make a go of it??? Is it possible with everything against it except physical passion and peaceful friendship? I don't know. In 3 years I shall be dead— suicide or death—or divorced again. Death, I hope. But what about Junie? He still needs me! Oh, dear! How sad and what a mess to thus dissolve a family.*

Dorothy's uncertainty about her future was never greater; she was bowing to inevitability. In the midst of a divorce, this period must have been terrifying for her, still questioning her future. *"There's much of me never leaks out or comes near the surface these days. I'm stifling and squashing a whole side of me forever. Life from now on will be very different, poorer, more suburban and certainly not so intellectually or socially exciting. Please God, may the other compensate!"*

Her own insecurity, bred by her mother, played a role. Dorothy questioned Eff's love for her, and worried if she was worthy: *"How can Eff possibly love me and want to <u>marry</u> me? He's so <u>young</u>, so free, so entirely undomestic and unattached? What can he see in me—older—life all messed, not beautiful—and only an income! I don't know really if Eff can remain faithful to just me after knowing so many women. And I never for a minute doubt my faith to him till all eternity."*

On the eve of her divorce, my grandmother was haunted by happy memories. She recalled with nostalgia Mount Whitney, Bend, Rocknoll, and the first herb garden George had planted. She had imagined that her final hours as Mrs. Putnam would be filled with relief. But eighteen years had solidified into something unforgettable. She could just remember the good times.

Still deeply uncertain about the divorce, Dorothy's final entry reads simply: *"Misery!"*

The only thing she was certain of was her need to be herself, and to know that in her heart, she was truly alive.

DECEMBER 19, 1929 *Couldn't sleep; couldn't eat! Mailed one letter early. Then to Court House of Washoe County in Judge George A. Bartlett's Chambers. All very simple and quiet. <u>It's done</u>. I'm <u>unmarried</u> from G.P.P. forever. How scared and empty I feel!*

PART FOUR

1930–1982

Life is an illusion – we get nothing that we hope to get; & if we get it, we never keep it . . . . no love lasts . . . And that is what we are wanting always . . . not only to get it, but to keep it.

There may be a perfect time; a perfect relation; but just as we grasped it & realize it; it begins to change.
  Does it always fade? And change?
  I'm afraid so. Yes

Life is an illusion. We get nothing that we hope to get.
Or if we get it, we never keep it. . . . No love lasts. . . .
And that is what we are wanting always. . . . Not only
to get it, but to keep it.
There may be a perfect time; a perfect relation; but just as
we grasped it, realize it, it begins to change.
Does it always fade?
And change?
I'm afraid so——yes.

D.B.P.

14

AN ORANGE GROVE FOR A GARDEN

DECEMBER 20, 1929 *So, I released him just so he could marry her. She's to get my husband, my house, my lovely garden—but not my furniture! Odd fate! The country has been whispering with suspicious gossip! Now it's over.*

M Y GRANDMOTHER WAS SICKENED BUT not surprised when she picked up the morning's paper in San Francisco to read the story about her divorce. It focused on the fact that George was finally free to marry Amelia Earhart. "Cupid Their Next Pilot" must have stung her, and may have provided the very reason she needed for marrying quickly. Her diary entry shows she was obviously hurt. She refers almost reluctantly to the news story: *"George got his divorce in Reno today."*

Leaving San Francisco and continuing on to Los Angeles by train, Dorothy was met at the station by Junie and his nanny, Mae Bergquist. They had arrived the previous day, and had already collected the dozen or so suitcases and delivered them to the *El Salvador.* *"L.A. by 9:30 and drove out*

167

to Wilmington docks instead of train. Just as well I went early for ship left at noon instead of 5:00 p.m. as posted."

Trying to elude photographers on the afternoon of December 21, Dorothy, Mae, and Junie boarded the ship and settled into their small first-class quarters. The nine-day cruise to Panama would eventually reunite Dorothy and Frank. *"Oh, the heavenly* <u>let down</u>. *Thank God, to be away from Reno! Don't know how many of the people aboard know I was on the front page of the L.A. and Frisco papers two days ago. But I don't care. We're off."*

On the first day at sea, Dorothy found a solitary spot on the promenade deck, and wrote that she was eager to see Eff.

DECEMBER 22, 1929 *Heavenly clear warm tropic day almost no motion at all. Have 2 deck chairs on secluded spot on "star deck" way off from everyone else. And just sit looking off at the horizon. I want—Oh, God how I want it! To go way off to far parts of the earth for a <u>year</u> with <u>Eff</u> to be with him, to see <u>together</u> strange places and people, to <u>weld</u> our lives together by our experiences as well as our emotions. Doesn't he feel this urge? I wonder? How does he see us growing together. In suburbs?*

DECEMBER 23, 1929 *Two weeks from today will I see the familiar and beloved back on the dock awaiting us at Balboa? I pray so. Up on my sunny top deck at a.m. Nap after lunch and then pleasant enough dinner and bed early. Watched sun set for an hour and had a plethora of thoughts that would sink an ordinary soul!*

Dorothy stood up from her deck chair and greeted the formally dressed purser who had come to deliver a radiogram. It was Christmas Eve. As she read the message, tears welled in her eyes. Deep down, George Weymouth was the only man she wanted, and she couldn't have him. What did it matter if she decided to marry? *"Adorable radio [gram] from G.T.W. 'Missing you terribly. Merry Xmas. Happy New Year. Greatest Love—Child' Bless him, anyway. I shall always love him,—always."*

At sunrise, the ship pulled along the rocky coast of the Gulf of Tehuantepec, and Dorothy, Mrs. Bergquist, and Junie prepared to go ashore and take the train ride from Champerico to Guatemala City. The irony of returning to her honeymoon location was not lost: *"Strange to be here! 18 years ago I began my married life here and am now ending it. Untangling the last skein of it. Bought some Indian textiles for a Spanish house of the future."* In the same country where she and George had ascended Mount Acatenango, Dorothy was now haunted by unhappy recollections of her first marriage. She even had rewritten her memories of that honeymoon voyage and reflected on what happened later. *"That other 'long-ago' wedding of mine seemed so unreal and as if it had never been. I remember the cold day, the swim! Red roses. Ugly trousseau clothes which distressed me. It wasn't very thrilling or romantic or pleasing."*

A week later, the *El Salvador* slipped through the Panama Canal and docked in the seaport town of Balboa. Frank Upton, a tall, muscular, dark-haired hero, was the first in line to welcome its passengers. He had arrived on the *Pennsylvania,* steaming across the Caribbean from Miami. Frank and Dorothy's relationship would no doubt be scrutinized by friends and family, but for now my grandmother believed she had found a man to save her from loneliness.

Barely a month after the divorce became final, Dorothy remarried.

JANUARY 12, 1930
Married: Exactly at sunset
Full moon rise
On the Star Deck, (above the bridge) of the S.S. El Salvador

To: Frank Monroe Upton
By: Capt. Henry Stephenson, Chief Officer
Elmer Abbott and Mae Bergquist and Eve Lundstedt, wit-
nesses
Dinner in Captain's Room
Danced late—At 2:00 a.m. a full rigged four masted schoo-
ner—near us in the moonlight.

Four days later, Mr. and Mrs. Frank Monroe Upton arrived at their new home. Back in Fort Pierce with its endless
stretches of serene white beaches, stately whispering coconut palms, and the Indian River that cut a blue swath between the barrier island and the mainland, Dorothy finally
seemed at peace. For years she had visited the little-known
citrus town with a mind to moving there one day. "A sleeping, sleepy little town," in the words of her sister, Helen B.
Kitchel. She recalled Fort Pierce in the early 1920s as described in Helen's book, *More Memories.*

> I remember vividly our arrival by train just before dawn.
> Enough daylight to see Bub on the station platform with his
> loving smile of greeting. A three or four block drive through a
> sleeping, sleepy little town toward the east. As we approached
> the Indian River, the sun rose and revealed Bub's ship, the *Flor-
> india,* moored to the crude dock. I remember Bub's obsession
> over the potentialities of the place, not only his land and
> groves, but the little town which consisted of a few blocks of
> houses and shops. He envisioned a thriving coastal trade in
> fruit and vegetables as well as other commodities.

At first, Dorothy's marriage was idyllic, and the sultry
days were filled with pleasure. Eff proved an attentive lover,
and a satisfying one:

FEBRUARY 12, 1930 *All these happy days are far too*
personal to write about. We're deliciously in love—the way

the kids are, only we mustn't let them know it. We read aloud in the evenings; I comb Eff's hair while he sits at my feet with his head in my lap. And he's a dear and satisfying lover—always.

The couple occupied two large adjoining apartments at the Casa Caprona, and Dorothy was content to call the Spanish-style complex home for the time being while she and Eff planned their permanent residence.

Before they had begun to look for land, they escaped into the winding waterways to enjoy some of their favorite sports. Dorothy had already bought a boat for both river and ocean fishing, and Eff's passion was his sleekly powerful bi-wing Standard airplane. Between the two activities, they were never at a loss for excitement. The highly charged couple never stayed in one place for long. They thrilled each other with their eccentricities and wild, spur-of-the-moment junkets.

It is not surprising, given my grandmother's love of the theater and her fascination with Spanish architecture, that she quickly discovered a movie house, the Sunrise Theater. (This early downtown landmark is now being restored as part of a movement to preserve the historic center of Fort Pierce.) One block west of the Indian River and across the street from the St. Lucie County Bank building, the Sunrise Theater would become Dorothy's local version of Broadway.

Arrangements were made for Junie to attend the nearby one-room school on Indrio Road, while Dorothy began to search for the perfect setting for her new home. In Reno while waiting for her divorce, she had clipped magazine photos and doodled sketches of houses. It had not taken long to find two separate forty-acre tracts, not on the water as one might expect, but in the wild, most heavily wooded acreage of undiscovered St. Lucie County, which suited Dorothy and Eff's sense of adventure. Few Floridians built in such an isolated part of the county, with the exception of her parents, who had done the same thing in 1913. The site the Uptons had chosen was four miles from the Binneys' farm and seven miles from Fort Pierce. In those days, this was considered extremely remote.

When Dorothy first saw the land, she chopped a narrow walkway into dense, steamy jungle. It was almost impossible to visualize it as a homesite, but it held a mystical allure for her. The adjoining acreage would be cleared for citrus trees and would surround the lush jungle hammock, which marked the future construction site:

MAY 5, 1930   *Drove all over Cobb's 40 acres again, measuring distances, etc. 3.8 miles from Florindia 7 miles from town. And each time the hammock seems thicker and full of finer big trees than I dreamed of.*

MAY 9, 1930   *Bought Cobb's 40! $2775. Started six men clearing the jungle "hammock" with grub hoes.*

MAY 14, 1930   *We're buying a 1-1/2 ton Chevrolet truck for the clearing at the place. And a 10–15 Caterpillar tractor. And we've cashed in the darling old 1928 Chrysler 75 "Blue Heaven." I shall get a new 77 in New York. And Eff has bought a little Ford Roadster, "Bouncing Bet."*

In the midst of preparing the woods, Dorothy thought of G.W., their "anniversary," and their love. Her memories would never die, and she decided to wire him a message. *"Wrote G.W. My little garden is prolific! And I'm giving away little table bouquets daily."* Even after her second marriage, this anniversary also drew a special notation in her diary.

MAY 19, 1930   *This day is "fixed" in my memory. It's an anniversary——an adorable and unforgettable one.*

MAY 23, 1930   *The new "40" is increasingly beautiful and each time I go there I find another big oak or fine tree!*

Yesterday a four foot oak entirely swamped *with air plants. There are thirty to forty oaks about 4' 5" to 5' 6" in diameter. And big pines and tall palms. I'm struggling to keep June's school work going. But it's hot and he's restless.*

MAY 30, 1930 *Tried to lay out house on our new "40." Packed up and tidied up my affairs so's to go north. There's water under the big central oaks. It'd be lovely for a lily pool. The woods are alive with new noises.*

I can imagine my grandmother during the first days of thinning out the land, her hair tied back with a scarf. Her hands must have been blistered and callused by the time the tangled thicket was tamed. She knew and loved every inch of the property, as my husband and I do now.

Dorothy selected Franklind W. Tyler as the builder for her home, then reluctantly left Eff, and traveled with Junie to New York in search of roofing tiles and furniture. Mugo Court had finally become her second home. *"To town again to get some rugs (3 big ones), three big comfy chairs and a sofa. A few small things for the new Florida house. Wrote Eff my daily scrawl. Read aloud to Junie on the couch in p.m. 'Ivanhoe.' It's quite like old times in Rye all that last year when he and I were alone together so much."*

She spent part of the summer in Old Greenwich, and the depression that had clouded her previous year lifted, much to the relief of her sisters and parents. They were reassured by the deep devotion she obviously felt for Eff. She seemed now to have put the relationship with George behind her. *". . . G.P. keeps phoning here—daily calls to David or Junie or about something. I'm glad to realize how totally detached I am for I never want to see him again as long as I live."* Dorothy was still in Sound Beach several weeks later when she wrote, *"G.P. had his Garrison bungalow last weekend for a pleasant two days with Amelia. (Well, I'm glad he has someone to sleep with and be 'gay' with occasionally.)"*

During her final days there, George Weymouth's parents and brother Bud spent the night with her and Junie in Sound Beach. It was on this trip that Dorothy renamed Mugo Court Journey's End. *"Mr. and Mrs. C. A. Weymouth and the handsome 'Bud' here overnight. My, they're a lovable family."*

G.W. also came to visit, accompanied by an attractive young heiress, Deo duPont. They had met the previous summer at a dude ranch in Montana and had fallen in love. Now he was anxious to introduce his future wife to Dorothy and the Binneys. *"George Weymouth and Deo duPont, Betty Chester. . . . A mob, a crowd, but all pleasant. Out on Bub's 'Dunworkin' for an hour, then home and music and cafeteria supper."* Though Dorothy was in love with her handsome new husband, she must have felt a twinge of envy in the presence of G.W.'s charming young fiancée.

One vacation day, Dorothy and Junie piled their usual stash of towels, books, and beach food in the rear seat of Bub's car and headed toward Rye. Junie had been invited to the ocean with a family called the Greens, and Dorothy planned to retrace her two-mile swim out to the lighthouse and back. *"Drove Junie to Rye to Greens. First time I've been down there and curiously enough felt no heartache, no longing for old times or the lovely gardens and home. G.P. sounds sick and blue on the phone. He is lonely, I know."* I am certain that my grandmother gained no pleasure in his continued suffering.

But Dorothy was homesick for Fort Pierce and missed Eff terribly. She writes of her frustration, waiting for his letters, which were rare. He was not the sort of man who communicated with words, and even his phone calls were few.

SEPTEMBER 13, 1930 *Eff phoned me last night and I loved hearing his blessed old voice. I believe he's actually, really in love with me. Yet for the life of me I can't understand it. Of*

*course, I do know perfectly that he wouldn't have married me
if I hadn't had money—couldn't have.*

Once back in Fort Pierce, however, she shared a passionate reunion with Eff and all her doubts dissolved. Both of
them resumed their work, wielding machetes and slashing
through the undergrowth, taking enormous pleasure in the
physical nature of the job. Dorothy was unfazed by the dis-
comforts, the snakes, insects, and poison ivy during those
blistering summer months. The palms, pines, and vibrant
blue and orange vines were marked to be saved. The giant
oaks were also tagged with bright yellow ribbons; Dorothy
rescued fifty small oaks and carried them to the perimeter
of the eighty-acre site. The young saplings were replanted
along the east and south boundary lines where she inter-
spersed each one with a clump of bamboo, planting them
side by side as windbreak for her future citrus grove.
*"Farm—picnic—home for swim. Moving lilies, putting giant
bamboo at North and West entrances. And every 100 ft. too on
south line. 1 bamboo, 2 water oaks. On East End (Lateral), 1
bamboo, 2 Australian pines."*

She had chosen pecky cypress, the old southern swamp-
land timber, to be used throughout her rambling house.
One of the new house's most distinctive features was the
roof of imported Italian tiles. Balconies and loggias were
fashioned at different levels and angles circling the house.
There were six fireplaces and four chimneys, with arched
openings to keep out the fierce Florida rains. From a short
distance, the creamy stucco reflected a soft pearly light in
the midst of the tropical umbrella. Dorothy had created a
fascinating treehouse, set snugly in a natural garden the size
of a public park. For her birds, she designed several water
fountains built into the exterior walls, and beside each one
stood screen-enclosed feeding stations. Finally, a decorative
balconet with the carved inscription "Immokolee" was

added onto the outside of the vaulted-ceiling living room beneath a miniature window.

The locals marveled as the Uptons' custom-made materials arrived on freight trains from Palm Beach and New York. They gaped to see such exotic furnishings, including cypress doors and one-of-a-kind polished brass screens. China and crystal in heavy barrels rolled off the train. Walnut plates and bowls and hand-hammered sterling silverware were among the items loaded onto a truck and delivered to Immokolee.

After a hard rain, Dorothy discovered a natural swale of groundwater beneath a circle of small cypress trees. Delighted, she roped off her future lily pond and designed the home's entrance around this low-lying feature.

Covered with mosquito bites, the Uptons returned to New York for two weeks. At summer's end, Alice and Edwin Binney organized a neighborhood reception to welcome Dorothy's new husband. *"Mother's big party—reception and music, etc. All the Binney Lane and Sylvan Lane neighbors in to meet us. And supper. Met the unhumorous and self-made Col. Schick of razor blade fame, also others. Worked on Journey's End most of the day."*

Frank returned to Fort Pierce while Dorothy remained behind to go over the Florida house plans with Robert Duncan, a local architect. She was also busy putting the final touches on Journey's End, which was exploding with summer colors from the garden beside the new swimming pool. The transplanted iris bulbs—so reminiscent of G.W.—had been the first to bloom.

AUGUST 18, 1930 *I'm happy to be returning to Eff for I've missed him tremendously of late. And I'm keen too, to see the Farm and what's been done. Eff has been living on black coffee during my absence! Not so good!*

AUGUST 20, 1930 *Eff met me at midnight all fresh and strong and tan. He's so utterly gorgeous looking always. He's*

the way God meant men to be I'm sure. Vigorous and healthy
and well muscled. Home and to bed in a leisurely adorable
way and we lay talking and chatting in each other's arms for
hours. Coffee at dawn! And another day.

Her life was spent in the "hammock" of snarled oaks
with tall, slender palms crisscrossing and snaking their way
upward into the sun. Dorothy relished the job of measuring
and marking trees while noting various species of birds. She
discovered nests and rare orchid sprays and had begun to
recognize Florida's colorful snakes. Wearing high-top boots,
she wasn't afraid of the rattlesnakes, corals, or water mocca-
sins. Just as she had done with George while building Rocknoll, Dorothy designed her Florida home to sit snugly
among the native trees without destroying the bearded old
giants that had originally claimed the land several hundred
years before she arrived.

SEPTEMBER 8, 1930 *Mon. Farm and picnic lunch.*
Trees, new part of road. Planted 10 papayas, tuberoses and
fragrant ginger lily. And on Saturday Mr. Hale brought a
dozen more vines to put in the trees. White jasmine, blue
thumbergia and brilliant yellow begonia. Dinner.

Dorothy insisted upon finding the perfect name for the
home and grove. She first considered naming it *Huimanu*
(which means "Rendezvous of the Birds"), as a reference to
the new couple's tropical nest. In the end, she chose *Immokolee*, the Seminole Indian word for "My Home Place." In
her diary for September 28, 1930, she noted: *"Up early again.
Out to '40' to set north line for a row of bamboo. It poured hard
and we were all entirely soaked! Home, dry clothes, dinner and
over to beach for swim (after a nap). 'IMMO-KO-LEE' Seminole (My
Home Place). Our grove name."*

Between the birthing of her new home and nurturing her
eight-year-old son, Dorothy felt richly rewarded. Her years

of pain and confusion had vanished; she had found a place
of her own.

SEPTEMBER 29, 1930 *Town early to start June at
school. He goes to 4A which is quite normal (and pleases me
as I taught him at home last year.) Farm for lunch. Very busy.
Plowing!! Set out 26 clumps of bamboo along north road. Killed
small rattler.*

The three Uptons were becoming comfortable with frontier Florida. Dorothy had already discovered the outdoor
wonders of her newly adopted state: excursions to the crystal pools at Silver Springs, exotic drives through marshlands
teeming with bird life, trips to the Everglades, and boat rides
through the Thousand Islands. By the time George Weymouth and his new bride, Deo, first came to Fort Pierce in
October 1930, Dorothy was intimately familiar with the
Florida landscape and took pleasure in serving as official
guide for her guests. *"George Weymouth and his bride of a
month, arrived at 11 p.m.! Great reunion."* It was during her
visit to Old Greenwich the summer before that the three-
some had planned their trip to Silver Springs. She and G.W.
had both found contentment in their marriages, but Dorothy still delighted in his company and thrilled to his laughter once again. *"Farm—to ocean, then a grand roughhouse
swim back at pool with the rubber animals and a BAND! Late
dinner and off at 5 pm for Silver Springs. Highballs at Hotel Mar-
ion, Ocala. G.T.W., Deo, Eff, D.B.U. Moon, long roads, chatter,
songs."*

Although Eff denied feeling jealous of G.W.'s wild sense
of humor and handsome physique (and his rather acrobatic
habit of walking on his hands), he could not hide his pos-
sessiveness. *"Breakfast in our room. Then all down to the
Springs. The glass-bottom boat, a swim. Drive in moonlight. Eff
hurt and obviously jealous which pleases me."*

But soon, Dorothy became aware that Eff's mood swings

were not as innocent as she first thought, and his jealousy was no longer flattering:

OCTOBER 7, 1930 *I shouldn't be pleased at his jealousy, but such fury and anger does mean he cares, and wishes to monopolize, despite all his protestations. And sometimes his silences and inarticulateness are a little disappointing. Moonlight drive and a romp on ocean beach. Bed, silently and apart. And still the resentment.*

OCTOBER 8, 1930 *Farm, picnic lunch and a sweet "make-up" but no admission of jealousy or hurt. Maybe he doesn't yet recognize the fact.*

That month, my grandmother—at the age of forty-two—thought she was pregnant. At first she was terrified, then as the possibility became real, saddened by the fact that Eff was not pleased. Indeed, he became even more sullen and distant.

She was anxious about her husband's reaction and could only wish for a change of heart. Once again, her insecurities were surfacing. *"I hope he cares."*

15

AMELIA AND GEORGE PUTNAM

NOVEMBER 14, 1930 *All local and N.Y. papers lately have been overflowing with news and conjecture about G.P. and Amelia. They evidently got a marriage license in Noank last Saturday, November 8th and it leaked out. Horrid pictures and insinuations. Too bad they just don't up and marry and have it over with. They'll fight like cats and dogs in a year. She's stubborn and cold bloodedly cruel and she'll soon tire of his indigestion and rotten, vile temper.*

ON A COOL AFTERNOON, DOROTHY SAT at the edge of the unfinished lily pond, poking a bamboo pole into the still water. She heard the muffled sound of a car on the sandy drive and looked up to find a delivery man bearing a telegram. She tossed the pole aside, and opened the sheer yellow envelope.

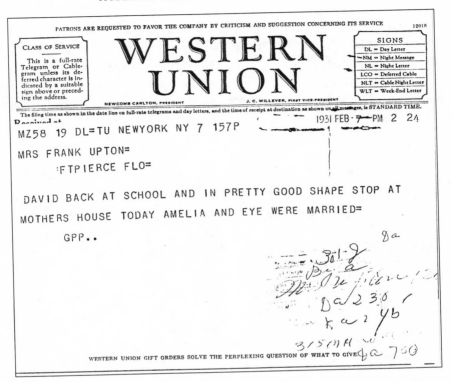

Dorothy caught her breath. She was stunned by the abruptness of the telegram, but relieved that George had shared the news personally. How alone she must have felt. Although she had asked for her freedom, his marriage to Amelia rekindled her insecurity. Her ex-husband was now married to her former friend and the most famous woman in the world. And despite my grandmother's doubts, she had to concede: The two were ideally suited for one another. At the same time, she must have been troubled by the vague sense that her own hasty marriage might have been a mistake. Amelia and George's celebrated union seemed in sharp contrast to her own. While she and Eff enjoyed a physical, almost earthy bond, George and Amelia shared a more cerebral relationship, one that was regarded by many as a business arrangement.

Only minutes before Amelia and George's marriage ceremony in his mother's home in Noank, Connecticut, Amelia had penned a prenuptial agreement, possibly the first in America's legal history. Written neatly on her future mother-in-law's white engraved stationery, Amelia set forth her requirements for the marriage:

Dear Gyp,

There are some things which should be writ before we are married— things we have talked over before most of them.

You must know again my reluctance to marry, my feeling that I shatter thereby chances in work which means most to me. I feel the move just now as foolish as anything I could ever do. I know there may be compensations but have no heart to look ahead.

On our life together, I want you to understand I shall not hold you to any medieval code of faithfulness to me nor shall I consider myself so bound to you. If we can be honest about affections for others which may come to either of us the difficulties of such situations may be avoided.

Please let us not interfere with the other's work or play. Nor let the world see our private joys or disagreements. In this connection I may have to keep some place apart—where I may retreat from even an attractive cage, to be myself.

I must exact a cruel promise and that is you will let me go in a year if we find no happiness together. (And this for me too.)

I will try to do my best in every way and give you fully of that part of me you know and seem to want.

A

February 7, 1931

This is an exact copy of the original agreement. My grandfather first published a second version in his biography of Amelia, *Soaring Wings*. This original draft is published for the first time, and having compared the two, I find it curious that two phrases were omitted from the sec-

PHONE MYSTIC 1016.
TELEPHONE NOANK

NOANK
CONNECTICUT

THE SQUARE HOUSE
CHURCH STREET

Dear Gyp.

Here are some things
which should be writ- be-
fore we are married - things
~~we have talked over~~ before
most of them.

You must know again
my reluctance to marry, my
feeling that I shatter thereby
chances in work which means
most to me. I feel the
more just now as foolish as
anything I ~~have ever do~~ could ever do. I
~~know there~~ ~~may~~ be compensations
but have no heart to look ahead

On our life together. I want ~~you~~
to ~~know~~ understand I shall not
hold you to any medieval code
of faithfulness to me nor shall
I consider myself so bound to you.
If we can be honest about af-

factious for actions which may come to either of us the difficulties of such situations may be avoided.

Please let us not interfere with the other's work or play, nor let the world see our private ~~joys~~ or disagreements. ~~In this connection~~ I may have to keep some place apart when I may retreat ⟨to be myself from even an adoring ~~one~~⟩.

I must exact a cruel promise and that is you will let me go in a year if we find no happiness together. (And ~~this~~ for me too)

I will try to do my best in every way and give you fully of that part of me you know and seem to want.

A—

~~February~~ 7, 1931

ond: "(and this is for me too)" and "affections for others."
In the first draft, it appeared as though Amelia was as concerned for her husband's well-being as her own. The fact
that she wanted to keep a place apart, however, still suggests
her need to be alone from time to time. The agreement reveals how resolute and focused the young flyer was. No personal affection would hinder her career, nor intrude on her
deep sense of privacy.

George has been portrayed as Amelia's Svengali, but the
unpublished document shows her to be very much in control. And despite her initial skittishness over marrying her
promoter, Amelia doted on his two sons. "Amelia was
deeply concerned with G.P.'s two young sons," her sister
Muriel Morrissey recalled. "When they came to visit at the
home in Rye, Amelia canceled all her outside engagements
and persuaded G.P. to do the same, so they could devote
their time to the boys—horseback riding, sailing on the
Sound, swimming and picnicking. Amelia's sincere interest
in them was repaid by their real affection for their famous,
fun-loving stepmother."

George and Amelia were the image of modern marital
bliss. They became media darlings, and were the subject of
gushing articles and often catty cartoons. Flying an airplane
had become secondary. It was Amelia's image as a feminist
that captured the nation's imagination, and George willingly supported it, becoming a role model for men as well.
In one article, he was quoted as saying, "Idleness is the
greatest damnation of married women!"

"Amelia was, of course, an early feminist," recalled Anne
Morrow Lindbergh. "With no hostility that I ever observed
towards men."

Reporters were coy about Amelia keeping her maiden
name. She was almost jokingly referred to as "Mrs. Putnam,
or rather Miss Earhart." In an interview for *Huntington Park
Signal*'s *Five Star Weekly* entitled "Why Their Marriage
Clicks," Amelia told the reporter, "I have done quite a bit of

observing, other than aerial observing. I think I'll know a matrimonial air pocket when I come to one. But we tried to avoid any such possibility in advance by having definite understandings. Our interests are similar and parallel. I've always been active and I've believed in a wife going right along with the activities in which she might have been interested. In fact, we figured on a very brief honeymoon—for work has a way of piling up on your desk."

I came upon pages from an old scrapbook quite by accident. They belonged to my grandmother and were found at Immokolee buried beneath stacks of black and white photographs. Dofry had obviously cut them out, but decided to keep them anyway. They had remained in dark storage bins of the "Captain's Room" for over sixty years, and were musty and torn. Staring me in the face were large pictures of my grandfather with his new bride, Amelia Earhart. The articles cover several years, and include the Putnams' Christmas card for 1932. Santa Claus is holding up a toy—half airplane, half helicopter—with the pair gazing out from the sky. The greeting reads: "Happy Landings, G.P.P. and A.E."

Other stories detail my grandfather's career at G. P. Putnam's Sons, and his decision to leave the company. Across the bottom of this article, in my grandmother's writing, is the date August 1930. The neatly overlapping collection is a fascinating piece of history.

I know from Dofry's diaries that her parents sent the clippings to her. How she must have flinched, seeing the smiling faces of her former husband and Amelia. I find it strange that she kept these pages, that despite her anger over their involvement, she still admired her former friend. By now, Amelia and George had become a much-sought-after couple for social events. But I doubt my grandmother missed the glittering life she had once enjoyed. In fact, she was deeply involved in the construction of Immokolee, and reveled in her privacy thousands of miles away, in her own remote retreat.

While Amelia was making personal appearances around the country promoting the safety of air travel, Dorothy had not abandoned her love of aviation. She organized several aviation clubs in Florida and became the governor of the East Coast Florida Women's Aeronautical Association. She also founded a local chapter of the Women's National Aeronautic Association (WNAA), and later started the first Junior WNAA in Florida to encourage young people to fly. As a member, Mrs. Olive Dame Peterson recalls traveling with Dorothy and the group to Vero Beach to see an air show. Olive described her first flight in a small open airplane as "a breathless adventure." Following the excursion the girls were entertained with a luncheon at Immokolee.

Like Amelia, Dorothy also pursued the theme of women's rights, speaking to various groups around the state. She was an expert on this controversial issue. In a newspaper article entitled "Hear Mrs. Upton Tell of Women Who Made Good," she was quoted as saying: "Women without beauty may have charm today and be popular through the power of their intellect. Not that beauty is not an asset, for it is. In olden days, however, physical beauty was the only point about women that counted. Women through the ages must have had some thrilling experiences in fighting for the right of intellectual recognition." In this same speech before the Stuart Women's Club, she cited Amelia as an example of outstanding womanhood. "I think Amelia has a 'worn' face, a *used* face. One that has been used for living, and laughing, loving and thinking, also feeling and suffering. But it's a face of quality and character. And unlike the *beautiful*, but bone-headed stupid Movie Star type."

Ever since Amelia had first crossed the Atlantic as a passenger in the *Friendship,* she had vowed to make the flight again, only this time piloting the plane herself. When Dorothy learned of the impending solo flight in May 1932, she reflected on her frenetic life with George four years earlier. *"News, Amelia is to fly Atlantic. Lordy, remember four years ago in Boston."*

Amelia carried on board her Lockheed Vega plane a red and white booklet for jotting down notes. Before safely reaching the coast of Ireland on May 21, 1932, she scribbled the following account, which has not been published in its entirety before. "Left 7:15 . . . Altimeter out 3:30 over fog 7:40 . . . rain . . . iceup 9:05 fish star."

And on the next tiny three- by two-inch page she wrote:

> 8:00 am. 13 hours on the way. If anyone finds the wreck know that the non success was caused by my getting lost in a storm for an hour and then the exhaust manifold, resoldered at St. John blew out and I have crawled near the water for hours dreading fire.

Once Amelia's safe arrival made the news, Dorothy was swept up in the excitement, and joyously recorded:

MAY 20, 1932   *She's done it! She flew across to Ireland. Solo. World Attention!*

JUNE 14, 1932   *A.E. decorated by Albert of Belgium. How she and G.P. must eat up all this!*

JUNE 15, 1932   *G.P. and Amelia en route to U.S.*

Sixty years later I found *The New York Times* front-page story of Amelia's solo flight folded up inside my father's childhood scrapbook. My grandmother had saved it for him. The headline, "Mrs. Putnam Flies Alone for Paris on 'Lindbergh Day,' " must have sent chills across Dofry's body when she first saw it.

After safely crossing the Atlantic, Amelia realized she had

left home without a passport, and before sailing back to the United States she obtained a new one in London. The maroon leather passport is dated May 27, 1932, and describes Amelia as five feet eight inches tall with light brown hair and blue eyes. On the line under place of birth (Atchison, Kansas) is the date of birth, July 24, 1898. It is believed that Amelia's actual birthdate was July 24, 1897. For some unknown reason, perhaps in 1919, she began to use 1898 as the year she was born. And written casually above the signature, Amelia Earhart Putnam, was her occupation: Flyer.

It is possible that Amelia presented her pilot's license to the consul general in London, and he simply copied the information from one document to the other.

Dorothy was relieved when she realized she was not carrying Eff's child after all, for she now knew he could never assume the responsibility of fatherhood. Frank Upton, decorated soldier and celebrated war hero, was an alcoholic. He must have succeeded in hiding this from his new fiancée and her family during their courtship. But now, having moved into Immokolee, it became obvious that his bouts of solitude and erratic behavior were a result of his drinking.

In 1930, Frank had designed his own private Captain's Room, an exact replica of the aft quarters of a Spanish galleon. Crafted with panels of polished mahogany and teakwood, it even included a porthole, and a single ship's bunk, as well as a fold-out desk and three brass antique ship's lamps that hung from the ceiling and walls. Inlaid in the center of the floor was a color-tiled compass the size of a sundial, and a fireplace was tucked in one corner. Dorothy's contribution to this sanctuary was two small bookcases on either side of the miniature picture window.

As a child, I recall being forbidden to enter the room. I always wanted to know what was behind that heavy cypress door, but my grandmother kept it locked. The prospect of some family secret only served to arouse my curiosity and my imagination knew no limits. It wasn't until years later that I finally learned her reason for keeping this room locked, and the bitterness she felt for providing her husband with such a haven.

Soon after moving into Immokolee, my grandmother's diaries begin to describe the slow deterioration of their relationship. *"Half the time Eff is overtired. He falls sound asleep on the floor in the evenings. He yawns from 7 p.m. on."* Dorothy had begun to record his drinking, rather cryptically at first. *"Dinner alone with Jr. Eff at Elks Club for 8 hrs.! He'll go stale above the ears as well as below if he keeps it up."* The private diaries were her most intimate confidences, and she could no longer deny the truth. *"Eff late for dinner. Odor—first time familiar."*

Dorothy's initial response was to ignore Eff's habit of coming home late, often drunk. She was acutely aware of his problem, but chose to hide it from her family and the outside world. Drinking was socially acceptable, and for some time she simply tolerated it, perhaps because their physical passion was still a source of intense pleasure. *"Calming down, controlling tempers, <u>not risking loss of happiness</u>."* In a way, the sense of danger and living on the brink may have fueled their insatiable desire for one another. *"Swam at noon with Eff. Cheers, Whoops, Cheerio! And the bed goes through the window! What a terrifying temper, yet—?"*

My grandmother spent part of each summer visiting her parents in Connecticut, and these vacations—a result of the divorce agreement—reunited George with his youngest son, June. In 1931, June stayed with George and Amelia at Rocknoll, and my grandmother was with her parents at Rocklyn, as she had been forced to rent Journey's End because of her financial losses.

Her diaries are now filled with anxiety over her stock portfolio and diminished income. *"Stocks still go lower! My income reduced a third and we're awfully in debt. It worries one.*

Banks are closing everywhere." Though it pained her terribly to let her home to strangers, she had no choice but to make sacrifices wherever she could. *"C.C. [Columbian Carbon] has been dropping, dropping. Way down to 83. That's ghastly, and it sinks me; especially as Eff was entirely opposed to my dabbling in the stock market at all."*

Like the summers of 1927 and 1928, Rocknoll had come alive again with children's voices. David and Junie loved spending these halcyon days with their father and Amelia, who now reigned as mistress of the Rye estate. Both boys clearly adored her, and she became a strong maternal influence.

But Dorothy did not feel neglected and arranged to meet George Weymouth in Manhattan for dinner and the theater. Whether or not she had confided in him about Frank Upton's drinking is not recorded in her diary. But I suspect that she did, for he made plans to travel to Florida with his wife, Deo, the following month. *"Sound Beach. In town for dinner and theatre with G.T.W. He looks thin and pale. Grand newsy visit with him. Dinner 'Divan Paris' to see 'Third Little Show.'"* The relationship with G.W. had mellowed into an affectionate friendship.

After a few weeks in Sound Beach, my grandmother once again yearned to be with her husband.

> JUNE 20, 1931   *On train with Mother. My ship sailed at noon. Dog and much baggage. Comfortable cabin, uninteresting crowd. Read "Juan in America" which G.T.W. gave. Delightful. Eager for Frank again.*

> JUNE 23, 1931   *Eff met me at 6 a.m. on dock! Such a thrill. Home, looks marvelous. New bird house is fine and lawns, groves, trees, etc. all growing splendidly. Baby quail.*

The warm reception was short-lived. With the arrival of the Hutchinsons and the Weymouths for a long weekend, Eff behaved abominably.

"Off at 8 a.m. for a weekend trip to Silver Springs. Wey-
mouths, Hutchinsons and Uptons. All afternoon, great swim and
boat trip. Hub swam under the glass boat in several big pools.
Such fun. Bok Tower at noon. Dude Ranch for dinner. Movies in
p.m." Immokolee echoed with sung duets and piano music,
which had always been a great source of pleasure for Dorothy, but Eff refused to join in. She had even avoided playing
her favorite word-guessing games to spare him from com-
peting against her more sophisticated young friends. Despite her ploy, Eff's jealousy erupted again. *"Eff in rude mood*
about guests and company and house full! He's not social or even
house broken! Guess I must change. He can't."

By now, Frank had attained a certain status in Fort Pierce,
and Dorothy was loath to ruin her husband's position
within the tight-knit community. He had earned a reputation as a civic leader and had recently been given the prestigious title of vice president of the St. Lucie County Bank.
But at home, he had become a different person, almost a
stranger. His drinking made him increasingly dangerous.
"Home—anger and threats. Scenes!—Rage—Drunk." She
makes passing reference to her husband's impaired driving
ability. *"Eff slept on couch last p.m. Eff to Palm Beach. (Auto*
smash)."

Upton was still in touch with many of his friends among
the aviation set, including Amelia's dashing former pilot
Captain Bill Lancaster. In the early summer of 1932, Lancaster made headlines in a lurid shooting that took place in
Miami. The British war hero was accused of shooting a
twenty-six-year-old writer, Charles Clarke, who had been
hired to ghost-write the memoirs of Australian divorcée and
Lancaster paramour Jessie ("Chubbie") Keith-Miller. It was
a classic love triangle, police said. Upton persuaded my
grandmother to donate money for Lancaster's defense, and
she did so without question. In August, the Uptons drove
to Miami to attend the notorious trial, which made torrid
headlines. Frank's loyalty was unswerving, and he was

called as a character witness to testify on his friend's behalf. The courtroom was packed, and my grandmother recalled the media circus of the event, which called into question the morals of this hard-drinking, fast-living clique.

No doubt Upton's nights in Miami did nothing to dispel his image.

When Lancaster was acquitted, he and Chubbie immediately drove to Fort Pierce to escape reporters. They spent the weekend with Dorothy and Frank at Immokolee before departing. (Soon after the trial, the government started deportation proceedings and the couple fled to England. Eight months later, while trying to set the flight record from London to Cape Town, Lancaster disappeared. His preserved body and Avro Avian 5, *Southern Cross Minor*, were discovered in 1962 in the Sahara Desert.)

By now, there were rumors swirling in aviation circles about Eff and Dorothy, possibly passed on by Lancaster, who must have been aware of his friend's drinking problem. In late summer, these rumors reached the *New York Daily News*, which printed a gossip item about an upcoming Upton divorce. Eff was furious and telephoned the paper, which printed a retraction. The apology appeared in the form of a telegram, dated November 7, 1932:

> To Captain Frank M. Upton, Fort Pierce, Florida . . . in an article published . . . October 30, 1932, referring to Mrs. Dorothy Upton, wife of Frank M. Upton . . . it was erroneously stated that she planned to obtain a divorce from Captain Upton on the grounds of incompatibility. . . .

It was signed, "D. A. Doran, *New York Daily News*."

This was obviously embarrassing for Frank. Nonetheless, it was clear the Uptons were going their separate ways.

Dorothy decided to concentrate on community work, and with the help of her new acquaintances, she began to enjoy the simple life she had always craved. Her routine was the same, but the people she associated with were townspeople, not celebrities. They were Garden Club members, local politicians, and environmentally minded folks committed to beautifying and protecting the burgeoning waterfront town. Dorothy was content in Fort Pierce. Her garden flourished year-round as she reigned over her small, private paradise. *"Off to Indian River Narrows in Bub's boat . . . on the river in the sun and wind . . . an outdoor Oyster Roast at Hale's. It's a good way to have a feast and an orgy of seafood. Big fire, outdoors, a grill and much food. Saw movie, Morocco, afterwards."*

She and Junie were brought together more and more as Eff's absences became routine. Her younger son had taken to his new home as if it were a summer camp. His yard was a zoolike playground that gave him enormous freedom. A dog, guinea hens, chickens, caged snakes, and a mule were permanent residents at Immokolee, all under Junie's care. His schoolwork revealed an intelligent, lively mind that delighted his mother. *"Jr. got twelve A's this last time!"* He and Dorothy fished together, either from the jetties lining the inlet leading into the Indian River from the ocean, or from her sixteen-foot fishing boat, *Mud Turtle*, which was noted for its uncanny nose in locating snook or grouper. *"Choppy sea, increasing wind. Rough. Only 3 groupers. Jr. grand at rod and reel."*

My grandmother volunteered as a speaker and writer on a variety of subjects, including aviation, gardening, birds, trees, and even snakes, which had fascinated her since discovering so many on her land. *"Wrote Rattlesnake article for paper. Fourth snake story. Bluebirds are here. Prepared vegetable garden for second crop."* A story in the *Fort Pierce News Tribune* headlined "Exhibits Snakes in Bank Foyer" described Mrs. Frank Upton as a scientist who was interested in teaching the locals to identify the differences between poisonous and nonpoisonous snakes. Dorothy arranged for eight specimens preserved in alcohol to be exhibited in the bank's lobby, much to the amusement of its customers. She even draped her pet python over her shoulders and brought it to the local high school. (Motivated by my grandmother's curiosity about snakes, I recall driving down U.S. 1 in Fort Pierce as a teenager with a six-foot boa constrictor wrapped around my neck, to the horror of drivers in the next lane.)

As Eff's behavior worsened, Dorothy's devotion to Immokolee increased. *"Am enjoying our new radio, at least I can hear concerts and I can dance by myself!"* The nights in Fort Pierce had grown violent, and Dorothy would bear this terrible secret and endure the terror for the next two years. While the country celebrated George and Amelia, Dorothy was terrified that the scandal within her marriage would be exposed, despite the *Daily News'* retraction.

Eff and Amelia are sandwiched together in her diaries only pages apart. From the depths of her disgust with her husband to her mixed admiration for the flyer, she felt torn apart.

"I wish I were going far away," she wrote.

I can't help but feel my grandmother was somehow testing her own strength. First she had made her decision to leave Rye, and now she was left with no alternative but to survive.

16

TORN OUT PAGES

"Without exception the most horrible and disillusioning experience of my life! Excruciating pain and horror! And from the man who promised to love and cherish me."

*I*T IS IMPOSSIBLE FOR ME TO IMAGINE my grandmother as a battered woman.

When I first read the diary entries recounting in detail her secret other life, I dropped the book to the floor and cried. The thought that anyone could abuse this gentle woman made me physically ill. For months I woke up in the middle of the night feeling the terror she had endured. She told no one, but at last she was able to reveal her secret shame to me through her diaries. It must have been an enormous relief. When I shared these pages with my husband, he also wept.

Living in her home now, there are times I can almost visualize her blood spilled on the tiled foyer floor and can hear Eff's angry threats.

This was the darkest chapter of her life.

JANUARY 1, 1933 *Drove north thro' rain after seeing David on train. (Childish, violent temper. Eff). It knocks the stuffing out of me. And I know, now, that it's not worth it to me. I must get out of it this year for I'll do better alone and not nagged!*

Yet throughout this ugly period, Dorothy hid her pain. In retrospect, I now understand why my grandmother decided that confronting her husband about his drinking would only make things worse. She knew that preserving his ego was her only chance. With Eff's election to the County Commission, Dorothy had further reason to protect him. She did not want to undermine his position on the board, especially because her father had taken Frank under his wing. On a deeper level, the insecurities that plagued my grandmother from childhood perhaps made her believe she deserved to be mistreated.

The development of Fort Pierce was very much a family affair. Edwin Binney had invested heavily in local real estate and was using his personal fortune to promote the harbor improvements. He later became the chairman of the Fort Pierce Port Commission. Though he had already given the St. Lucie County Bank a personal check for $186,000 in 1929 to keep its doors open, the bank still needed additional funds to stabilize its weakened financial base, caused by the Depression. Two years earlier, Frank Upton had been involved in drumming up funds for the bank's dwindling reserves. *"Well, he did it; he got a large loan (for now!) On my 1400 Columbian Carbon stock and mortgaged this house, etc. $65,000 which is marvelous—for the bank."*

Dorothy was also involved in helping her father secure funds for the financial institution, and had mortgaged Immokolee as collateral for the St. Lucie County Bank. With Edwin as the bank's board chairman and Frank as its newly appointed vice president, Dorothy was determined to hide Eff's problem and help carry the bank through its continuing crisis.

In the year 1933, Eff's monstrous behavior escalated, prompting his wife to write: *"I swear I'll divorce! And I ought to. Contrite all day, hanging around—sad and quiet."*

Whether Eff knew at this point that Dorothy planned to leave him is unclear. What is clear from her diaries is that the violence was unrelenting. He seemed determined to punish Dorothy, perhaps as a result of his own insecurities. At one point, this burly man resorted to grabbing a bull-whip in rage; he was even spotted by a neighbor chasing my grandmother through the orange grove, brandishing the whip. She was helpless to fend off his blows, and after one beating tearfully sought refuge at the downtown home of her close friend, Franklind Tyler, and his wife, Bess.

MAY 29, 1933 *Ill in pain and miserable beyond words. Horsewhipped—19 lashes. To bed at Tylers all afternoon, in agony.*

MAY 30, 1933 *Just dragging myself around. 19 great black and blue swollen welts across my body—bleeding open wounds on ribs and thighs and buttocks. Moved downstairs to red room [downstairs guest room] Monday. In pain, went to doctor again.*

My grandmother wrote of the beatings in her diaries, but Eff, determined to destroy the evidence, tore out the incriminating pages. The only way she could record this horror was by backdating her entries and mixing them with earlier years. She hoped he would not destroy her hidden notes. Lost somewhere in the pages ripped out by Frank is the full story of her humiliation and suffering; the severity of her abuse will never be known. *"He's torn out all these pages because they were too frank about his rotten behavior. Not in to dinner—at 12:30 came in, drunk and repulsively amorous. I loathe it, loathe it!"*

Dorothy knew that the drunken rages would be followed by urgent apologies the following morning. Frank would beg for Dorothy's forgiveness, and his repentance seemed genuine. Over and over again she forgave him, wanting to believe his anger stemmed from his passion for her. She was both ashamed and afraid at the same time, and would "go thro' hell" before finally admitting her mistake and seeking the help she so desperately needed.

Alice and Edwin Binney were unaware of the trauma being inflicted on their daughter, but they must have begun to suspect something. *"Mother and Bub arrived by boat from New York. So glad to have them! Yet tongue tied and embarrassed."* Edwin had just named Frank president of the St. Lucie County Bank, making the situation even more delicate and embarrassing for his daughter. Soon, Frank turned his temper on her parents.

JUNE 22, 1933 *The most revolting evidence of bad taste and no breeding! Quarrel, then downstairs and insulted Mother—yelled at her. Woke up Bub. Maudlin. Cried!! No apology! He just won't do what nice people do, nor their customs! Oh, so sorry for Mother and Bub. So completely ashamed of him. I feel sunk and pep-less. I mustn't let him crush me; it's weak of me.*

JUNE 28, 1933 *Mother and Bub moved over to Casa [Caprona] yesterday. Don't blame them. It can't be very pleasant at Immokolee. At 1:45 a.m. Eff left for Washington on business—cross and angry at me. God help us.*

Dorothy was afraid of public disgrace. Women of her time were ashamed to report to the authorities such spousal abuse, especially forced sex within a marriage. In July she wrote: *"Had to submit tonight when Eff came in late—he'd been drinking. So disgusting."*

JULY 18, 1933 *Sun. 16th: Terrible scene with Eff—drunk. He pretended to shoot himself, tore off my clothes, etc. Called servants; lay shivering with fear rest of night.*

SEPTEMBER 9, 1933 *(On 10th, pages torn out!) A ghastly scene and quarrel. Oh, it's too awful! Nowadays they occur every two weeks or so. "I began too late. I ought to have horsewhipped you two years ago."*

For the first time, my grandmother feared for her life. *"Another terrible night, from 10 to 4 a.m. And this time: 'I'll kill you, and I'll kill myself!' And nine times my throat is held, vice-like and my hair pulled. Parapet on deck."* Between this entry in October 1933 and February of the following year, Dorothy's diary pages were blank. She was afraid to write the truth.

On February 4, 1934, Frank and Dorothy had been arguing earlier in the day when she pleaded with him to stop drinking. He ignored her tearful request and set out by himself for a local bar. Several hours later she heard a car pull up to the front door. The headlights were dimmed. She peered through the window, expecting to see Frank stumble inside, and braced herself for another night of terror. Instead, she saw a figure emerge from the driver's seat and walk around to the passenger side. Now there were two silhouettes in the dark, one struggling to hold the other's dead weight. Dorothy drew in her breath and realized that the crumpled figure was her husband. He had been shot twice in the head.

Dorothy bundled Junie into a coat and rushed from the house, but not before calling for medical help. *"Brought home at 10 p.m., Jr. and I fled Ghastly. Doctors. Blood."* Whoever the assailant—perhaps as inebriated as Upton—he had failed in his mission. The bullets only grazed the target. Dorothy does not name the shooter and took this secret to her grave. *"He shot him twice in the head, but too drunk to be aimed right. Bed, two doctors. Loss of blood. I shall be 24 hr. Nurse. Must lie about it all. Still dangerously weak. Bed. Dr."*

The following day she returned to Immokolee from town, and found Frank lying in the red room where she had left him the night before, and where she herself had often gone to recuperate from his lashings. She served him meals from her delicate tea tray, not bothering to hide her disgust. The room was dark and hot, and Frank brooded, anxious for a drink. Leaning against the mirrored door, staring at the blood-stained sheet, Dorothy wondered how she had gotten herself into such an ungodly mess.

On Valentine's Day, Dorothy was clearly shattered: *"I shall burst emotionally soon! Dead."*

Two weeks after the shooting, when Eff was well enough to drive himself into town, she walked outside and headed for her swimming pool. The night before, she had fallen asleep with the knowledge that her son David would arrive the next afternoon. She knew help was on the way. For the first time in over a year she slept peacefully; in the morning she stretched out in the warm sun to wait for him.

David was now twenty-one, a physically imposing young man, six feet four—and utterly fearless. Dorothy once described him as *"the kind of boy I saw in my secret heart when he was conceived—high in the western mountains. Tall blonde clean cut and alive to people."* He was living near Portland, Maine, and flying for the Boston and Maine Airways. Someone—perhaps his grandfather or even Dorothy herself—had called him about the terrifying situation. Throwing a few belongings into the open cockpit of his Kinner biplane, he had notified his fellow air-mail deliverers, sent a radio message to his mother, and taken off. David planned to land in Fort Pierce between 4:00 and 5:00 P.M. and would circle Immokolee several times to announce his arrival before turning east in the direction of the grassy airstrip.

Hearing the distant hum of the plane's engine, Dorothy stood and waved frantically, both arms outstretched above her head. She turned and ran down the steep concrete steps, gripping the rail. *"Dave arrived by plane! At 5 p.m. Much excitement!"*

Frank Upton knew that his marriage was over. Whether or not he was confronted by a furious David is not recorded.

It seems very likely. I recall my mother telling me that Dad went out to Immokolee in a rage and "ran Eff out of town." Dorothy explains his abrupt departure from Fort Pierce in very terse terms: *"Eff to Washington. (In silence and anger.) David here!"*

Her oldest son had always thought of his mother as invincible. To find her in such a broken state was deeply painful, and he felt a strong sense of guilt for living so far away. He also worried about his younger brother, imagining what the thirteen-year-old must have witnessed. David had been spending most of his free time at Rocknoll with G.P. and Amelia, and on several occasions he had accompanied his stepmother on trips, acting as her bodyguard. Now it was his mother who needed protection.

The Florida sun streamed into the living room as David watched his mother at the piano. The slow, soft music reflected her grief and David knew how deeply she regretted her marriage to Eff.

David's visit had another historic consequence. That week a family friend invited him to meet a young woman visiting from Georgia, Nilla Shields, who was staying at the nearby Casa Caprona. A blind date had been arranged with Nilla—who had just graduated from Duke University—to attend a dance at the Breakers Hotel in Palm Beach.

Blond, petite, and beautiful, Nilla Shields had gone to visit a medium two weeks earlier on a whim with her three sisters. They giggled when the psychic predicted that Nilla would meet a tall, handsome man who owned his own plane. She had never met a flyer, let alone someone her age who owned his own plane. The psychic also predicted she would fall madly in love with this stranger and marry him.

She must have grinned when David Putnam arrived to pick her up and, on the drive down to Palm Beach, told her about his life. He was instantly attracted to Nilla's southern beauty, but it was her sense of humor that ultimately stole his heart. They arrived at the dance, and onlookers could not help but notice the couple. He towered over her by a foot and a half, and she seemed to disappear when he wrapped her in his arms. *"Kids at 'Casa' for swim and cock-tails. To dance at Palm Beach. And David took Nilla, a 'blind date.' "*

Forty-eight hours later, they eloped, and with David's marriage a miracle occurred: Peace returned to Immokolee.

MARCH 4, 1934 *Fished till 3 p.m. Home, swim and Ramseys [Nilla's hosts] and Nilla out for evening. Nilla is charming and beautiful.*

MARCH 5, 1934 *David married Nilla while I was at hospital and Angler's Club Meeting! Too exciting. Gave them my room.*

My grandmother learned later that the couple actually had to wait a whole day for the justice of the peace to return from vacation to perform the hasty ceremony; otherwise the lovebirds would have married after a twenty-four-hour courtship. Rather than feeling cheated out of a formal wedding, Dorothy was thrilled by the romance and gave the newlyweds her treetop bedroom as their bridal suite.

At night, lying under a cool sheet in the treetop bedroom, I imagine my mother and father starting a life together in the same room. I laugh when I think that my parents forced me to wait a whole year before marrying my own husband, Jack.

Several days later, David had to leave Fort Pierce to resume his job in Maine, but not before stopping briefly in Rye to tell his father and Amelia the news. His new bride remained with Dorothy at Immokolee for several days before returning home to Georgia, where her family was understandably shocked by this turn of events, but still thrilled for their youngest daughter. Her new in-laws were equally surprised and delighted, judging from a letter she received from George Putnam, her father-in-law, accompanied by a note from Amelia.

March 11, 1934

Dear Nilla,

Dave has just shoved off for Boston. We had a fine day with him most of which, curiously enough, was devoted to his telling us about a gal he met and married down south!

This is just a hasty note to say hello and send my love. I was sorry that it happened so suddenly, as a little delay would have been fairer all around and better for you and for him in the long run. But that is water over the dam, and all that counts now is for you both to be happy and to move wisely. Dave knows that you both can count upon me for every bit of help I can give—although the real test is for you to help yourselves. Anyway, I'm eager to see you, and you'll find a full measure of affection in your new dad. What's more, you'll also find here another friend who will do her part and more. For Amelia is devoted to Dave, understands him well, and knows with me that you must be just the kind of girl we both can love.

When Dave gets squared away again on his new job, we'll know more about your plans. It would be fine if you can stop off here on the way to Boston, assuming Dave could come down. That would give us a chance at a little visit. And by the way, I suggest that you do not try to buy much in the way of clothes down there. That will be more fun and better, in New York. And Amelia and I would enjoy fitting you out with a few duds you'll likely need for a northern spring, as a sort of left handed wedding present. So count on that.

I want you to know that I know it was hard to let Dave go so soon, and hard for him. That was playing the game—and courage helps a lot. Also separation makes reunions all the happier.

Please feel sure that you have two good friends here, and that everything will be easy as can be.

> *Affectionately,*
> *David's Dad*

And I echo all that "David's Dad" has said.

> *Amelia Earhart*

Dorothy, Junie, and Frank "Eff" Upton during the Sarasota/Silver Springs trip (1929).

Dorothy and Sen. Fred Walcott sailing on Long Island Sound (1929).

Adm. Richard Byrd presents the Explorers Club flag that flew over the South Pole to G.P.P. (VP of club), with Clarence Chamberlain (second from left), Amelia, and Bernt Balchen (1930).

Eff during Immokolee's construction in 1930.

G.W. at Casa Caprona pool (1930): *A grand roughhouse swim back at pool with rubber animals and a band!*

Junie, Alice and Edwin Binney,
Dorothy, and Eff at Florindia (1930).

Don Blanding and Eff (1930): *Don's
undersea panels for the new house are
colorful and original.*

G.P.P. and Amelia (portrait by
Ben Pinchot, 1931).

G.P.P. and Amelia, shortly after their wedding in 1931, in their New York apartment.

Amelia and G.P.P. in Paris after Amelia's historic flight (1932): *She's done it! She flew across to Ireland. Solo. World Attention!*

Amelia and David with a model of a Lockheed Vega (1932): "David had been spending most of his free time at Rocknoll with G.P. and Amelia."

Eff, Dorothy, and Junie outside Immokolee (1932).

G.P.P. and Amelia at home (1932).

Dorothy with a giant sea bass (1933).

David, Nilla, Amelia, and "Philbert," Amelia's gift to the newlyweds (1934).

The stairs leading up to the loggia at Immokolee (1935).

1935: "IMMO-KO-LEE," Seminole (My Home Place). Our grove name.

Amelia at the Double Dee Ranch (1935).

Amelia and G.P.P. (1937)

Amelia and G.P.P. at a Japanese tea ceremony in Hawaii (1935).

Amelia with her Cord and Electra (1937).

Nilla, G.P.P., and Amelia, May 31, 1939: "The day before the flight, Mom accidently walked into their room to discover them in a warm embrace, reassuring one another that the daring attempt would be a success."

These were the last photos of Amelia taken by G.P.P. before her flight on June 1, 1937, in Miami.

A week after this photo was taken, Nilla woke from a dream seeing "Amelia through a thick pane of glass in deep water pleading for me to help her."

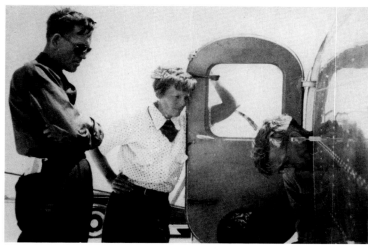

G.P.P. photographs Amelia and Fred Noonan with their mechanic.

G.P. to A.E.: "Once this is out of your hair, what a very happy interesting time we can have. We can have it, too, should you for any reason decide to quit."

George ("Junie"), Dorothy, and David dressed in the standard Immokolee chef aprons and hats (1940).

Dorothy sitting at the Driftwood (1940).

Don and Dorothy at Immokolee (1942): *2nd anniversary. Filled house with orchids. Set a beautiful South Sea Island table.*

G.P.P. with Nilla in Fort Pierce to welcome his first grandson, David B. Putnam, Jr. (1942): *A major in the Air Corp., more power to him.*

Alice Binney with David (1944).

G.W. as a colonel with the Air Transport Command (1940).

Nilla, David, and Jean Marie Putnam (1940).

Peg and G.P.P.'s wedding day, San Marino, CA (1945): Recalled Robert Lee, "She loved G.P.P. for both his strength and his idiosyncrasies."

Dorothy and Lew Palmer (1949): *I'm trying to think why I deserve so much joy and happiness after all the turmoil in my life so far! But I love it!*

Dorothy with a rickshaw driver in Africa with Lew (1945): "Perhaps those ebony blacks of Africa and the white-robed Mohammedans of far off Arabia or the coastal islands of Africa should have a right to their way of thinking, too."

Lew at the site of their Smokey Mountain cabin (1949): *Cabin. A 'Smokey' day and cool. Planted azaleas on hillside below porch. Hope they grow.*

Lew at his Spanish garden wall at Immokolee (1950): *At sunrise in the garden, I said a prayer, and gave my Beloved forever to Immokolee, which he loved!*

Dorothy at seventy-five (1963): *Time is learning to accept a few defeats. But it's rather fun frustrating the old monster.*

Dorothy at eighty-one with Binney Putnam (1969).

17

NILLA'S DREAM

"Children and work, maybe, are all that matter. Tho' of course, close contact with friends goes a long way to help. So we have to have our children."

ON DECEMBER 17, 1934, EDWIN BINNEY died of a massive heart attack. Dorothy's sister Helen described the events surrounding their father's death in her book, *Memories:*

> When he [Bub] and mother left for the South the middle of December they stayed overnight at the Hotel Iroquois. Because I felt very depressed when they left Old Greenwich, I decided I must see them again. So, when Cotter [the Binneys' chauffeur] took off the next morning to pick them up, I went along. They gave me a warm welcome and seemed delighted when they knew that I had arranged to drive as far as Washington with them. . . . Instead of leaving for home early, I had to go to the capitol with Bub, as he had conferences with several Senators about his inlet project in Fort Pierce. . . . But I remember most, my distress at his shortness of breath and persuaded him to use the elevators. Cotter drove us to the station for my noon train, and we parted affectionately with a big hug and my urgent admonition, "Take care of yourself—I love you."

On December 17, 1934, he died of a heart attack in the car before he had reached his beloved Fort Pierce. Certain memories do not fade.

Heartsick and grieving, Dorothy retreated to Immokolee following the funeral. It was a painful blow coming so soon after her split from Eff. However, she was not the sort of woman who stayed inactive for long. Edwin Binney had been a towering figure in Fort Pierce, and now his daughter would assume some of his responsibilities. With Bub dead and Eff gone, Dorothy felt a profound attachment toward her hometown. But the greatest boost to her spirits was the news that David and Nilla had decided to move down to Florida, planning to build a house across the road from Immokolee on land Dorothy had given them.

On July 6, 1935, Dorothy became a grandmother. David and Nilla Putnam named their daughter—my older sister— Binney. From the moment that Dorothy held the tiny baby to her breast, she felt renewed. Her grandchildren would prove to be an overwhelming source of pride and pleasure, and she vowed to make up for the times she felt she had neglected both David and June.

The young Putnams were still living at the Casa Caprona in Fort Pierce during the construction of their home when Amelia and her cousin Lucy Challis flew down to see the baby. David left for the airport immediately after hearing the roar of the Lockheed Vega as it swooped down so close to the rooftop that he later recalled seeing Amelia's freckled cheeks through the plane's window. Driving south on U.S. 1 beneath the shadow of the low-flying plane, David chased the airborne visitors, laughing as he attempted to beat them to the dirt runway.

It is possible that Amelia and Dorothy took the opportunity to become reacquainted during Amelia's brief stay in Fort Pierce, for I suspect that the two women (who now shared a grandchild) met privately. There are, however, no diaries for this time.

Though the two old friends had traveled a different road, they still had much in common. While Dorothy had felt little pride as G.P.'s subservient wife, she would eventually become the powerful matriarch of the entire family, with Immokolee as its "home place."

It was a misty morning in May 1937 and the evening showers had paved the way for a low-lying fog. From the loggia on the second floor, Dorothy spotted David as he appeared through the cloudy trees that circled the lily pond. Five minutes along the woodsy trail beside the honeybell trees was all it took to walk from the clearing where David and Nilla lived. No sooner had he loped up the outside staircase, two steps at a time, than his mother welcomed him with her traditional glass of freshly squeezed orange juice.

David was preparing to leave for Miami, where he would spend the following week at the Columbus Hotel with his father and Amelia. Over the years, the relationship between Amelia and her stepson had deepened into a close friendship. She admired his adventurous spirit as a young author and explorer. David was a kindred spirit and Amelia loved him as a son. "She was wonderful to me," he recalled. "From the age of fifteen to eighteen, a whole three-year period, I flew all over the country with her as part gofer and bodyguard. She was absolutely delightful, friendly, a real sharp gal and everybody loved her." My father always described her to me as a shy woman, not seeking publicity, and he regarded his father George as being protective of Amelia almost to a fault.

My grandmother not only understood David's bond with Amelia but encouraged it. She knew that Amelia had given David his first flying lessons, had bought him his first car, and that she had attended several of his football games with G.P.

On this morning in May, he had come to tell his mother everything he knew about Amelia's highly publicized attempt to be the first person to fly around the world. My grandmother had read about a first attempt, and had been concerned when Amelia and her crew, Captain Harry Manning and navigator Fred Noonan, crashed on takeoff in Honolulu. David had heard from his father that the Lockheed Electra was being repaired in Oakland, California, and that Amelia—along with Noonan—planned to try again.

A former navigator on the Pan American Pacific Clipper routes across the Pacific, Noonan had made a number of trips in this area and had experience in celestial navigation. It was rumored that the darkly handsome Noonan drank heavily, but coworkers said it had never interfered with his job. At forty-four, he was newly married and planning to start a navigation school, and the free publicity from the round-the-world trip with Amelia Earhart would be invaluable.

In my grandfather's private papers is a wealth of material never before published. It includes Amelia's papers as well: letters (both personal and business), photographs, publishing documents, speeches, cartoons, and other memorabilia. For years I have studied them, searching for answers to questions about his marriage to Amelia and their vastly different personas. For instance, I have read that my grandfather was a cold and calculating husband and that they did not have a loving marriage. In the privacy of their home, however, Amelia spoke of his public image but felt helpless to soften it, trying to give him credit for his efforts whenever possible.

He was a sensitive man and must have suffered a great deal. I know he was impatient and often irritating, and he did not suffer fools gladly. But he adored Amelia, and she knew the depth of his love for her. Among the unpublished papers she saved were letters from George written to her during the around-the-world flight that were sent back to him for safekeeping prior to her disappearance. One reads:

> . . . I have carefully analyzed our situation and appraised the last several days in your company. My considered conclusion is that I love you very much and would rather play* and work with you than with anyone I have yet encountered or could imagine—comb that out of your carefully tousled hair.
>
> G.
>
> *Open to several interpretations, and applicable to all.

The reference to their lovemaking will probably come as a shock to many who believe the couple did not share a physical relationship. As my mother and father reminded me so often, "in the privacy of their home, they were lovingly demonstrative."

Included in these papers is a poem submitted for publication and rejected. As a budding writer, Amelia used the pen name "Emil A. Hart." There are also cartoons that she placed in an envelope; in pencil she had written, "For A.E.'s funny scrapbook—made while sitting by the fireside someday." I have held her passport in my hands and stared at the weary-looking young woman whose dark circles under the eyes are testament to a record-breaking Atlantic crossing and a willful determination to prove that women were not the weaker sex.

In their correspondence, my grandfather and Amelia usually divided their letters into two halves. The first portion was devoted to their business affairs; the second half was reserved for their personal sentiments for one another. In their private vows to one another, they promised never to expose their personal lives. Thus my grandfather never published these or other letters. But one letter to Amelia, written shortly before her final flight, reveals a sensitivity that belies his stiff public image.

It is clear that the decision for her to take this trip was a joint one.

Sunday evening.

Dear Hon:

I have been thinking a lot about your book. There is such a wealth of material. Probably the right thing for this book to concern solely "world flight," if, or, and when! Possibly it might embrace a chapter each on the Atlantic, first Pacific, and Mexico. These flights by themselves, with us as a background or in between. Which would leave for another (and more important book) the rich material of these full five years ("A Full Five Years" is a possible title)—people, places, lecturing, Purdue, education, modern flying, philosophy, politics, women, etc. Anyway, the immediate chore is to get down on paper, even roughly, a graphic record of what you've just done. Likely it breaks up somewhat thusly. 1. Planning; 2. Oakland-Honolulu; 3. Birchlots, of which #2 is the one to tackle immediately, while it is warm in your mind. Then #3. I'll get together the fabric of #1. At the end I may do a chapter myself regarding the business end. Much of all this we can serialize in advance of book, hon, if we wish.

Hon, I miss you.

I alternate between spasms of contentment and of worry. I'm so happy with you and we really do have such a swell time together, in all ways. And I wish this flight wasn't hanging over us. You know I sympathize fully with your ambition and will abet it, and 98% I know you'll get away with it. But we both recognize the hazards, and I love you dearly—I don't want to run the risk of perhaps having to go on without you—that makes me terribly sorry for myself? (Entirely disregarding your end of it!)

But gosh, once this is out of your hair, what a very happy interesting time we can have. We can have it, too, should you for any reason decide to quit.

Love you lots,
G

In another letter, my grandfather seems depressed and worried.

Hon;

I'm just recovering from a slump! Two days of feeling punk + mental depression—the one produces the other, but at the time that's hard to rationalize.

Please, Ma'am, know that I am deeply in love with you. . . . Hon, I've been having the heebies a lot again . . . it is wearing—this waking up and countering the dangers the gal I love is preparing to face again. By the way, thanks for the generous paragraph in your last story as to the help I give.

I'll be so happy when it's over. I want peace—and you. I'm never really content anymore, when I'm away from you. So face the horrid likelihood of being mighty close to me the rest of your days! Please love me a lot.

G

George and Amelia's kind of equality of the sexes was unusual for the time, although their union was a forerunner of "power marriages" today. "I loved his humor and could see why A.E. was so attracted to him," Amelia's sister Muriel told me. "It was a difficult role he had to play, being the husband of a famous person, but there was never any bitterness or antagonism." The playwright Robert E. Lee said, "Husband and wife both knew they had a good thing going. I suspect she probably needed him more than George needed her."

Having studied their private papers for twenty years, I don't believe this was the case. I think they both took advantage of each other's skills, and were equal partners in their loving and adventuring.

During an interview in 1978 with Cap Palmer, my grandfather's former business associate, he described his experiences with George. "There's a general impression that he was a supreme egotist. That he was all for one and that one

was himself . . . that when he promoted Amelia, he was promoting himself," Cap told me. "But in fact he had no conceit on his own or about himself. He knew his notoriety,
which is a better word for George than fame. He was very
much like Cecil B. DeMille, always selling tickets, never
himself."

Cap Palmer added, "He promoted Amelia, not for the
glory of the country, he just loved to promote things. . . .
Amelia was older than her years. She was a very mature, balanced person. She was the only person who had George
under complete control. He was dominant by nature,
but Amelia was someone in her own right. She could
handle George. When he would get a little expansive,
Amelia would catch his eye, lift her eyebrows a little and go
pphhhsss and George would cool it."

I have also learned that my grandfather was the more
cautious of the two. The legend that his P.T. Barnum instincts forced the trip is a false one.

In an article dated September 26, 1937, he recalled that
"we seriously discussed abandoning the flight. This she was
unwilling to do."

Amelia's response to G.P. would not surprise anyone
who had ever met the headstrong aviatrix. She was eager to
take the risks as a final coup in her career. The *Milwaukee
Journal* quoted Amelia telling her husband, "Please don't be
concerned. It just seems that I must try this flight. I have
weighed it all carefully. I want to do it. There's just about
one more good flight left in my system. I'm getting old and
ought to make way for the younger generation before I'm
feeble."

A month shy of her thirty-ninth birthday, Amelia had
begun to consider her own mortality. In one handwritten
poem found among her papers, she writes: "Merciless life,
laughs in the burning sun, and only death, slow circling
down, Shadows."

Earlier that spring of 1937, while visiting the noted flyer

Jackie Cochran Odlum's ranch in Indio, California, she had met a psychic called Eldon Smith. The unconventional and spirited Cochran was absorbed by "thought transference" and confided that she herself had such a power. Amelia also felt she was blessed with psychic gifts, and the two women became confidantes.

I was fascinated to read the penciled document written in Amelia's own handwriting. The notes summarize a brief question-and-answer session with the medium. She asks him if there is any way to get "explanation of world" and if "table tapping" is the only means to conjure up the spirit of the dead. He answers, "Develope [sic] more right thinking."

A.E.: I asked if he meant higher minded thinking.
E.S.: Yes.
A.E.: I asked if broad minded attitude meant [sic].
E.S.: Yes, very vehemently. We fly with you.
A.E.: Fly with me?
E.S.: Yes, very vehemently.
A.E.: How can I get the message.
E.S.: Concentrate. Vision will come. Follow your hunches.

While her plane was being repaired at the Lockheed Factory in Burbank, California, Amelia received a letter from another psychic.

Dear Miss Earhart,

I hesitate to write you this letter, but the urge comes upon so strongly, that I feel I must write. Do not make another attempt to fly around the world, you will not make it. You will meet with accidents, and you may loose [sic] your life through them. You have finished in the flying world; Let others do, what you have achieved.

I am writing you this, that you may enjoy a long life, and have a happy future. Higher powers rule our destinies, and we cannot go beyond them, we can get so far, and then we cannot go any further, you are entering into a critical period.

Yours very truly,
Miss E. M. Blair

As if tempting fate, Amelia left behind a lucky rabbit's foot someone had given her and took off with Noonan on May 20, this time flying from Oakland toward the East Coast. My dad had received a message from his father to come down to Miami, the third stop along the new route, and help with the loading of the plane. Since both my mom (Nilla) and he would be making several trips to Miami before the takeoff, Dad had arranged for Dofry to baby-sit my three-year-old sister, Binney, at Immokolee during their absence.

Mom and Dad joined Amelia and my grandfather in Miami. The day before the flight, Mom accidentally walked into their room to discover them in a warm embrace, reassuring one another that the daring attempt would be a success. Neither had pulled apart as my mother stood there. Recalling the intimacy between G.P. and Amelia, my mom, who was five months' pregnant with me at the time, wept when she later described the scene to my father. They had shared so many wonderful times over the past two years and had been among the few to witness George and Amelia's intimacy, something the couple protected with a vengeance.

Although Amelia had a reputation for aloofness, my mother found her to be a tender and affectionate woman. She was touched by the flyer's sensitivity. As Amelia prepared to depart, she reached down, gently placed her hand on Mom's swollen belly, and whispered, "Take care of yourself, little one." Amelia also spoke to my father, "David, please keep an eye on your dad for me."

On sheets of lined school paper, my mother scribbled down details of the historic departure from Miami on the morning of June 1, 1937:

> . . . I was there several times during the week or so of preparations. But I had to leave one little girl at home (well cared for) and had another with me soon to be born.

It was an eerie feeling being awakened at 4:00 a.m. for departure for Amelia's flight, from the 36th Street Airport. We stopped en route for coffee and donuts to take along the way.

Once at the airport, there were things to be gone over and final arrangements to be made. The plane was ready and sitting on the runway. Amelia and Fred Noonan walked to the plane. There was a faint light in the morning sky when the two engines were fired.

Dave, G.P., and I stood alone on the upper deck of the airplane hangar as the plane took off . . . Amelia was on her way around the world. G.P. flew back to New York, and Dave and I came home to Fort Pierce. In the middle of the night a week or so later I woke Dave and told him that I had seen Amelia through a thick pane of glass in deep water pleading for me to help her. I knew I could never reach her, nor help her, nor ever see her again.

My mother later recalled, "we watched until she faded in the east. It was kind of an eerie feeling you had, mysterious or scary in a way."

Amelia eventually flew over 22,000 miles, down the coast of South America, across the Atlantic, over the heart of Africa, and over India and Indonesia, stopping along the way whenever she needed to sleep, to take on fuel, or make repairs. Once, at the end of June in Bandoeng, Java, in the Dutch East Indies, a crew of mechanics worked three days on the Electra's engines. In a telegram, Amelia asked George to send thank-you notes to the hosts who had housed her along the way.

It seemed that Amelia's fame preceded her and she was amused by the lack of red tape. "No one has asked for passports. No customs, no inspections. We signed the police register in St. Louis, that is all. Better not mention this 'till it's all over as someone might get in trouble. . . . Lots of love, A."

The entire world was riveted, as newspapers and magazines followed Amelia's progress. At every stop along the way, she collected gas and mechanic receipts, weather reports, and notes, which she sent back to my grandfather. He carefully saved them for her upcoming book. They fill a brittle manila envelope and are the tangible and fragile evidence of the flight.

In several handwritten notes, Amelia addressed him by her affectionate nickname, "Mugs." Before publishing another highly publicized letter following the Pacific crossing in 1935, George edited out this closing: "Well, anyway, here's hoping and cheerio to my Pugs. A.E." Both husband and wife were intent upon keeping their affections to themselves. (It is curious that Amelia called George both Mugs and Pugs.)

On one page, torn from a spiral notepad, Amelia sounds frustrated and anxious: "I certainly wish I were alone. Oh well I'll try to do a good job anyway. Not that Freddie is not okay. He is in many ways. But I do better alone whenever possible. I wish you were here, so many things you would enjoy. Perhaps someday we can do a pleasure trip. . . ."

The most difficult leg of the trip lay ahead: 2,556 miles of Pacific blue between Lae, New Guinea, and Howland Island, "an almost microscopic bit of land," the final destination. Among these same papers is a Western Union telegram Amelia sent from Lae on July 2, 1937, while she and Noonan waited to take off. The dispatch, which runs to seven pages, begins with Amelia's concern over the method of navigation she had chosen.

ANY LACK OF KNOWLEDGE OF THEIR FASTNESS AND SLOWNESS WOULD DEFEAT THE ACCURACY CELESTIAL NAVIGATION HOWLAND SO SMALL SPOT TO FIND THAT EVERY AID MUST BE AVAILABLE.

DESPITE RESTLESSNESS AND DISAPPOINTMENT NOT GETTING OFF THIS MORNING WILL STILL RETAINED ENOUGH ENTHUSIASM

During the layover, the pilot and navigator spent their time in coconut groves and picturesque villages. Amelia pays one of the natives two shillings for a dictionary of pidgin English and tells her husband she's "up." The natives refer to her Lockheed Electra as "Biscuit Box" because the smooth metal resembles the tins of imported crackers from England.

Amelia begins the final page of the communication:

I HAVE WORKED VERY HARD LAST TWO DAYS REPACKING PLANE AND ELIMI-
NATING EVERYTHING UNESSENTIAL HAVE WEIGHT WE HAVE EVEN LEFT OUT
AS MUCH PERSONAL PROPERTY AS WE CAN DECENTLY AND HENCEFORTH
PURPOSE TO TRAVEL LIGHTER THAN EVER I RETAIN ONLY ONE BRIEF CASE IN
WHICH ARE PAPERS AS WELL AS CLOTHING AND TOOTH BRUSH HE HAS SMALL
TIN CASE WHICH PICKED UP IN AFRICA I NOTICE IT STILL RATTLES SO CAN
NOT BE STUFFED PARA

WISH COULD STAY HERE PEACEFULLY AND LEARN TO KNOW SOMETHING
OF COUNTRY STRANGE THINGS TO ME HAPPEN FREQUENTLY . . .

Amelia and Noonan finally lifted the gleaming silver bird over the sea at 10:00 A.M. local time in a spectacular takeoff, beating the end of the runway by fifty yards. The flight was expected to take eighteen hours. Seven hours later, she reported by wireless that they were flying at an altitude of 7,000 feet and at 150 miles per hour. My grandfather arrived at the Coast Guard headquarters in San Francisco to wait for her radio messages and plan her joyous homecoming in a few days. For the last month he had maintained a close connection to his wife through her regular dispatches radioed back to him in the United States from the well-publicized stops along the route.

But on the afternoon of July 2, he received the disturbing news that contact with Amelia's plane had been lost. In a radiogram sent from the Coast Guard cutter *Itasca*, which was cruising just to the north of Howland Island, the dispatcher begins by saying, ". . . Broadcasting to Steamers but few in this area." The weather was overcast and cloudy, and "Earhart's direction finder apparently not functioning well."

The radiogram also said, "She had barely sufficient fuel under the conditions to make Howland." The Coast Guard believed that Earhart had passed "close to and to northward of Howland," but Amelia only acknowledged receiving the *Itasca*'s signals once and did not answer questions as to her position or course. Fearing the worst, the ship said it was using "every resource to locate plane."

From Oakland, California, my grandfather immediately wired William D. Leahy, the chief of naval operations at the Pentagon:

TECHNICIANS FAMILIAR WITH MISS EARHARTS PLANE BELIEVE WITH ITS LARGE TANKS CAN FLOAT ALMOST INDEFINITELY STOP WITH RETRACTABLE GEAR AND SMOOTH SEA SAFE LANDING SHOULD HAVE BEEN PRACTICABLE STOP RESPECTFULLY REQUEST SUCH ASSISTANCE AS IS PRACTICABLE FROM NAVAL AIR CRAFT AND SURFACE CRAFT STATIONED HONOLULU STOP APPARENTLY PLANES POSITION NOT FAR FROM HOWLAND.

He requested government assistance and heard from the commandant of the Fourteenth Naval District, who replied,

PEARL HARBOR HAS BEEN DIRECTED TO USE IN ANY PRACTICABLE WAY THE FORCES UNDER HIS COMMAND TO AID IN SEARCH FOR MISS EARHART. WILLIAM D. LEAHY, CHIEF OF NAVAL OPERATIONS.

Stamped in half-inch black letters across this telegram is the word: PRIORITY.

On July 3, G.P. also wired Daniel Roper, the secretary of commerce, that a signal should be broadcast every hour asking that Amelia should

CONCENTRATE ONE WORD "LAND" OR "WATER" SETTLING WHETHER AFLOAT OR ASHORE ALSO WORDS "NORTH" OR "SOUTH" DEFINING POSITION RELATIVE TO EQUATOR STOP THANKS
     PUTNAM

The next morning, the world learned what a heartsick George had known for the last twenty-four hours: Amelia Earhart and Fred Noonan were missing.

At the very end of my grandfather's biography about Amelia, *Soaring Wings*, he recalls a poignant conversation:

It was wintry blue dusk, and all around us buildings were checkered with gold when AE stopped her car at a traffic light. The wheels were still rolling just a trifle when a man—an old man, ragged, weary, pale—stepped out from the curb. . . . We went home, and nothing more was said about the old man through dinner or the evening. But later, when the world was closed down and still, Amelia said, "It is hard to be old—so hard. I'm afraid I'll hate it. Hate to grow old." . . . And then, as one who may be imagining or simply comprehending a fact, she said slowly, "I think probably, GP, that I'll not live—to be old."

In Fort Pierce, Dorothy and her two sons had been mapping Amelia's world flight since her departure from Miami. From San Francisco, George wired David and Nilla with the devastating news. David immediately wired back his love and support, and received his father's reply on July 3: "Thanks dear boy. It helps. There's plenty hope yet. Love, Dad."

David packed hurriedly, drove to Immokolee to say goodbye to his mother, and left for the West Coast. For days, David and G.P. went without sleep, my grandfather weeping at times. Their mood veered from cautious optimism to despair, but G.P. knew that he was the only one who could direct the massive search for the missing plane. They had known the flight was dangerous and had weighed the odds. Still, it was impossible to believe that the plane could disappear without a trace. My grandfather held the telegrams and said a silent prayer. He kept returning to one line in the first Coast Guard dispatch: "Earhart apparently handicapped through night by cloudy weather . . ."

On July 5, three days after communication had been lost, the *Itasca* wired:

1904 0700 TO 0704 HEARD FOUR SERIES OF DASHES FROM 0714 TO 0716 HEARD FOUR SERIES OF DASHES FROM 0727 TO 0731 HEARD EIGHT SERIES OF DASHES FOUR OF WHICH WERE VERY STRONG VOICE INDICATED BUT NOT DISTINGUISHABLE ALL ON 3105 KCS 2045.

Then, only silence.

18

TRANSITIONS

"An old photo album: and each picture is a tomb where a dead heart lies buried."

MORE THAN HALF A DOZEN WARSHIPS, countless airplanes, and thousands of naval and Coast Guard officers were involved in an effort to locate the missing aviatrix. Wireless operators were ordered to stand by. There were news reports that the search for Earhart was costing $250,000 a day. Franklin Roosevelt defended the cost of the mission, and joined the nation in prayer. The Coast Guard cutter *Itasca* radioed back to my grandfather that they thought they saw flares from the downed plane, but that slim ray of hope vanished with the news that the flash was only lightning.

For the next two weeks, radio messages spawned countless rumors about possible sightings, and my grandfather, exhausted and emotionally spent, moved with David into the home of close friends. Back in Fort Pierce, my mother's dream of Amelia kept her awake at night. She desperately wanted a better ending than the one that haunted her sleep.

On July 18, the U.S. Navy abandoned its search, having covered 360,000 square miles of sea and coral islands.

My grandfather's private search was just beginning.

George was aware of Amelia's interest in the supernatural, and he was not surprised to receive a letter immediately after news of her disappearance from a medium saying that the famous flyer "knew her end was inevitable that the fall was the worst part owing to fear. She then floated for hours . . . clung to a wing . . . until the last moment a big wave . . . swept her into a new life. She describes it as a last breath being the first for a baby it was so swift."

There is a second typewritten, unsigned letter. For years I wondered who might have written it. At first, I thought it was from some unknown psychic, but now I believe it may have been written by the flyer Jackie Cochran, and that my grandfather—in order to protect her identity—may have destroyed her original notes and retyped them. Cochran had requested that he "keep her name out of it." At that time, "channeling" was considered bizarre, and my grandfather himself did not want anyone to know that he too had resorted to such unorthodox measures to aid his desperate search. In this letter, the author claimed to have connected with Amelia's spirit.

> I want you to tell Mr. Putnam there are no regrets and none should feel that way a bit about this. He must go on and live as he always has to try and know in his soul that I am alive and will now do a greater work than I ever dreamed was possible to do. . . . Not for one moment did I lose consciousness. I know that we were hit by lightning. We were heading north again and I believe that I might have made it, but when the ship was struck I slowly went into the water. . . . I felt that I had fallen asleep—just dreaming—dreaming that I was flying, going higher than I had ever gone before. . . . If Mr. Putnam would sit in our room alone, I shall try and make my presence felt and try to impress him with my thoughts. May all the good things of this earth come to you, my dear friend.

How this letter must have torn him apart, sitting alone for hours. Waiting.

Notes and papers from Amelia mailed after her departure from Lae continued to arrive at George Putnam's office. Among them was a silver cigarette case etched with a map. It was a gift for David—engraved "D.B.P. from A.E." (My father later gave this to me when I made my first solo flight.)

A month after Amelia's disappearance, George still refused to give up hope that his wife was alive, and continued his search, following any leads. He was contacted by another psychic, J. Lacey, who advised him of the downed plane's position, and invited Putnam to a séance. In his reply, my grandfather informed the psychic that the detailed position given matched exactly the location of an uncharted island on the eastern fringe of the Gilbert Islands.

Lacey also told my grandfather that telepathic messages were being received and that

> the plane was damaged in the forced landing as undership caught on reef. High winds and rough seas later released plane which floated out to sea and sank in deep water. It has been definitely given to us that only hope of rescue will come from help of natives in surrounding islands and Japanese fisherman now in those waters. Some of these natives who are very psychic know of the plight of the castaways and by some means of telegraphy have broadcast the news throughout the islands. Noonan was badly crippled in landing and little hope is held for him. Rescue must come long before your expedition could reach those waters or the worst can be feared.
>
> Yours very sincerely and in full sympathy,
> J. Lacey.

George frantically wired Undersecretary of State Sumner Welles, who sent a telegram to the American Embassy in London asking that the British join in the search, concentrating specifically on the Gilbert Islands. "It is of course a forlorn hope," my grandfather wrote Welles, "but one which, you will understand, is of utmost concern to me."

Three days later, he wired Welles again. "Forgive me for being a nuisance," he wrote, "I expect to leave for Coast

Tuesday. . . . Is there any possibility of getting definite word from British. . . ?"

On August 24, Welles replied that "all Gilbert Islands" had been searched, but that another cutter had been dispatched to the position recommended by the psychic. "I am sorry that this whole matter has caused so much trouble to you," my grandfather responded; ". . . it was impossible for me to rest until this specific matter had been run to earth, remote as is any hope that it could produce results."

But the British were unsuccessful in their search.

Growing more desperate, he offered a cash reward of $2,000 to anyone who could provide information on Amelia's whereabouts. This naturally resulted in a succession of false leads and my grandfather—vulnerable and willing to stake everything on getting his wife back—became the victim of several cruel hoaxes. In one, a Bronx janitor sent him a note at the Hotel Barclay in Manhattan where he was staying, claiming to be a crew member of a gun-running ship that had rescued Amelia and Fred Noonan in Pacific waters. My grandfather met the man at two in the morning. The next day, accompanied by an FBI agent, he met the man again: He produced a brown and white scarf that Amelia's secretary (Margo de Carrie) later recognized as belonging to Amelia. He said he was holding Amelia—ill and malnourished—on his ship, and would release her for $2,000.

Investigators determined that the man had not been to sea in twenty-two years. He was later arrested and charged with extortion. In his confession, he admitted that the scarf was one Amelia had lost during takeoff several years earlier and that he had found it on the dirt runway and kept it as a souvenir. Desperate for any connection to his wife, George nonetheless paid him $50 for the scarf, against the advice of the authorities.

My grandfather could not bring himself to return to Rocknoll, and decided to sell the rambling estate. He never returned there after Amelia's disappearance. The house simply held too many memories—a wall of one room papered with aviation maps, the trophies and her mementos, the gardens where they walked together planning their next adventure. (Some of their treasures had been destroyed in a 1934 fire, including autographed pictures, first editions, and a collection of Rockwell Kent paintings. My father's room was also badly damaged, and he lost many of his souvenirs from his Arctic trips, as well as a model of Amelia's plane.) What was left in the house was packed into storage boxes and sent to California, where George would remain for the rest of his life.

During the construction of Immokolee in 1930, Don Blanding had visited Fort Pierce. Dorothy had hired her friend to paint a colored version of his trademark Hawaiian fish mural on two paneled doors in one of the guest rooms. *"Don's undersea panels (really on guest room doors) for the new house are colorful and original. They work out very well. He's going to do one <u>Florida</u> one, a silhouette of live oak, air plants and Spanish moss. On the specially fine fir doors with their beautiful grain in the wood."*

In the summer of 1937, Dorothy took Junie and returned to the Hawaiian Islands to visit Don. She had long admired his work from the time they both lived in Bend, Oregon, and it was during her first trip to Hawaii, when Junie was recuperating from a long illness, that Dorothy realized the depth of affection Don felt for her. As she wrote now: *"Mt. Haleakala. A strange talk with Don last night, as tho' we'd stayed exactly as we were 14 years ago. He swears I've influenced him more than any human being and that things now he knows he took from me. He's been very unhappy and is just finding himself again."*

His book of poetry, *Vagabond's House,* was published in 1928. In a subsequent printing (1943), he dedicated the book to Dorothy: "The Lady of Vagabond's House Who Was the Inspiration for the Dream That Made Itself Come True."

Blanding was a dapper, highly sophisticated man with a courtly, gentle bearing. After the ambitious George Putnam and the abusive Frank Upton, his sensitivity appealed to Dorothy's creative side. He had been dubbed the Poet Laureate of Hawaii, and once described himself as "a painter, poet, vagabond, and lusty liver of the physical and a tireless aviator among the higher, luminous clouds of idealism." Extremely handsome, he still possessed an athletic physique and his year-round tan lent him a certain exotic masculinity. Dorothy, acting as a sort of benevolent patron, once again found herself falling in love. The fact that they were simply good friends should have affected her judgment, but she was facing middle age alone and longing for companionship.

My grandfather declared Amelia legally dead in 1939, two years after her disappearance. That year, he published *Soaring Wings*, which sold well and received good reviews as well as bringing in much-needed income (he had received an advance of $1,000 from Harcourt Brace).* The income helped restore his financial security, but the book did not earn as much as he expected.

With a nearly depleted bank account as a result of his ongoing search for his wife, G.P. accepted a job from Paramount Pictures as a story editor. I was saddened to find among his papers a 1938 letter of resignation from the Explorers Club in New York.

Gentlemen:

Inasmuch as I have moved permanently to the coast, and due to recent events it is necessary for me to economize pretty drastically. I am regretfully obliged to discontinue my membership in The Explorers Club. This is my resignation, effective immediately.

Very Truly Yours,

G. P. Putnam

*Amelia's final dispatches had been published in 1938 as *Last Flight*.

Severing ties with his fellow members must have been painful for my grandfather. I know how deeply he valued his association with the club and its purpose. In 1926 he carried the Explorers Club flag on board the *Morrissey* to Greenland. On March 22, 1997, at their annual dinner, it was my privilege to return this flag to the club.

At fifty-one, my grandfather was lonely and in need of companionship.

In 1938, he had met Jean Marie Consigny, a petite blonde with blue eyes and finely chiseled features. The twenty-three-year-old Hollywood socialite told my grandfather that she wanted to write a book on small gardens, and he offered to publish it. They were soon seen together at Hollywood parties, but both denied any romance, apparently because Jean Marie was still married to her first husband. Her mother objected to the relationship because of their age difference, but in May 1939 newspapers reported an engagement. Three weeks later, the couple were married at the Boulder Dam Hotel, eluding reporters who were led to believe by my grandfather that the ceremony would take place in Las Vegas.

It was during his marriage to Jean Marie that my grandfather wrote his autobiography, *Wide Margins.* In recalling Amelia, he did not disguise his feelings for her, saying "In life she denounced the difference between men and women. She wanted an equal chance in the air, the right to fly wing to wing with other pilots, to go where they went, take the risk that they took, and, if necessary, to die as they died."

The book was dedicated "For Jeannie."

Although my grandfather rarely spoke of Amelia, Jean Marie felt her presence. She once said that she lived in fear the famous aviatrix would walk in the door any day. It must have been an impossible position for any woman, let alone one so young and rather shy. How could she compete with a ghost?

George was much in demand on speaking tours, and the couple needed the income to finance their lifestyle, which included talked-about dinner parties with my grandfather's coterie of famous friends. Several years later, Jean Marie announced to George she wanted a divorce. In an interview with Mary Lowell in 1988, published in *The Sound of Wings*, she said, "I always loved him . . . I've never stopped loving him. I should never have divorced him!" The divorce, after only five years of marriage, came as a complete surprise to George. Acquaintances had noted their opposite personalities, however, and were not so surprised by the breakup.

Dorothy's life as a single woman was anything but dull. In 1939 she penned her own lyrics for the song "Thanks For the Memories." My grandmother did not identify the poem's recipient, but knowing the name behind the verse would do little to enhance the clever joy found in her words.

> Thanks for the memory of candlelight and wine
> Of roads and jasmine vine
> Of starlit nights together, your cigarettes and mine
> How lovely it was!
>
> Thanks for the memory of sunny afternoons
> And singing theme song tunes
> And motor trips and burning lips
> And your morning toast and prunes
> How lovely it was!
> Many's the time we feasted
> When we really should have fasted
> Gee it was swell while it lasted
> We did have fun, and no harm done
>
> And thanks for the memory of that connecting door
> And lovemaking galore

You might have had a headache
Thank God you never snore
So thank you so much!

Thanks for the memory of a cathedral's moldy wall
And an early morning call
That weekend on Long Island
When colors screamed of Fall
How lovely it was!

Thanks for the memory on the City of Mexico
Tela Rancho Telva, perched up in the mountain at Taxco
Strolls of window shopping
Just happily on the go
Then peaceful the hours of musing
When adolescents would be twosing
But that's all right: we'll love tonight
And thanks for the memory of glaciers in the park
And trout fishing after dark and startled deer at Granite
And a wrestle with that shark
I thank you so much!

    D.

As president of the Fort Pierce Garden Club, Dorothy traveled throughout the state lecturing on the use of native materials in arranging flowers. One project undertaken by her Garden Club was planting royal poincianna trees throughout the town. Among those dozens of bright orange-red beauties, only a few survive today. Ironically, three of them, though chopped off across the top, still mark the entrance to Immokolee Road.

On the society pages of the *Fort Pierce News Tribune* dated June 18, 1939, an article appeared announcing Dorothy Binney Putnam's invitation to present a flower arrangement at the New York World's Fair. (Since Dorothy's divorce from Upton, she reverted to using the name Putnam.) Her prize-winning exhibit was made from local flowers, leaves, and other tropical vegetation. Dorothy named her arrangement

"Blue Summer." I still have a postcard of the exotic display: The blue-ribbon arrangement is perfectly balanced, and beneath the tall pottery vase it reads, "Greetings from IM-MO-KO-LEE."

In 1940, Dorothy was the subject of another story in the *Miami Daily News* claiming that she was "the leading spirit of the movement to keep the roadways beautiful. To this end she led the women of the city in a raid against unsightly billboards and pulled up over 1,000 of them herself!"

During that same summer in 1940, Don Blanding came to Immokolee for what was planned as a brief visit. The inevitable occurred, and what had been a warm friendship over the years blossomed into love. On June 13, less than three weeks after Don's arrival, he and Dorothy were married. The previous day she had written in her diary, *"I'm deeply in love with Don and I know he is with me. Why don't we marry and go the rest of the road together."*

Blanding evidently agreed. *"This a.m. at 10:45 I said 'yes' to Don. Hurried excited lunch and then—marriage license, family—and Dr. Howard married us 6:30!"*

Although they had been friends for years, the decision to marry was an impulsive one for my grandmother—still the incurable romantic. It would be impossible to estimate which of the two had the stronger ego. Both were stubborn, independent, highly critical, and sharp-tongued. Rather than mellowing with age, both seemed more set in their ways, and for Don to suddenly find himself with a wife as formidable as Dorothy must have required a considerable amount of patience. Don's long bachelorhood had left him with an inflexibility that would threaten this newly discovered ardor. Nonetheless, Don had seized on Florida as a suitable place to inspire his next book of poetry.

The flamboyant artist was introduced to Dorothy's long-time friend A. E. ("Beany") Backus, another talented young painter. Dorothy had discovered Beany's landscapes in Fort Pierce and had become one of his supporters. She arranged for him to share Don's "Floridays" studio, and the sun-filled space was often the meeting place for an eclectic group of artists and writers. It was here Don began writing his chatty column, which appeared daily in the local newspaper.

"Don absorbed in his new studio. It's good for him and will give his ego a chance. Sally swims alone! Aged 4, 22 strokes! Whoops."

As a child, I can remember calling my grandmother's new husband "Pappy Don." My earliest memories of Don center on birthday parties and diving lessons, but he wasn't at Immokolee long enough to be thought of as part of the family. Looking through his tenth book, *Floridays,* I am always delighted by one verse dedicated to my sister, Binney, and me.

WATER HYACINTHS
for Binney and Sally
When they're about five years older.

. . . With water-bugs for pirates and pollywogs for whales,
You search for high adventure, tiny pixie vagabonds . . .

With silken banners flying, frail bright banners yet untried,
you are like the thoughts of children, innocent and young and brave.

May the kindly God of Children let his friendly power guide
'Til you find snug harbor waiting in a world that's dark and grave.

Aside from his newspaper duties, Don devoted his days to painting black and white silhouettes and writing poetry. The whimsically illustrated *Floridays* is a result of his love for Immokolee, and Don dedicated it

TO DOROTHY
"Thy People Shall Be My People"

I said I'd love this land because of you. I love it for itself . . . for it has brought haven and peace to you when your heart sought surcease in beauty from the pain you knew.

The very early days of their marriage were blissful, at least according to my grandmother's diaries. *"Sabal palm in bloom and loveliness everywhere. Each day a little sweeter and happier than its predecessor."* On one of her regular trips to New York, where she loved to walk and attend the theater, Dorothy was delighted to see her husband's new book displayed: *"New York. Errands at Wanamaker's. Don's 'Floridays' out today. Fun to see it in the shops."*

But while Don's literary accomplishments appealed to my grandmother, his presence at Immokolee was to become more and more of a strain. He simply was not the outdoor type, and there were quarrels over the most innocent housekeeping and gardening decisions. My grandmother tried to appease him by building a studio at Immokolee, and she organized a grand party for its opening, attended by three hundred friends and supporters.

Don resented his lack of authority in Dorothy's world and, increasingly frustrated, resorted to penning her a witty but stinging evaluation of their lopsided arrangement:

Dear Gal,

Let me draw you an amusing, but serious little picture, and don't look for hidden barbs because there are none. But I believe this little picture will help you to see us in clearer perspective and clear the way to a better understanding of problems we have to meet. Immokolee is a charming little kingdom by itself, or rather it is a charming little Queendom owned, ruled to The last inch and operated by that charming, generous and lovable benevolent dictator, Queen Dorothy (that's not politically correct language, but you know what I mean). I am nothing but The Queen's consort . . . It's a gracious job and my Queen is generous, lovable, passionate, everything a Queen should be, and also everything that a Queen is . . . Imperious, accustomed to giving absolute orders, which it is her right to give, while she's a Queen alone. But when she takes a consort she has problems. The Queen's consort is and always has been a faintly ridiculous figure in The eyes of The rest of The world. And in his own eyes because he is given a little scepter to play with (but mustn't make any serious gestures with it). He can even have his small toy army, but he must just parade it and blow little trumpets to scare The guinea hens. He mustn't be a serious threat to The absolute power of The Queen.

Now, if he was raised for that kind of job he is content with his little toy army and his little toy scepter, but you see, I've been King Don in my own little kingdoms, and I think I've done a damned good imitation of The ideal Queen's consort, seldom stamping in public or in any way appearing to usurp The Queen's powers. . . . In the whole of Immokolee there's just one small space, about The size of a grave, where I by God have authority and that's The studio . . . I'm just not The material for Queen's consort, and if I were, you'd be very disappointed because you do not like spiritless men. . . . You've made quick decisions (had to make them) so long in running your life and The homes, etc., so that action and reaction are almost simultaneous. . . . Just something to think over.

With love and kisses,

Don

Dorothy hastily scribbled her reply to the letter on the outside of the envelope: "Very excellent and tastefully said. I agree, but it was a *shock* as I had not realized it." Predictably, she assumes responsibility for his criticism.

This missive was enough for my grandmother to admit that while he was a solution to her loneliness, an enduring union required more. *"Blue—disheartened: Things go wrong. Two Egocentrics! Vanity and personal conceits clash. You hurt my pride!"*

Few of Dorothy's intimates were surprised the marriage didn't last. "Don Blanding was a man who wore Hawaiian shirts and wrote poetry, none of which endeared him to George [Putnam], who saw him as ridiculous," Cap Palmer later recalled. "We were together once speaking on a panel and I thought George was going to take off on the guy."

By now my grandmother was considered one of the most influential grove owners in St. Lucie County, despite the fact that her acreage was small in comparison to the larger commercial ones. Managing her grove was the only job in her life that gave her such a feeling of accomplishment. Even now, as I survey the clean, straight rows of trees surrounding our home, I can imagine her overseeing the picking crews. In a letter written to a friend she boasted. "Have run and managed a citrus grove at Fort Pierce (Indian River Fruit!)." Don was right; Immokolee was her Queendom.

DECEMBER 7, 1941 *At dawn Japs bombed Hawaii. Terrible excitement. Radio all day. 16 to curry supper and Special Game here in p.m. Everyone talked war.*

Don left Fort Pierce immediately to enlist in the service. Like most women at the time, Dorothy was proud that her husband and two sons had joined the military. *"Dave accepted as Ferry Pilot for Pan Amer. Co.!! Sad for me, but what he wants. June and Rene [his wife] late last p.m. June goes to Navy tomorrow! Both my sons at once. And a snotty letter from Don— all in one day!"*

At the age of fifty-five, my grandfather also enlisted in the army air forces. The old warrior who had reupped was the quintessential patriot whom Dorothy had so admired thirty-six years before. Major Putnam—an intelligence officer—was assigned to the task of planning attacks and briefing combat crews in a Superfortress operation headquartered in India. In a strange twist of fate, both my grandfather and G.W.—a major in the same Air Transport Command—were involved in ferrying planes between Taspor, India, and China ("over the Hump," as the dangerous mission across the Himalayan Mountains between China and India was called).

"George was the type of guy who could never stand something exciting going on and not be in it. . . . His job was to debrief the crews when they came back, and then translate the stuff," recalled Cap Palmer. "He flew one mission. A rather hazardous one in fact. But they got back all right."

As the war raged on, my grandmother waited for news of her loved ones. The Fort Pierce beaches were closed to civilians, having been taken over as the new U.S. Naval Amphibian Training Base. But Dorothy could still wander through her groves and along the shores of the Indian River.

One spring night as the moon cast its light across the river's surface, she was reminded of G.W. Standing at the water's edge in the dark of the town's shadow, Dorothy had driven in from the country and had tried to leave the burden of the world's warring behind. Fifteen years before, she and G.W. had created an anniversary she obviously would never forget:

MAY 19, 1942 *This day of all days to me and yet it's now more than 10 years ago! A brown thrush!*

Dorothy would become a grandmother again when her youngest son, George Junior, and his wife welcomed the third George Palmer Putnam. *"I drove to Valdosta! A baby son and June there!! To see Rene at hospital then drove home all day with June. Grand visit with him."* Three years earlier Junie had given his mother a namesake, Dorothy. During these trying war years, Dorothy lent her growing family a sense of strength and comfort. In October 1942 my father, David, left Pan American's ferrying service and enlisted in the U.S. Army Air Force. A few months later, on February 19, 1943, my mother gave birth to my brother David, Jr. *"Nilla has a six pound baby son born 5 a.m. today! Champagne toast to David Binney Putnam, Jr.! Binney and Sally overnight with me. Ten of us to supper. . . .*

"More war news and I know both June and Dave are en route to North Africa. June by tanker, Dave in his plane. Waffle supper at Ruth's."

With the opening of the Naval Amphibian Training Base, Fort Pierce—a town of less than eight thousand residents—was invaded by hordes of servicemen. My grandmother knew how the parents of these young sailors must have felt, and she opened up her private pool, preparing home-cooked meals for hundreds of navy men at a time: *"Served at U.S.O. after working at Red Cross. Sundays are invariably full-up with boys. A mob to cook for, etc. But it means much to them and I'll do it if it kills me."*

The wounded servicemen were all heroes to Dorothy and she ached as they were brought to shore from ships attacked by German U-boats off the Florida coast. Her admiration for their courage was boundless: *"Wounded men being brought home to U.S.A. and many heroes decorated, we have several in Fort Pierce. Fine records of merit."*

In 1944, when her last two grandsons, Douglas and Richard, were born, both their fathers were still overseas. Fatherhood afforded them a brief leave of absence from their duties, and my grandfather, who was stationed in India, arranged to meet his two sons in Miami. *"G.P.'s 57th birthday and he is with B-29s superbombers in Burma. A major in Air Corp., more power to him."* Dorothy clearly admired George for his courage, but it was G.W. who was now returning to her thoughts. *"Gorgeous moon these nights. I will always remember The 'October Full Moon.' Oh, please, won't this war ever end!"*

On April 12, 1945, Dorothy heard the stunning news that Franklin D. Roosevelt had died: *"President Roosevelt died at 4:30 p.m. and nation is shocked! We heard it at dairy, 5:30 en route home. The whole world is shocked and mourns the loss of great allied leader. All 'commercials' off radio and beautiful tributes from everywhere."*

Servicemen returning home were moving slowly across the country, and Dorothy's own prayers were answered when at last she received word from her sons. They had both survived the ordeal and were coming home. *"A won-*

derful heavenly month. The war over and our men returning, and safe—Praise God."

MAY 7, 1945 *Peace in Europe! 8:45 a.m. radio report. Rheims, France. Unconditional surrender to Allies! V-E. Great news. Thank God.*

In a radio broadcast delivered in Fort Pierce at the end of the war, Dorothy spoke of hope for the future, and a desire for a better city to raise children in:

> We have just passed through four bitter years of work and worry. Our sons and husbands have come home from war (thank God) and once again we can bend our efforts not to destruction but to construction and civilian achievement. Now is the time to show our returning men that we want them to come back to a better world and city. We want a better state and a better city for our families, for our children and our grandchildren to grow up in.

It was the last weekend in June 1945, and Dorothy had made plans to travel to New York, leaving Immokolee at dawn on the first train north. The ride that morning seemed interminably slow, but Dorothy's heart was racing and a secret rendezvous had called her back.

July was stifling and Grand Central Station was teeming with sailors and soldiers returning from duty. There was only one soldier Dorothy wanted to welcome and she worried if he would be there, as the train was three hours late. Spotting him across the terminal, she caught her breath. He walked slowly at first, then began to run; they embraced and were together at last. The tall man and woman left the station arm-in-arm, oblivious to the hectic rush of traffic and crowded sidewalks.

In my grandmother's diaries, she does not recount details of the postwar rendezvous, nor does she identify the person by name. This is the only time she ever deliberately omitted naming the person with whom she was staying. I can only surmise from her cryptic notes and the small hints she gives that it was G.W. It had been sixteen years since their first days in love, and the reunion must have been glorious. *"Sunday. New York. Nice cozy breakfast late, and a visit to The Museum of Natural History. Chinese food later. I refuse to think!"* By 1945, the Museum of Natural History housed a permanent Arctic exhibit from the Putnam Baffin Land Expedition of 1928.

Though Dorothy wrote the following words in 1928, she could just as easily have written them at the end of her stay in New York: *"Why should one need to apologize for loving people; why this 'guilty' passion. And why do one's knees feel empty. Is our morality kept there that they shake and give way so?"*

Their friendship had stood the test of time and war.

An extraordinary man, George Weymouth lived his life fully. He became a founding partner in a prestigious investment firm, and took his greatest pleasure in his children and grandchildren. George Weymouth, Jr., G.W.'s namesake, once said of his father, "George told his children that a polar bear chewed his thumb off, when in fact, it became infected on the expedition when he cut it on a can." And in another story, "They were playing parlor games . . . my dad walked down the stairs on his hands and put his feet right through the chandelier. He could walk on his hands up until he was in his fifties or sixties. . . . None of us could do it."

George Weymouth's first wife, Deo duPont, died in 1961 after thirty years of marriage. In 1963 he married Kathy du-Pont, a distant relative of Deo's.

In one piece of writing toward the end of his life, G.W.'s sentiments seemed to mirror Dorothy's own outlook: " . . . If age and experience have taught me anything, it is that money doesn't buy the most important and best things . . . a sense of humor, the desire to do something to leave your mark in the world, and above all, to be loved and love.''

On a scrap of paper I discovered my grandmother's sentiments. ''Probably the best portion of a good man's life; his little, nameless, unremembered acts of *kindness* and *love.*''

19

ONCE MORE FOR LOVE

"If I saw a beautiful sunrise or sunset or moonrise, I would stop to enjoy it: or the lovely lilt of a bird would make me stop or I would pick a beautiful flower. And why not?"

I FOUND MY GRANDMOTHER'S MISSION-style kitchen table in a storage area underneath the outdoor pool. It was laced with spiderwebs and had not been used for twenty-five years. My heart leaped when I spied it, the familiar blue trim barely visible after half a century of use. These same slabs of oak had served up my earliest memories of tangerine juice and history lessons. Jack and I hoisted it onto a wheelbarrow and brought it inside to the kitchen, where I began writing this book. As I sat every morning in the darkness, hours before dawn, I could almost see Dofry across from me, guiding me through her story.

From this point on, remembering her will be easier than the seventeen years I spent trying to interpret her words and thoughts. She was a deeply loving woman, intensely passionate and unable to resist the attentions from men. She was also a risk taker, a life sampler, and in the end she discovered that by loving herself, she was capable of profound love for others. This perhaps was her greatest lesson.

As an older woman, my grandmother became self-assured. She often spoke of a woman's struggle, reminding me that peace only comes with age. "I didn't even know there was anything attractive or likeable or even acceptable until I was over forty," she once wrote to me.

In July 1946, still officially separated from Don, Dorothy turned fifty-eight. Although they had corresponded for a while, *"his letters are impersonal and no pleasure to receive,"* she wrote in her diary. *"He's been pretty lousy to 'duck out' the way he did. And he intends to remain west. So be it!"* She had been alone for five years and had grown to believe that she was fully capable of (and had a right to) enjoying a complete life without the male partner she once believed essential. However, the years of hardship and self-discovery had not been wasted.

In 1947, she decided to travel to Central America, one of her favorite destinations, with her good friend Ruth Yonge. The trip was being organized by the Fort Pierce Garden Club, and as its president for the past sixteen years, Dorothy would be a lecturer for the group of two hundred women. The day before she left, she received news from a family friend of the whereabouts of Frank Upton. *"Funny after years of silence and mystery Red Ramsay brings word of Frank M. Upton. He's at Cardiff [Wales]—land job of Marine Cargo, etc., and doing well."*

Waiting for Ruth one morning, a few days before their departure, Dorothy swung easily in the cotton hammock on her screened loggia. It was her favorite spot to await visitors as she watched for them to turn into the narrow, sandy drive. Her steady, clear whistling filled the air and on this still day she could hear her songbirds respond. Following

Dorothy's familiar notes, Ruth Yonge made her way up the outside stairs. So often the two had begun or ended their days with a swim, walking down from the loggia, taking the narrow, bamboo-lined path to the pool. The friends were excited about the trip to Guatemala, and Ruth was her favorite traveling companion.

They arrived in Guatemala City on February 14, where the organized tour offered the group an opportunity to study exotic private gardens as well as the seldom-visited hinterland. *"Guatemala. 'On our own,' shops and passport photos. Banquet. Flower arrangements! Whoops—Flop. But adore this country. Textiles."*

Before leaving home she had prepared well, and knew that her assignment as featured speaker would be demanding. But Dorothy was confident on her feet. She had not anticipated any other challenges, and the last thing on her mind was the thought of falling in love with another man.

FEBRUARY 24, 1947 *Guatemala City: Sightseeing, Palace, Cathedral, Residential, gardens, etc. Walk after dinner. Fine meals (29 gals in town). Met Lew Palmer.*

Far from his birthplace in Denver, Colorado, Lewis Hamilton Palmer had settled in Guatemala after a tour of duty with the Royal Air Force. Now managing a large coffee plantation in the Sierra Madre Mountains on the outskirts of Guatemala City, he was a dark-haired, ruggedly handsome figure. With his bold, sunburned cheekbones, he could have been a native. He was rather small, but strong and fit, with powerful hands. Earlier in his life Palmer had been a barnstorming pilot; now, at fifty-one, he was flying machine parts to mountain farmers who were cut off from roadways. During Dorothy's visit, he was also lecturing on the country's history and coffee production at the Sierra Madre plantation.

Dorothy brought her group to the plantation and was

instantly infatuated with the kind-hearted flyer who served as their tour guide. In turn, he was impressed with this soft-spoken, inquisitive woman, who stood out from the rest of the crowd. Lew knew nothing of her background or wealth; she was direct and confident and it did not take long for a relationship to blossom. He accompanied them on the remainder of their trip. *"Off for Antigua. Stopped at Lake. Lunch. Alcazar, shops, park, etc. and sightseeing. Lew Palmer with Ruth and me. Marimba and danced with our guide."*

Lew Palmer was not the sort of man my grandmother would have been attracted to earlier on. He was uncomplicated, simple in his tastes, and a relief after the years of emotional chaos. *"Atitlan: boat across lake to Indian village Sandiego. (Lew P.) Left Cantenta after fine lunch, for Guatemala City—8 in car! (L.H.P. to our room.)"*

I was not surprised when I read that Lew Palmer had become infatuated with my grandmother. Though she was approaching her sixtieth birthday, she was still a seductive woman and her charm and intelligence were irresistible.

Two weeks after returning to Fort Pierce, she received a telegram from Lew accepting her invitation to visit Immokolee. *"A wire from Lew, he'll be here on the 19th. Nilla, Rene and the four boys out for lunch and a short visit. They are such dears!"* She could hardly wait for Lew to arrive, but she worried whether Immokolee would intimidate him.

APRIL   19,   1947   *Town to meet Lew. He's nicer than ever and so easily "fits in to the picture" here. Most helpful and very efficient.*

Lew's total dedication to his hostess came as no surprise. *"I'm happy and life is full of joy and for the future too."* Roaming about the eighty acres, Lew easily assumed the role of grove manager. *"Lew is 'taking over' on grove work. A big relief to me."* He painted and plowed, and carried flowers and morning coffee to her bedside. *"I'm trying to think why I de-*

serve so much joy and happiness after all the turmoil in my life so far! But I love it!"

In Lew, my grandmother had discovered those qualities she had always desired, and had wished for ever since 1928, when she wrote in her diary: *"I should have married a farmer—lived on a big ranch and had 6 children! How different it all might be. . . ."*

Fascinated by him, the Putnam grandchildren could not stay away. To all of us, he was the big-hearted man who bounced us through the woods on the back of his motor scooter and made us squeal with laughter. His skin was silky-smooth, and I recall seeing little hair on his strong, tanned arms. His eyes squinted naturally; his square jaw reminded me of a Native American, determined and focused. He was a thoughtful man and always invited the grandchildren to drive with him to town to collect the mail. Often, I saw my grandmother and Lew kneeling in the garden together planting flowers. From the rear, they appeared the same size, shoulder to shoulder.

In June 1947, Dorothy's divorce from Don was granted, and it was obvious to David and George that their mother was in love with Lew, still a guest at Immokolee after two months. At first, they were concerned that he might be taking advantage of her generosity; but after spending several weeks getting to know him, they were reassured. Marriage was being mentioned. After three failures, my grandmother was torn. *"I wonder, do I dare to try again for personal happiness after three failures? It's a question, yet I'm strongly tempted!"*

At the time, there was a waiting period in Florida for licenses, but none in Georgia. A steady stream of nervous brides and grooms made the drive north to cross the state line, in search of an accommodating justice of the peace. On July 21, 1947, Dorothy's heavy blue Lincoln crept slowly by the still pond in the early morning darkness. Hearing the crunch of tires in the driveway, the bullfrogs launched into their morning chorus, which startled the eloping couple. *"Off at 5 a.m. with Lew. Drove all day. Lunch at Folkston. Married Lew today and find happiness and completeness at long last. Overnight Silver Springs and delish dinner. New moon."*

Two weeks later, my sister Binney and I tossed our bags into the trunk of Dofry's car. We had no idea that our grandmother and her "boyfriend" were taking us with them on their honeymoon to New York and Old Greenwich. *"Lew, Binney and Sally off in Lincoln to New York and Old Greenwich for two weeks. En route; gorgeous mountain drive, but overcast and in the clouds. Natural Bridge. Log cabin for night. Skyline Trail to Endless Caverns."*

At the age of fifty-nine, a bride again, my grandmother was a stunning and provocative woman. Her eyes, weary with a telling sadness, were still as crystal clear and blue as a pool of bright water. Her languid stride, though a bit slower, was deliberate and confident.

I remember this time of her life as a tranquil one. She and Lew shared a quiet affection for one another, and I knew that she not only relied on him but respected him. Here at last was the partner she had always needed, and she was thrilled at having met such a man, she once told me, "before I was sixty!" My grandmother seemed ageless, and with Lew at her side she returned to Immokolee with a heightened sense of purpose.

Sharing her "home place" was her fondest wish. *"Weather is ideal and each day very lovely. I don't deserve to be so contented and happy. Lew is a darling, always."*

My grandmother had always wanted a "Spanish" walled garden in her yard to protect her flowers and vegetables from ground-grubbing intruders. Wasting no time, she and Lew designed a two-tiered fountain with a constant flow of warm water for the birds and for irrigating the plants. Lew hoped to find tiles with giraffes and zebras to decorate the back splash when he and Dorothy traveled to Africa the following year.

"Still grateful for Lew and his really deep love and concern about me. Each day so much real happiness." She was content. *"I've never known before what perfect companionship and congeniality meant over a whole year! Thank God for it! Yes: I was right, a thousand times. We are congenial and happy and very much in love."*

As 1949 ended, my grandmother's diaries express her complete fulfillment: *"The miracle continues! Only finer and deeper than ever. We are increasingly <u>closer</u> and love is deeper."* They dined casually whenever the mood struck, either on the back terrace seated on the cobalt blue Venetian fountain, or at the old Mission table, and called these their "in time" meals. There were also early suppers at the beach, and I recall them lingering on a blanket over dinner after a cool ocean dip.

To an old friend, Dorothy wrote of her marriage and new life: "We grow oranges on an eighty acre grove: We fish and garden as hobbies. Last summer we spent five lovely and thrilling months circumnavigating Africa on a Dutch freighter. We saw lions and rhinos and hippos, elephants, etc. to last a lifetime. And we've written a small book on the subject, too!"

African Overtones is a collection of several newspaper articles woven together into a single essay. Written with my grandmother's usual flair for dramatic narrative and vivid imagery, the booklet gives a colorful account of her trip; more important were her opinions on the rights of the people of Africa:

> Lew and I agreed that probably the most terrifying thrill of all Africa was seeing a huge bull elephant, one that stood ten feet in his stocking feet, and carried eighty pounds or so of precious ivory in each gleaming tusk. And all of this tonnage not more than seventy feet from our lorry. . . .
>
> As we sailed out at night, a full moon, the stars, the soft swish of the sea all combined to make one think rather deeply. One wonders why any place so utterly enchanting and lovely

could be called the pest hole or the cesspool of the world? The world today with its airplanes and quick service grows smaller and smaller. We in this part of the globe feel one should have his own ideas and mode of life and live it according to his own ideas and ideals. Perhaps those ebony blacks of Africa and the white-robed Mohammedans of far-off Arabia or the coastal islands of Africa should have a right to their way of thinking, too.

20

THE LEGACY

George dared. He had power, knew it, used it, enjoyed it. If GPP had been on the bridge of the *Titanic,* that iceberg wouldn't have had the gall to collide with him. Or if it had, he would have sunk the iceberg!

—Robert E. Lee

I DIDN'T KNOW MY GRANDFATHER AS WELL as I would have liked to. His visits to Fort Pierce were brief, and I was usually too preoccupied with building huts and fishing to spend much time with him. Our last visit together in 1947 was a stroll (a stroll for him; for me, an adolescent jaunt) along the water's edge. On that particular Saturday, he walked to the Sunrise Theater to meet me when the western double feature let out. We held hands and talked about boats and cowboys. We caught a few horseshoe crabs and carved knives out of the palm fronds. And when we finally reached our driveway, I remember leading him around the backyard to see my fort beneath the Hayden mango tree.

He was a serious man, always dressed in coat and tie, even on weekends exploring the woods with me. In a lecture he once gave years later, he said, "There is no book I would rather write if I were able than a book whose title

247

would be 'How to Be Happy Without a Future.' . . . We're going to learn to get what we can out of the simple things, out of the present. Security is such a fleeting thing anyway."

By the late 1930s my grandfather had started a small publishing firm, George Palmer Putnam, Inc., operating from the study of his North Hollywood house. "He needed an editor because he was creating books all the time," remembered Cap Palmer. "Everyone he ran across, he said, 'Why don't you write a book?' They'd turn out some stuff, but it was seldom publishable. My job was ghostwriter. We did twelve books in eighteen months. George would market the books." *Duration,* "a novel of war on the Washington front," and *The Man Who Killed Hitler* were two of Putnam's books written during this period.

The firm grew, and they took an office on Sunset Boulevard above the Tick-Tock Restaurant. "He created books, causes," Palmer added. "His effort was entirely to push that. He just loved to promote. Promotion was his creativity."

Amelia's disappearance continued to haunt him. "From time to time," Robert Lee recalled, "bottles with notes enclosed, cruel hoaxes, would turn up in our mail at the Sunset Boulevard office." Eventually, my grandfather disbanded the company and retired to the rural outskirts of the city.

I never visited his homes in California. During the summers, he lived in Lone Pine at the foot of Mount Whitney, in a rustic mountain chalet dubbed Shangri-Putnam. Later, he owned and operated the Stove Pipe Wells Hotel in Death Valley, with his fourth wife, Margaret Haviland Putnam. Peg, as she preferred to be called, was from Michigan City, Indiana, and, much like Dorothy, was a college graduate and honor student. Unlike Dorothy, however, Peg made a career for herself that began at her alma mater, Western College, in Oxford, Ohio. Peg met George at the USO in Salina, Kansas, just prior to his being sent overseas. They remained in touch during his active duty and became reacquainted when he returned home. After a brief courtship, they were married at the home of friends in San Marino, California. The new Mrs. Putnam began her married life at the foot of Mount Whitney at Shangri-Putnam.

The wedding, in 1945, took place a year after George's divorce from Jean Marie. This marriage would be a happy one. "She loved GPP for both his strength and his idiosyncrasies," recalled Robert Lee, George's best man at the wedding. "Peg was staunchly at his side—sharing his frustrations, compensating for his cantankerous bent, and in a strange way, it was almost a mirror image of the A.E. situation, with the roles reversed."

George and Peg were of different temperaments. While he enjoyed the mountains during the winter season, she preferred the warmth of the desert and the house-party atmosphere of the hotel that he had purchased for her comfort. He, on the other hand, still loved to rough it. Even in middle age he was seen snowshoeing down the mountainside for supplies and mail, going back up the same strenuous way.

In 1946, my grandfather described his life in a letter to a friend: "Book publishing and Forty-fifth Street seem far away and long ago. For some years now I've been dug in here out in California at a storybook little place 8300 feet high in the Sierra, and having myself a pleasant existence doing some writing and radio work."

He worked on various literary projects, published five more books, and continued to correspond with old friends and acquaintances who contributed to his various endeavors. Guests were always welcome at Shangri-Putnam. Among his papers is a file of letters from celebrated artists, including the composer Leopold Stokowski, who wrote: "It sounds wonderful where you live. You are still in the world and yet you are withdrawn to perfect privacy."

As my grandfather would tell a newspaper reporter, "Everyone who is not shackled solidly to the city at some time nurses a dream that he'll get away from the pavements.

I contrived to put my dream into practice. . . . A friend of mine says that I read a book I had written and believed it."

In another piece of correspondence he offers sympathy to a friend whose husband just died: "Death is the one inevitable thing in life which cannot be combated. At least it is true that time heals the wounds, desperate as they seem. I know for I have been through all that, as all of us have."

On January 4, 1950, my grandfather died in a California hospital. He was sixty-three.

TUESDAY, JANUARY 10, 1950　*"G.P. was cremated . . . & asked autopsy on his body to try to find out <u>what</u> cause death."*

He had become ill in China while serving in the army air forces and was given a medical discharge. Peg recalls, "When GPP was at that miserable air base in far western China, they had to eat whatever food the peasants put before them—diseased pork—rotten food of all kinds, day after day . . . bowls of cereal with maggots in them. . . . They all got sick but the young men in their late teens and twenties could throw off the effects. But G.P.—then between fifty-five and sixty years—could not . . . he just got sicker and sicker. . . ." My grandfather never recovered from the deadly parasite that invaded his kidneys.

Even in death, his name was synonymous with his famous wife. Newspaper headlines identified him as "Mate of Late Amelia Earhart."

George Palmer Putnam was eulogized as a generous, if somewhat difficult, man by his friends and family. An intellectual, he was often misunderstood by those who sought his approval and envied his success.

As Robert Lee recalled,

GPP is remembered more for his eccentricities than his virtues. His fame is clouded by the clout of his candor. He was a genius at befriending large people and offending small ones. Yet, as in our case, he was our staunch friend because of a shared admiration. He dismissed stupidity. He was no celebrity-chaser. One of his best friends was a forest ranger at Whitney Portal named Shorty. . . .

Although he had written twelve books, and been one of the world's foremost publishers, my grandfather was never a wealthy man. He left Peg with debts, and she single-handedly operated the Stove Pipe Wells Hotel for many years after his death to satisfy creditors. "When G.P. was buried early in January 1950, there was nothing I could do but go back to Stove Pipe and carry on. The place was much smaller then . . . I had a big mortgage to confront and no money in the bank," Peg recalls.

Peg later married Willard Lewis, a pioneer land developer in Bel Air, California.

My grandmother had always fantasized about a log cabin life. During the early days of her marriage to Lew, they sketched plans for their handmade "dream" cabin. In the fall of 1950, following the birth of Dorothy's granddaughter Cynthia, they drove north to the Smoky Mountains to examine the piece of rocky terrain they had acquired the previous spring. It would be the site of Sundown, a forty- by forty-foot poplar log cabin that would sit dead end at an almost inaccessible road. *"Cabin. A 'smokey' day and cool. Planted azaleas on hillside below porch. Hope they grow. Read aloud to Lew. 'Bright Feathers.' "*

The following year, they christened their hideaway. Like children playing house, each with their own specific chores, the couple basked in the seclusion of their bungalow, gathering blackberries, cutting wood, baking pies, and reading aloud to one another. *"There are myriads of gay yellow helianthus all around the cabin and blue ague, purple iron weed, yarrow."*

The cold creek was dammed up in the backyard to form an icebox for the milk and butter. It often broke loose during the night after a hard rain. *"Nice lazy day just the two of us. Samba and marble games. Lew 'chinked' holes in the walls and painted outside of east windows."*

It was sad at the end of each season to board up for winter. The trim little log house appeared abandoned from the bottom of the drive. Leaving was particularly hard for Lew, a man who was never happier than when he was chopping wood or hauling brush. A tireless worker, he was rarely unable to perform any task my grandmother wanted. But in 1951 there came a first sign that he was not well. *"Lew sick: His left side 'asleep'—called Dr. C in a.m. Put him to bed. Quiet and rest."*

Two weeks later, Dorothy took him to see a doctor in New York. She herself had lost weight and was worried about her heart. Lew carefully tended to his wife and brushed off any suggestion of his own ill health. *"My Lew is much better. Never mentions aches."*

The following month they returned to the cabin one last time before boarding it up for the year. The car got stuck on the hilly driveway and my grandmother writes in her diary that Lew carted everything up to the cabin by hand. He must have had to struggle as he rounded the sharp curve, tripping over loose stones. I cannot imagine anyone with the strength to haul their supplies up such a steep hill, but he never complained.

A few slivers of sunlight still sneaked in between the logs. There were paintbrushes with robin's-egg blue smeared up the handle that matched the door and window trim, and the bird feeders were hung and filled one last time with sunflower seeds. The stone chimney was cold for the first time in ten days, but Lew's cord of wood would be seasoned by the following spring. Closing the gate, they said their goodbyes to Sundown.

The drive back to Fort Pierce was always a separate vacation in itself, and my grandmother was an enthusiastic tourist, visiting anything of educational interest en route: caverns, gardens, Rock City, tobacco fields, Marine Land, and so on. She was unable to waste a single minute, and as children we all benefited from her insatiable curiosity.

The Palmers had barely returned home before packing up again, for Dorothy had ordered theater tickets and was planning a celebration in New York City. *"Everyone all okay. While George [Junior] and Rene take baby for a ride, two boys stay with Lew and me."*

After a brief stay to put Immokolee in order, they left for their Manhattan interlude. *"George took us to the noon train for New York. Bedroom and played canasta. Dinner early and bed twelve hours! Wonderful rest."*

New York was exactly what they needed, and the Bristol Hotel was a simple but comfortable alternative to their rustic cabin. After breakfast in bed, Dorothy and Lew took their morning walk, followed by a Broadway matinee. A few popular musicals and a museum or two rounded out their indulgent days before they drove to Old Greenwich to visit the Binney clan.

My grandmother had never lost her desire to return home, sleep in her childhood bed, and gaze with nostalgia at the unchanging sea from the small window of her room: *"Old Greenwich. Alice D. in for tea. Cards with Mother in p.m. Very nice day and Mother very gay and chipper! Fine."*

The grouping of family photos on the mantelpiece was a collection of Alice and Bub's favorites. In the center was the white-haired patriarch, whom Dorothy missed terribly. Picking up an old photo of her father, the one in which he was standing beside his three young daughters, Dorothy felt her mother's arm as she also lifted a photo taken recently of Dorothy and Lew in Africa. As Dorothy replaced the framed image, her mother looked directly into her daughter's eyes and said, "You were a sweet child, Dolly dear, and what a beautiful woman you are today."

However tender, her mother's words could never make up for the lifetime of insecurities, and Dorothy choked back her tears.

At this point my grandmother writes in her diaries of feeling tired and ill. She had lost twenty pounds and had undergone a battery of tests. She and Lew returned to New York for a few more days. The first afternoon, they walked along Fifth Avenue before attending the theater. *O.G. [Old Greenwich] Helen over for lunch 'Happy' to say goodbye. Cotter drove Lew and me to N.Y. City in afternoon. Saw 'Stalag 17,' prisoner of war show (Germany). Excellent."*

That evening, they walked in the bitter cold air and Lew wrapped his arm around Dorothy to keep her warm. Catching smiling glimpses from passers-by, they were blissfully happy.

Returning to their hotel suite, Dorothy soaked in a tub of hot water and was grateful to be alone with her husband. Dusting lightly with a rose-scented bath powder, and tying her freshly combed hair back with a thin blue ribbon, she slipped on her new satin nightgown, an anniversary gift from Lew. She had been saving the white peignoir for a special occasion, and excitedly she opened the bathroom door.

In that second, her world collapsed.

Lew was lying motionless on the bedroom floor, his face an ashen mask. Her husband had suffered a fatal heart attack and the grim scene left Dorothy in a near-paralyzed state. She stood frozen for several seconds before falling to her knees weeping, taking his head in her arms and calling his name. The gentle and loving man who was my grandmother's best and last partner was gone.

NOVEMBER 16, 1951   *My Beloved died at 11:10 p.m.?! So without warning—so cruelly quick.*

She immediately notified her family, and Cotter, the faithful chauffeur, was sent to the city to bring her back to

Rocklyn. *"N.Y.—Old Greenwich all night! Police and doctors. Etc. Red tape. Cotter came. . . . 'Ferncliff' crematory. Service 4 p.m. . . . Many wires and phones and letters, etc. from all over the country. Such loving messages about Lew. Family over. Gill called from Canada."*

NOVEMBER 18, 1951   *Dr. Vincent Daniels gave the service and a beautiful personalized prayer. White chrysanthemums. Only family and Louise at service.*

NOVEMBER 20, 1951   *Old Greenwich. A dull sad day, and endless. Yet I can't sleep at night. Gill came to be with me and go home with me. So glad to have her.*

Gill Bignell, Dorothy's college friend, came down from Montreal and escorted her home on the train. *"O.G. to N.Y. in car (Cotter). And nearly missed our train. Drawing room, and just sat quietly all day. So sad!!"* Her grief was overwhelming. As she sat watching the same scenery she and Lew had passed on their way north, she questioned whether she could go on without him: *"How will I live the rest of my life?"*

The quaint clapboard railroad station with the bold block letters FORT PIERCE was a welcome sight. Following along beside the hissing train until its caboose had cleared the Orange Avenue crossing and the Pullman car had jerked to a stop, David and George watched for their mother. When she first appeared, her sons realized that they had never seen her dressed completely in black. They had just learned to accept their mother as an older woman in love. Now suddenly she was a widow.

At dawn on December 2, my grandmother buried Lew's ashes inside the pale yellow walls of his Spanish garden. She knew this was where he would have wanted to rest. Closing her screened door, and clutching a small white embroidered handkerchief, Dorothy took the rear stairs down from the loggia. She spotted first the top of the garden wall, beaded with silver bubbles reflecting the morning sun. The tall bamboo held back a wide patch of sunlight, and behind the fountain—guarded by the zebra and tall giraffe tiles—stood a nubby old avocado tree. The upturned soil was softly shaded by wide, draping banana branches.

Opening the spring latch, she remembered the rainy day when the two of them had completed their secret garden. Allowing her tears to run freely now, she wept for the future she had lost with Lew.

"At sunrise in the garden, I said a prayer, and gave my Beloved, forever, to Immokolee which he loved!" On her left hand gleamed a gold wedding band, and beside it was the one belonging to her devoted husband. From that day on, she wore the two rings together, side by side. They would never be separated again. *"It has been a year of great contrasts—yet loving happiness too. Loss and a heart full of precious memories."*

Dorothy accepted that her brief love had been richly rewarding and she took comfort in the peace that it afforded her. She vowed: *"Try to be extra sweet to all the others, to make up my own loneliness."*

Having researched my grandparents' lives over the years, I find it sad that they could not have found a way to stay together. In the end, on opposite sides of the country, they both found peace in the simple life they once shared in Bend, Oregon, and so loved. They never lost their passion for the outdoors, and I believe that had there not been an explosive period in the 1920s when the age of aviation sparked the constant challenge of breaking barriers, they might have remained together.

In August 1960, Dorothy returned to New York from a North Cape cruise with two of her grandsons. As usual, before taking the train to Florida, she was picked up by Cotter and driven out to Old Greenwich to see her family. Her mother was ninety-four years old, bedridden and quite frail after a long illness.

On the first day back in Fort Pierce, there was news of a hurricane brewing to the south. *"Storm coming and already has hit E. Cuba. Only wish it could blow Fidel Castro off the map!"* And on the following morning, September 7, in the midst of a howling storm, Dorothy received a phone call from her niece Hyla Kitchel. *"Hyla phoned: mother is sinking. . . . Later Allan called; she died 3:10 p.m. quietly and in her sleep—Thank God . . . glad she died peacefully."*

Great-Grandma Binney was a gifted pianist and composer. In 1927, she wrote her own creed. As a child I recall seeing it framed, hanging in our kitchen. When I first began to read my grandmother's diaries, I discovered that she had transcribed her mother's creed across two pages, under "Memoranda":

MY CREED

> I think that many a soul has God within,
> Yet knows no church nor creed, no word of prayer,
> No law of life save that which seems most fair
> And true and just, and helpful to its kin
> And kind; and holds that act alone as sin
> That lays upon another soul its share
> Of human pain, of sorrow, or of care,
> Or plants a doubt where faith has ever been.
> The heart that seeks with zealous joy the best
> In every other heart it meets, the way
> Has found to make its own condition blessed.
> To love God is to strive through life's short day
> To comfort grief, to give the weary rest.
> To hope and love—that surely, is to pray.
>
> —Alice Stead Binney

As the years passed, my grandmother remained an invet-
erate traveler and offered many opportunities to her children and grandchildren. Several times each year we had the
good fortune to explore faraway places through Dofry's
eyes. She boasted of introducing all of her "Grands" to the
two extreme poles of the earth, and hoped that in the end
they would remember the difference between them! *"New
York—Hotel. Davey and Rick. Busy, over to ship, all excited.
North Cape Cruise on 'M/S Gripsholm.' Sailed at 10 p.m. Sally
and Jack to see us off."* Unwittingly, she had passed on to all
of us her irresistible wanderlust. *"At sea, foggy and cold. Binney and Sally Hammerfest Village a.m. Bird Rock (auks, puffins
and murres) N. Cape 1 p.m. Gals climb it. Great thrill."*

The music room at Immokolee remained alive with the
sounds of piano and singing. *"Family picnic here—all Putnams 11, 3 Yonges. Swim for kids. Binney and I played, <u>whistled</u>
and lovely <u>flute</u> music."* In the springtime of each year, the
brightly colored painted buntings left Immokolee and returned to their northern climate just as the whippoorwills
began to serenade in the dark. Gardenia petals fell by the
handful and lay bruised beneath the huge bush inside the
protected garden. Looking down from her bedroom window, Dorothy could see the blooming shrub Lew had
planted fifteen years earlier. She often reminded us that she
wished to be buried within close distance of its fragrance,
beside her husband.

It was also toward the end of the spring season each year
that Dorothy left Fort Pierce to open up her cabin. In the
summer, when the blackberries were ripe and the sun had
replaced the wood-burning fires, she would return. In later
years, even as her strength faded, she returned to Sundown
with her grandchildren. *"Cabin. Indigo buntings, <u>thrushes</u> and
catbirds all singing."*

A warm and faithful correspondent, Dorothy continued

to marvel at nature's hand. Her letters to my mother reflect a childlike appreciation for the simple pleasures in life, the joy of a gently aging woman who still regarded wildlife and all animals with innocent wonder.

Nilla dear;

Gosh, how many times these past few days Ruth and I said, "Oh, I wish Nilla were here with us!" The birds are simply marvelous, songs all the time, and thrushes come to bathe in the tiny streams at the back door. Song sparrows keep up their dear little notes and every once in so often I hear a cardinal whistling, but so far I've not caught a glimpse of him, but he is nearby. There are now three "runs" under the house of some critter, maybe a hedgehog, or a rabbit, but we have not seen him either. The sheep and the cows come "belling" down the mountainside each evening, and stare at us with wonder near the fence.

Bye and all my love dear,

Mom

The following are a few of my grandmother's random thoughts; they are among my favorites. Her own words offer the best view into her keen mind.

"Why, oh why, is kindness always whispered while anger is so loud? And how delightful it would be if people shouted 'I love you' as though it were an insult."

"Grasshoppers converse by rubbing their back legs together. (I kinda wish we did too.)"

"There is a definite knack in discovering the best in people's character, instead of the worst!"

"The stronger the sex urge, the less friendship. Guess friendship and admiration (or respect?) is what holds marriages together. Look around at the older couples near you, their compatibility, yes, sex was there, but the other qualities have taken over and lasted."

My grandmother never remarried, although she was amused to have several suitors in her later years. She had learned to find happiness in solitude. I will never know whether her life after my grandfather was as rich as she imagined it would be. I believe, though, that her hard-won freedom had been easier to achieve than was the heavy task of sustaining it. *"Time is learning to accept a few defeats. But it's rather fun frustrating the old monster."* The hallmark of my grandmother's philosophy was her undiminished optimism, and her relentless pursuit of knowledge and adventure. This was her personal bequest to all of us.

As I came to the end of Dofry's story, I reread two letters she wrote me three years before her death. "To you, probably forty seems ancient—and so OLD. To *me* however, you're still in your 'salad days'—just really starting to know yourself—and what it's all about!! Then you'll spend the next forty years trying to find a satisfactory answer. . . . Nowadays I'm learning about the birds, the bees and a few 'buntings'—always so much that is fascinating. By the way, it takes ten years to have a friend."

In the second letter she thanked me for the banana bread I had baked, reminded me of her photo albums and clippings saved over a lifetime, and described her garden in Rye, where she and Junie buried one hundred daffodil bulbs throughout the woods. In the same letter, she responded to the idea of my writing her story, "It's real work and I've done all the 'dirt' and research on two books for G.P. years ago! And I know! . . ."

At the age of ninety-three, she began to fail, but she continued to keep up her diary entries.

JANUARY 5, 1982 *The pain is always present now: there used to be periods without it, & I could draw a breath in without being conscious of my "insides"—it's the lower right side . . . a diseased ovary? It's in that area . . . even at night when I rouse for a few minutes it's there.*

JANUARY 8, 1982 *Too much pain & distress—so lie down on my bed for 2 hours. Only the 2nd time I've really caved in with pain.*

The following day, the pain grows worse. *"How much longer. How much? I am now nearer 94 than 93 & <u>weary</u>. Read more than ½ a book 'Heat' by Ed McBain. So much better than sweet old Agatha Christie!"*

She writes of her concerns with the citrus crops and a possible freeze, about the birds at her feeding stations, and the fluctuating value of her family-owned stocks. The month of February is a blank, except for two doodles showing a stick figure with a rod, reeling in a fish.

MARCH 3, 1982 *Pain increases once in a while but when it does return it is more intense.*

MARCH 7, 1982 *It's a pleasure to see folks & no [sic] someone still cares that I'm alive. But also it wears me out, & by late afternoon I'm SUNK.*

Her handwriting appears fainter with each entry. By now, she was attended by a twenty-four-hour nurse whom she describes with typical candor: *"Practical nurse, 4 yrs. experience as a 'Field Nurse.' In Korean War. (Short, heavy, kinky <u>red</u> hair—husky & able. Also <u>common</u> background.)"*

That month she learned her granddaughter Cynthia was pregnant. She wrote of her excitement over the news, but complained of too many caretakers, "and no one really 'in charge.' "

MARCH 25, 1982 *Sometimes the pain is more than I can bear! So what? <u>Surgery</u> at 93??? <u>No</u>, definitely. No.*

The following day my grandmother for the first time saw her death as a welcome release. *"Is there NO END to this? Why? Why?"*

On April 2, her writing appears bold and strong. Not surprisingly, one of her final entries is devoted to her birds at
Immokolee: *"Buntings still here—but fewer and fewer. Perhaps
some flocks have already gone N. to Va. . . . Dry weather—we
need rain. . . ."*

In those final days, my grandmother's memory was still
sharp. Closing her pale blue eyes, she rested peacefully as
faded snapshots from the years past filled her dreamlike
state. Blue satin ribbons and long cotton dresses, the thrill
of grandchildren swimming the full length of her pool for
the first time, the smooth warmth of her father's hand in
hers. The essence of orange blossoms, pine needles in the
sun, and the predawn singing of the thrush. The splendor
of Mount Whitney, the endless blue horizon that hot summer day as she flew above the clouds with Amelia, laughing
wildly. The infinite pride in her two sons, the sound of
piano music, and those carefree, childlike days playing
house in the Great Smoky Mountains.

And always, she remembered G.W., and daisies from the
garden. Lying on Laddin's Rock, singing "Blue Skies."

His inviting smile, his clean, strong hands, his intimate
knowledge of her hidden private self that belonged to him:

> *. . . I should like to find myself with him on some golden rain
> drenched day where I could completely ignore or forget age,
> distance, and geography, society—all the controlling influences
> of my everyday life. To be held warm and responsive—
> completely feminine—in arms strong to the point of hurting.*

On Sunday, May 9, 1982, Dofry died. It was Mother's
Day.

Only an hour earlier, my father arrived and was upstairs
alone with his mother, holding her frail hand. As if to be

certain that he had come, and with just a hint of a smile, Dofry opened her eyes one final time, and then let go with a long sigh.

George Junior arrived soon after she had passed away. For over fifty years the magnificent wooded garden had held Junie's childhood memories, and on that exact date he had also celebrated his birthday. Wandering through the dark hammock of trees, he was stunned by the absence of any other living soul and by the deadly silence. The usual drone of crickets, frogs, and whippoorwills, the roaming raccoons and possums, the barn and screech owls, and the occasional fox and bobcat were hushed. There had come an eerie quiet that George had never known before. Looking up at the closed blinds and sensing the reverent stillness of the home place, he knew why.

When I arrived in Florida the following day, I was met at Miami Airport by my father. We drove north to Fort Pierce, both of us overcome by sadness. Struggling with his own grief, yet wanting to share his mother's last moments with me, he described every detail of Dofry's passing. I can still see his enormous hand trembling as he wiped his tears away. And then, after taking a long, deep breath, he added: "You know, Sally, leaving us on Mother's Day was just like Mother."

MEMORANDA

*I*N APRIL 1985, ALMOST THREE YEARS AFTER my grandmother's death, my husband Jack and I, with our sons David and John, were invited to Tampa to attend a party being given by our third son, Steven, and his business partner, Tom duPont. The event was to launch their new automobile magazine, the *duPont Registry*.

Jack and I arrived early, and John and David were the first to meet us outside the rented airplane hangar. We were all thrilled that Steve's concept had become a reality. Inside, glaring spotlights bounced off the polished bumpers of the rare classic automobiles. The formal party featured a million-dollar Duesenberg; I was nearly blinded by the hot lights from television crews filming the event. Steve had told us all about these plans excitedly weeks before. But what he had not told me and could not possibly have known was that a strange twist of fate that evening would pull me directly into the heart of my grandmother's past.

Steve was waiting inside the door, along with Tom and his parents, who had also flown in for the occasion. "Sally, I would like for you to meet my mother, Kathy," Tom said. We greeted each other warmly as two very proud mothers. Then he turned to his stepfather and said, "George, I don't believe you have met Steve's mother, Sally Chapman."

There was a slight pause before he turned back to me. "Sally, this is my stepfather, George Weymouth."

I was stunned. Standing before me was the romantic figure with the same blue eyes my grandmother had so often described in her diaries. Looking up into his distinguished face, I flushed with emotion, the power of their unconventional love so fresh in my mind from reading her words. The tall, still handsome eighty-one-year-old gentleman took my hand tenderly in his. My eyes filled with tears.

"Mr. Weymouth, do you know who my grandmother was?" I asked.

"No," he responded softly. "Who was she?"

"Her name was Dorothy Binney Putnam," I said.

He looked down at me for what seemed like an eternity, and then slowly turned to his wife, standing beside him. "Dear," he said with quiet dignity, "do you remember only yesterday I told you of a woman who whistled like a bird?"

Immokolee
January 15, 1997

BIBLIOGRAPHY AND
ADDITIONAL SOURCES

Backus, Jean. *Letters from Amelia, An Intimate Portrait of Amelia Earhart.* New York: Beacon Press, 1982.

Bartlett, Captain "Bob." *Sails Over Ice.* New York: Charles Scribner's Sons, 1934.

Beebe, William. *The Arcturus Adventure.* New York: G. P. Putnam's Sons, 1926.

Blanding, Don. *Floridays.* New York: Dodd, Mead & Co., 1941.

——. *Vagabond's House.* New York: Dodd, Mead & Co., 1943.

Chronicle of Aviation. Jacques Legrand, 1992.

Cochran, Jacqueline, and Maryann Bucknum Brinley. *Jackie Cochran. The Autobiography of the Greatest Woman Pilot in Aviation History.* New York: Bantam Books, 1987.

Crowell, James LeRoy. "Frontier Publisher: A Romantic Review of George Putnam's Career at the *Bend Bulletin,* 1910–1914, with an Extensive Epilogue," Master of Science thesis, University of Oregon School of Journalism, June 1966.

Dunne, Colin, et al., eds. *Rye in the Twenties.* New York: Arno Press, 1978.

Earhart, Amelia. *The Fun of It.* New York: Brewer, Warren & Putnam, 1932.

——. *Last Flight.* New York: Harcourt, Brace/Harrap, 1938.

——. *20 hrs. 40 min.: Our Flight in the Friendship.* New York: Grosset & Dunlap, 1928.

Edgar, Bob, and Jack Turnell. *Brand of a Legend.* Basin, Wyo.: Wolverine Gallery, 1978.

The First Hundred Years of American Yacht Club. Centennial Book Editorial Board of the American Yacht Club, 1983.

Ford, Corey. *The Time for Laughter.* Boston: Little, Brown, 1967.

——. *Salt Water Taffy.* New York: G. P. Putnam's Sons, 1929.

Greenwich. The Historical Society of the Town of Greenwich and Greenwich Time, Connecticut, 1990.

Hutchinson, Hubbard. *Far Harbors Around the World.* New York: G. P. Putnam's Sons, 1924.

Kitchel, Helen B. *Memories*. Self-published.

——. *More Memories*. Self-published.

——. *Oaklyn*. Self-published.

Lindbergh, Anne Morrow. *Hour of Gold—Hour of Lead*. London: Chatto & Windus, 1973.

Lindbergh, Charles A. *We*. New York: G. P. Putnam's Sons, 1927.

Lovell, Mary S. *The Sound of Wings. The Biography of Amelia Earhart*. New York: St. Martin's Press, 1989.

Milestones of Aviation. Washington, D.C.: Smithsonian Institution National Air & Space Museum/Crescent Books, 1991.

Miley, Charles S. *Miley's Memos*. Indian River, FL: Indian River Community College Historical Data Center, 1980.

Morrissey, Muriel E. *Courage Is the Price*. Wichita, Kan.: McCormick-Armstrong, 1963.

——, and Carole Osborne. *Amelia, My Courageous Sister*. Santa Clara, Calif.: Osborne Publishers, 1987.

Oakes, Claudia. *United States Women in Aviation 1929–39*. Washington, D.C.: Smithsonian Institution Press, 1978.

Putnam, David Binney. *David Goes Voyaging*. New York: G. P. Putnam's Sons, 1925.

——. *David Goes to Greenland*. New York: G. P. Putnam's Sons, 1926.

——. *David Goes to Baffin Land*. New York: G. P. Putnam's Sons, 1927.

——. *David Sails the Viking Trail*. New York: Brewer, Warren & Putnam, 1931.

Putnam, George Palmer. *The Southland of North America*. New York: G. P. Putnam's Sons, 1913.

——. *In the Oregon Country*. New York: G. P. Putnam's Sons, 1915.

——. "The Putnam Baffin Island Expedition," *Geographical Review*, vol. XVIII, no. 1 (January 1928), 1–40. Reprinted by the American Geographical Society.

——. *Soaring Wings*. New York: Harcourt, Brace & Co., 1939.

——. *Wide Margins*. New York: Harcourt, Brace & Co., 1942.

——. *Mariner of the North. The Life of Captain Bob Bartlett*. New York: Duell, Sloan & Pearce, 1947.

——. *Up in Our Country*. New York: Duell, Sloan & Pearce, 1950.

Railey, Hilton Howell. *Touch'd with Madness*. Carrick & Evans, 1938.

Thadden, Louise. *High Wide and Frightened*. Stackpole Sons, 1938.

Who's Who in America. New York: A. N. Marquis Company, 1897–1947.

PERIODICALS

Rye Chronicle
The New York Times
New York Herald Tribune

MULTIMEDIA

Sierra Club. Microsoft Encarta, Microsoft Corporation, 1993; Funk & Wagnall's Corporation, 1993.